Measurements, Attacks, and Defenses for the Web Workshop 2021 (MADWeb 2021)

AA005367

Online
25 February 2021

ISBN: 978-1-7138-3765-7

Printed from e-media with permission by:

Curran Associates, Inc.
57 Morehouse Lane
Red Hook, NY 12571

Some format issues inherent in the e-media version may also appear in this print version.

The Internet Society
11710 Plaza America Drive, Suite 400
Reston, VA 20190
U.S.A.

Phone: (703) 439-2120
Fax: (703) 326-9881

www.internetsociety.org

Additional copies of this publication are available from:

Curran Associates, Inc.
57 Morehouse Lane
Red Hook, NY 12571 USA
Phone: 845-758-0400
Fax: 845-758-2633
Email: curran@proceedings.com
Web: www.proceedings.com

Proceedings of MADWeb 2021 – Workshop on Measurements, Attacks, and Defenses for the Web

Table of Contents

Proceedings

MADWeb 2021

Workshop on Measurements, Attacks, and Defenses for the Web

February 25, 2021
Virtual

Published by the

Internet Society

Internet Society
11710 Plaza America Drive
Suite 400
Reston, VA 20190

Address your correspondence to: NDSS Program Manager, Internet Society, 11710 Plaza America Drive, Suite 400, Reston, VA 20190 USA, tel. +1 703 439 2120, fax +1 703 326 9881, ndss@elists.isoc.org.

Internet Society
11710 Plaza America Drive
Suite 400
Reston, VA 20190
tel +1 703.439.2120
fax +1 703.326.9881
http://www.internetsociety.org

Program Committee Chairs' Message

The web connects billions of devices, running a plethora of clients and serving billions of users every single day. To cope with this widespread adoption, the web constantly changes with a stream of new technologies to develop web applications and ever-more complicated web browsers to render them. These rapid changes of the web's ecosystem are not always studied from a security perspective, resulting in new attack vectors that were never observed before.

The Measurements, Attack, and Defenses for the Web (MADWeb) workshop aims to attract researchers that work on the intersection of browser evolution, web security, and large-scale measurements. Our goal is to create and sustain a new venue for discussing the rapid changes to web technologies from a security perspective, how we can protect users, and how we can make future browsers more secure without hindering the evolution of the web. To this end, we invited researchers to contribute to the third Workshop on MADWeb, co-located with NDSS Symposium 2021. This year the workshop received 25 submissions (56% more submissions than last year), which indicates the excellent growth and confirms our intuition that the research community wants a security and privacy workshop dedicated to the web. More specifically:

- 25 papers were submitted to the workshop, out of which the Program Committee selected 9 (36% acceptance rate).
- 33 Program Committee members supported the reviewing process, including prominent representatives of academic and industrial research.
- 1 paper was selected for the best paper award based on its outstanding review scores, and 2 additional papers were selected for the best paper runner-up award.
- One author of each submitted paper was offered financial support to cover the cost of workshop registration.
- 2 invited talks were scheduled (from academia and from industry) on the crucial topics of browser security and measuring and defending against phishing

The wide range of topics covered by the accepted papers is remarkable, as it indeed covers all the three thrusts of the workshop, i.e., measurements, attacks, and defenses. In fact, we see that in addition to securing browsers, researchers focused on core infrastructure security (e.g., encrypted DNS), and on studying various new attacks, including cookie exfiltration and malicious content in social media platforms. We had a large number of attendees (more than 50 present online at each talk and Q/A session) and a very productive discussion at the workshop, and we expect that the number and diversity of web-related research topics will keep growing in future editions of MADWeb.

MADWeb's paper awards and financial support for registrations were possible thanks to the sponsorship and generous support by Palo Alto Networks, Inc.

Oleksii Starov and Roberto Perdisci
Program Committee Chairs, MADWeb 2021

Organizing Committee

Program Committee Chairs

Oleksii Starov, *Palo Alto Networks*
Roberto Perdisci, *University of Georgia*

Program Committee

Adam Doupé, *Arizona State University*
Adam Oest, *PayPal*
Amin Kharraz, *Florida International University*
Antoine Vastel, *DataDome*
Ben Stock, *CISPA Helmholtz Center*
Billy Melicher, *Palo Alto Networks*
Christo Wilson, *Northeastern University*
Cristian-Alexandru Staicu, *CISPA Helmholtz Center*
Gianluca Stringhini, *Boston University*
Gunes Acar, *KU Leuven*
Jason Polakis, *University of Illinois at Chicago*
Konrad Rieck, *TU Braunschweig*
Kyu Hyung Lee, *University of Georgia*
Leyla Bilge, *NortonLifeLock*
Louis DeKoven, *Facebook*
Luca Invernizzi, *Google*
Lukas Weichselbaum, *Google*
Nataliia Bielova, *INRIA*
Octavian Suciu, *University of Maryland, College Park*
Peter Snyder, *Brave*
Phani Vadrevu, *University of New Orleans*
Sajjad “JJ” Arshad, *Google*
Sebastian Lekies, *Google*
Steven Englehardt, *Mozilla*
Tamara Rezk, *INRIA*
Thomas Vissers, *Cloudflare*
Tom Van Goethem, *KU Leuven*
Walter Rudametkin, *Polytech*
Lill Weihang Wang, *University at Buffalo*
Yinzhi Cao, *Johns Hopkins University*
Yuchen Zhou, *Facebook*
Zachary Weinberg, *University of Massachusetts Amherst*
Zubair Shafiq, *University of Iowa*

Steering Committee

Alexandros Kapravelos, *North Carolina State University*
Nick Nikiforakis, *Stony Brook University*

HTTPS-Only: Upgrading all connections to `https` in Web Browsers

Christoph Kerschbaumer
Mozilla Corporation
ckerschb@mozilla.com

Julian Gaibler
Mozilla Corporation
jgaibler@mozilla.com

Arthur Edelstein
Mozilla Corporation
arthur@mozilla.com

Thyla van der Merwe†
ETH Zürich
tvdmerwe@ethz.ch

***Abstract*—The number of websites that support encrypted and secure `https` connections has increased rapidly in recent years. Despite major gains in the proportion of websites supporting `https`, the web contains millions of legacy `http` links that point to insecure versions of websites. Worse, numerous websites often use `http` connections by default, even though they already support `https`. Establishing a connection using `http` rather than `https` has the downside that `http` transfers data in cleartext, granting an attacker the ability to eavesdrop, or even tamper with the transmitted data. To date, however, no web browser has attempted to remedy this problem by favouring secure connections by default.**

We present *HTTPS-Only*, an approach which first tries to establish a secure connection to a website using `https` and only allows a fallback to `http` if a secure connection cannot be established. Our approach also silently upgrades all insecure `http` subresource requests (image, stylesheet, script) within a secure website to use the secure `https` protocol instead. Our measurements indicate that our approach can upgrade the majority of connections to `https` and therefore suggests that browser vendors have an opportunity to evolve their current connection model.

I. Introduction

The Hypertext Transfer Protocol (generally displayed as `http` in a browsers address-bar) [10] is the fundamental protocol through which web browsers and websites communicate. However, data transferred by the regular `http` protocol is unprotected and transferred in cleartext, such that attackers are able to view, steal, or even tamper with the transmitted data. Carrying `http` over the Transport Layer Security (TLS) protocol (generally displayed as `https` in the address-bar of a browser) [11] fixes this security shortcoming by creating a secure and encrypted connection between the browser and the website. More precisely, TLS enables the browser to authenticate the identity of the web server to the browser, and ensures that messages sent between the browser and the server are kept confidential from all other parties. Browsers typically display the lock icon (🔒) in the address-bar to indicate that the connection is an `https` connection and therefore encrypted and secure.

Over the past few years we have witnessed tremendous progress towards migrating the web to rely on `https` instead of the outdated and insecure `http` protocol. Efforts like HTTP Strict Transport Security (HSTS) [14] and the vitally important *Let's Encrypt* initiative [21] have helped to accelerate this migration. HSTS informs the browser that a server prefers secure connections, and *Let's Encrypt* [21] allows web servers to automatically obtain a browser-trusted certificate, enabling secure connections over `https` between browser and server. Importantly, the majority of websites already support `https` connections, and those that do not are increasingly uncommon. And yet, regrettably, the web contains millions of legacy `http` links that point to insecure versions of websites. Additionally, websites frequently fall back to using the insecure and outdated `http` protocol. Web browsers traditionally do not make any effort to adjust this security drawback by trying to upgrade the request and establish a secure connection instead.

As of December 2020, all major browsers (Chrome, Firefox, Edge, Safari) do not attempt to upgrade the scheme of a URL when the user clicks any outdated legacy `http` link. Additionally, all browsers default to using `http` when the user enters a scheme-less URL, (e.g., typing `example.com` into the address-bar). They also do not attempt to upgrade the scheme of a URL to `https` when the user enters or pastes an `http` URL into the address-bar. This industry-wide browser preference for `http` connections has been the status quo since the inception of the web and has not changed even after the introduction of `https`. Browser vendors are understandably hesitant to upgrade connections when such upgrades could downgrade a user's experience in any form.

On the server side, converting all legacy `http` links to `https` in websites is time-consuming and expensive. To successfully migrate a whole website, it's necessary to serve not only top-level documents but also all subresources (such as images, stylesheets, or scripts) over `https`, to make sure that no page content is blocked by web browsers' Mixed Content Blocker [36]. Thus it is also not surprising that not all websites have yet fully migrated to `https`.

To compensate, we present *HTTPS-Only Mode*, a new security feature that tries to upgrade all connections (top-level and subresource) to rely on the secure `https` protocol. The principle idea behind the *HTTPS-Only* approach is that resources are increasingly likely to be available over `https` as the web progresses towards `https`. *HTTPS-Only* first tries to establish a secure `https` connection to a website. If and only if that secure connection cannot be established, our algorithm presents the end user with an exception page, explaining the security risk and giving the user an option to either abandon the connection attempt, or to connect using the insecure and outdated `http` protocol. Our approach aims to pave the way for a reform in industry-wide browser design to make `https` the default protocol for the web.

†Work completed whilst this author was employed by Mozilla.

Workshop on Measurements, Attacks, and Defenses for the Web (MADWeb) 2021
25 February 2021, Virtual

https://dx.doi.org/10.14722/madweb.2021.23010
www.ndss-symposium.org

The remainder of this paper is structured as follows:

- In Section II we provide background information on the related mechanisms HTTP Strict Transport Security and Mixed Content Blocking.
- In Sections III and IV we present the design and implementation details of *HTTPS-Only Mode*, a browser security feature which upgrades all connections from `http` to `https`, implemented in Firefox (v.83.0).
- In Section V we examine the effectiveness of the proposed *HTTPS-Only* approach by evaluating real world data reported by Firefox end users.
- In Section VII we discuss the feasibility of changing the industry wide default to use `https` instead of `http` in all web browsers.

II. Background

Before presenting the design and implementation of *HTTPS-Only Mode*, we give an overview of two relevant security technologies: (a) *HTTP Strict Transport Security* and (b) *Mixed Content Blocking*. Both technologies are essential to the *HTTPS-Only* approach and to the objective of making the web rely on secure connections only.

A. HTTP Strict Transport Security (HSTS)

HTTP Strict Transport Security (HSTS) [14] is a browser security mechanism that allows a website to signal that the browser should only interact with a website using secure `https` connections and never with insecure `http` connections. For HSTS-enabled websites, the browser will require an `https` connection to a website even when the URL the browser is following is a non-secure `http` URL.

A website implements an HSTS policy by sending the `Strict-Transport-Security` response header in `https` server responses during `https` connections. The presence of the header indicates that the browser should automatically upgrade `http` links to resources on the website to the corresponding `https` links. Because browsers will ignore the header if it is sent over non-secure `http`, web servers utilising HSTS first have to redirect and upgrade the non secure `http` request to a secure `https` request. The header can further provide a `max-age` directive specifying how long the browser should cache the provided HSTS information.

When the browser receives an HSTS header, it caches the fact that the sending website wishes to be upgraded, and upgrades future requests to the website. This allows the browser to automatically turn any non-secure `http` link for a website into a secure `https` link. For example, suppose `https://siteA/index.html` embeds a script from `http://siteB/widget.js`. If `siteB` deploys HSTS, and the browser has previously visited `siteB` and additionally received an HSTS header, then the browser will load the script over `https` despite the `http` link.

HSTS has a vulnerability, however: before a browser has visited a website and received HSTS information, a request may still occur using plain `http` and is therefore still be vulnerable to downgrade attacks by tools such as SSLStrip [22]. To decrease the risk of any kind of downgrade attack, modern browsers introduced the *HSTS Preload* mechanism - a compiled list of HSTS supporting domains which is shipped with the browser [1], [23]. The browser will only make secure `https` connections to websites on the *HSTS Preload* list. Unfortunately, the web contains billions of websites [16] and hence scaling such lists remains challenging. For example, as of December 2020, the Firefox preload list contains roughly 100,000 entries.[1]

B. Mixed Content Blocking

The *Mixed Content Blocker* [36] is a browser security mechanism that blocks insecure content on pages that are supposed to be secure. That is, if the top level page is `https` then a browser's *Mixed Content Blocker* blocks requests for non-secure subresources within that page. The mixed content specification distinguishes between active (blockable) and passive (optionally-blockable) content.

a) ***Passive Mixed Content:*** Content, such as images, audio, and video resources, cannot alter other portions of a website page. For example, an attacker could replace an image served over non-secure `http` with an inappropriate or deceptive image, but could not otherwise change the behaviour of the page. According to the mixed content specification [36], blocking such content is optional and browser vendors may decide whether to block or allow such content. For a long time all major browsers followed the suggestion of the specification and loaded mixed passive content, additionally providing an indicator in the browser UI signalling that mixed content had loaded. More recently, the successor specification named *Mixed Content Level 2* suggests that browsers should auto-upgrade passive mixed content [39].

b) ***Active Mixed Content:*** In contrast, blockable content such as scripts or stylesheets have access to all or parts of the Document Object Model (DOM) [34]. Loading active mixed content into an otherwise fully `https` compatible website allows an attacker to change the behaviour of, or even steal sensitive user information from, the `https` website. For example, if a script were loaded over non-secure `http`, an attacker could inject a modified script that would log the user's keystrokes to an attacker's server. This is why modern browsers now warn users when a non-secure website page has a password field, even if the password is submitted over `https` [24]. Because of the high risk posed by active content, the mixed content specification suggests that browsers always block mixed active content.

We recognise that both of the aforementioned technologies are critical security enhancements to the browser ecosystem. Nevertheless, HSTS and Mixed Content Blocking do not fully solve the problems posed by web connection security. More precisely, if a website does not get upgraded to `https`, then the Mixed Content Blocker has no effect and if a website gets upgraded to `https`, then the Mixed Content Blocker might block relevant resources necessary for the functionality of the website, therefore potentially downgrading the end user's experience.

[1] https://searchfox.org/mozilla-central/source/security/manager/ssl/nsSTSPreloadList.inc

III. Design

The fundamental security problem of the current browser practice of defaulting to use insecure `http`, instead of secure `https`, when initially connecting to a website is that attackers can intercept the initial request. Hijacking the initial request suffices for an attacker to perform a man-in-the-middle attack which in turn allows the attacker to downgrade the connection, eavesdrop or modify data sent between client and server.

Using `http` as the browser default was sensible when the bulk of websites supported `http`. In 2020, however, we see that the majority of websites support `https`. Regrettably, misconfigured websites frequently default to the insecure and outdated `http` protocol even though they already support `https`. Worse, the web contains millions, if not billions, of legacy `http` links that point to insecure versions of websites. When a user clicks on such a link, a browser traditionally connects to the website using the insecure `http` protocol. To overcome this legacy problem and to establish a secure-by-default connection mechanism, our proposed approach attempts to silently upgrade connections. More precisely, when the user clicks an `http` link or enters an `http` URL in the address-bar, *HTTPS-Only* first tries to establish a secure connection to the website using `https`.

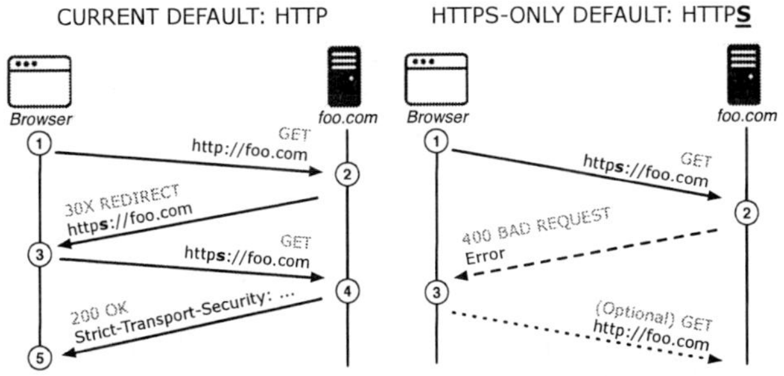

Fig. 1: Current browser behaviour defaulting to `http` (left) vs. *HTTPS-Only* behaviour defaulting to `https` (right).

Current best practice to counter the explained man-in-the-middle security risk primarily relies on HSTS (see Section II). However, HSTS does not solve the problems associated with performing the initial request in plain `http`. As illustrated in Figure 1 (left), the current browser default is to first connect to `foo.com` using `http` (see ①). If the server follows best practice and implements HSTS, then the server responds with a redirect to the secure version of the website (see ②). After the next `GET` request (see ③) the server adds the HSTS response header (see ④), signalling that the server prefers `https` connections and the browser should always perform `https` requests to `foo.com` (see ⑤) .

In contrast and as illustrated in Figure 1 (right), the presented *HTTPS-Only* approach first tries to connect to the web server using `https` (see ①). Given that most popular websites currently support `https`, our upgrading algorithm commonly establishes a secure connection and starts loading content. In a minority of cases, connecting to the server using `https` fails and the server reports an error (see ②). The proposed *HTTPS-Only Mode* then prompts the user, explaining the security risk, to either abandon the request or to connect using `http` (see ③).

IV. Implementation

In brief, our proposed security-enhancing feature internally upgrades (a) top-level document loads as well as (b) all subresource loads (images, stylesheets, scripts) within a secure website by rewriting the scheme of a URL [8] from `http` to `https`. While this overall approach is simple in principle, implementing a product-ready version of the presented upgrading algorithm entails many corner cases and potential pitfalls, which we describe in detail in this section.

We implement our upgrading mechanism within Firefox (v.83.0) which enforces a Secure by Default [18] loading mechanism and attaches meta-information to every resource load. Building on these efforts, we implement *HTTPS-Only*, by instrumenting and subsequently encoding additional information into the meta object attached to every single request. This encoding of additional information in a request's (top-level or subresource) meta object allows us to silently upgrade any connection from `http` to `https` in Necko, the network layer in Firefox.

A. Upgrading Top-Level (HTML Document) Loads

Upgrading a top-level request (that is, the top-level HTML document [40] of a web page) with *HTTPS-Only* entails uncertainties about the response that the browser needs to handle. If everything works optimally, then Firefox using *HTTPS-Only* simply connects to a website using `https` and the browser proceeds to load the web page securely. If, however, connecting securely to the web server fails, then *HTTPS-Only* prompts the user with an exception page, explaining the problem and the security risk, and provides an option for the end user to *'Accept the Risk'* and connect using `http`. Our approach supports this fallback mechanism because at present not all websites on the Web support `https`, and simply blocking any connection to those websites would downgrade the end user's experience. To accommodate for websites which do not yet support secure connections, we distinguish between the following two error cases:

*a) **Immediate Errors:*** If there is an error response, either from the remote server itself or a firewall, then our approach can instantly respond to that error. Error responses can range from a `TCP Reset packet` to server responses with some type of TLS error. Therefore, our approach interprets all errors reported by the networking code as an *HTTPS-Only* error. If detected, our approach prompts the user with an exception page that explains the problem and the security risk, and provides an option to connect to the website using `http`.

*b) **Timeouts:*** A non-responding firewall or a misconfigured or outdated server that fails to send a response can result in long timeouts which ultimately downgrade an end user's experience, forcing the user to wait a long time for the exception page to appear before they can continue browsing. When testing *HTTPS-Only* we experienced timeouts taking as long as 90 seconds. To mitigate this problem, *HTTPS-Only* first sends a top-level request for `https`, and after an N-second delay, if no response is received, sends an additional `http` background request. If the background `http` connection is established prior to the `https` connection, then this signal is a strong indicator that the `https` request will result in a timeout. In this case, the `https` request is canceled and the user is shown the *HTTPS-Only Mode* exception page.

```
1  void PotentiallySendBGRequest(nsIChannel* aOrigChannel) {
2    // if not top-level load, then there is nothing to do
3    nsILoadInfo* loadInfo = aOrigChannel->GetLoadInfo();
4    if (loadinfo->Type() != TYPE_DOCUMENT)){
5      return;
6    }
7
8    // if already https, then there is nothing to do
9    nsIURI* uri = aOrigChannel->GetURI();
10   if (!uri->SchemeIs("http")) {
11     return;
12   }
13   NewTimerWithCallBack(3000, SendBGRequest(aOrigChannel));
14 }
15
16 void SendBGRequest(nsIChannel* aOrigChannel) {
17   nsIURI* uri = aOrigChannel->GetURI();
18   uri->StripPathAndQuery();
19
20   uint32_t loadFlags = LOAD_ANONYMOUS
21                      | LOAD_BYPASS_CACHE
22                      | LOAD_HTTPS_ONLY_EXEMPT;
23
24   nsIChannel* bgChannel = NewChannel(uri, loadFlags);
25
26   BGListener *bgListener = new BGListener(aOrigChannel);
27   bgChannel->SetNotificationCallBacks(bgListener);
28   bgChannel->AsyncOpen();
29 }
30
31 void BGListener::OnStartRequest() {
32   if (mOrigChannel->IsLoading()) {
33     return;
34   }
35   mOrigChannel->Cancel(POTENTIAL_TIMEOUT);
36 }
```

Listing 1: *HTTPS-Only Mode* trying to establish top-level `https` connection while simultaneously connecting using `http` in the background to avoid long timeouts.

Whenever a user enters an insecure URL into the address-bar, or clicks a legacy link, our *HTTPS-Only* approach upgrades the connection to `https`, but subsequently calls the function `PotentiallySendBGRequest()`, providing an `nsIChannel` argument which is Firefox's internal representation of a network request in Necko. The function `PotentiallySendBGRequest()` determines if our mechanism should send a background request so that end users do not have to wait for a connection timeout in case the website does not respond to the upgraded `https` request (thereby improving the user experience of our *HTTPS-Only* mechanism).

As illustrated in Listing 1, this function first queries the `nsILoadInfo` of the `nsIChannel` (Line 3), a data structure which provides varied loading information [18]. Amongst other things, the `nsILoadInfo` object conveys the load type. Since our approach only performs a background request for top-level loads it can immediately return if the load type of the request is not `TYPE_DOCUMENT` (Line 5). Similarly, if the request is not `http` (Line 10), meaning the user has already entered an `https` scheme, then there is no need to send a background request and the function can return. If, however, the checks have not caused the function to return, then we send a background request by calling the function `SendBGRequest()` using an N-second delay (Line 13). Using a delay is crucial because we need to account for enough time such that the browser and the web server can negotiate parameters, perform the TLS handshake, and establish a secure connection. We empirically found that setting N=3000 milliseconds allows for the best results on Desktop and Mobile (please see Figure 6 in the Evaluation section).

Path and query information is irrelevant in determining whether a server responds to a connection request, and users browsing using *HTTPS-Only Mode* expect the browser to not leak any user sensitive information. Therefore, in the first step in the function `SendBGRequest()`, we strip any path and query information from the URL (Line 18). While our approach strips user sensitive information from the background request so as to not reveal any user data by default, we also provide an option for cautious users to opt out of sending the background request.[2] The downside is that such cautious users will have to wait until the request times out before the exception page appears.

Next, we equip the new background network connection (Line 20) with three flags: `LOAD_ANONYMOUS`, `LOAD_BYPASS_CACHE`, `LOAD_HTTPS_ONLY_EXEMPT`. These three flags ensure that we (a) perform an anonymous request by not attaching any cookies, (b) ask that the request does not end up in our cache, and (c) exempt the load from *HTTPS-Only*, otherwise our upgrading mechanism would upgrade the connection to `https` later in Necko which we explicitly want to avoid for sending the background request.

Before opening the background channel and connecting to the server (Line 28), we have to create a Listener (Line 26) and set the Notification callbacks (Line 27). These two mechanisms allow our code to track progress of the original, upgraded top-level channel. In particular, within the function `OnStartRequest()` on Line 31, we check if the original channel has already started loading by consulting `mOriginalChannel->IsLoading()`. If that function returns true, then we know that the original channel, which was upgraded to `https`, is already loading. If that function returns false, however, meaning that the upgraded channel encounters a problem, then we cancel the original channel (Line 35). This causes the exception page to appear and signals to the end user that the server has not responded to the `https` request. The user then can then to choose to connect to the website using plain `http`, if desired.

B. Upgrading Subresource (Image, Stylesheet, Script) Loads

Any given web page consists of many different resources that are fetched by the browser as requested by the top-level HTML document [40], including images, stylesheets, scripts and other content linked via URLs [8].

Upgrading the top-level document only to use `https` would provide limited security guarantees because an active network attacker could still eavesdrop and tamper with subresources loaded over `http`. Additionally, not upgrading subresources to `https` results in mixed content (see Section II), and a browser's implementation of the *Mixed Content Blocker* starts blocking active content like scripts, thereby downgrading an end user's experience.

Instead of only upgrading top-level requests, our holistic approach also upgrades subresources by rewriting the scheme in the URL. However, if loading a subresource over `https` fails, then in contrast to the handling of top-level loads, our

[2] security.https_only_mode_send_http_background_request

approach does not provide any kind of fallback mechanism. Instead *HTTPS Only* logs a message to the *Browser Console* indicating that the upgrade attempt failed but, as previously mentioned, does not fall back to trying to load the request using insecure `http`.

In addition to comprehensively enforcing `https` for subresources, *HTTPS-Only* also accounts for WebSockets [13]. A WebSocket provides full-duplex communication channels over a single TCP connection and enables interaction between a web browser (or other client application) and a web server with lower overhead than half-duplex alternatives such as `http` polling. Similar to other subresource loads, *HTTPS-Only* upgrades a WebSocket's scheme from `ws:` to `wss:`.

It can happen that a website itself is available over `https` but resources within the website page, such as images or videos, are not available over `https`. Consequently, such websites may not look right or might malfunction. To compensate, our implementation provides an option which allows users to disable *HTTPS-Only* for a website that has been loaded with `https`. For any website that has been upgraded by *HTTPS-Only Mode*, Firefox shows a user-interface widget in the security doorhanger, accessed by clicking the lock icon (🔒) in the address-bar, which allows the user to temporarily or permanently disable *HTTPS-Only* for that website.

Beyond these considerations, a practical implementation of *HTTPS-Only* also needs full integration with two critical browser security mechanisms related to subresource loads: (a) *Mixed Content Blocker*, and (b) *Cross-Origin Resource Sharing* (CORS).

a) Interaction with the Mixed Content Blocker: As explained in Section II, the *Mixed Content Blocker* blocks `http` subresources within a top-level `https` page. Since our approach upgrades resources in Necko, the networking layer in the Firefox web browser, we have to adjust the *Mixed Content Blocker* implementation to not block the potential mixed content subresource load, relying on Necko to upgrade the load later.

```
1  bool BlockMixedContent(
2    nsIURI* aTopLevelURI, nsIChannel* aSubresourceChannel) {
3    if (!aTopLevelURI->SchemeIs("https")) {
4      return false;
5    }
6
7    nsIURI* channelURI = aSubresourceChannel->GetURI();
8    if (!channelURI->SchemeIs("http")) {
9      return false;
10   }
11
12   if (Preferences::HTTPS_ONLY_MODE_ENALBED()) {
13     nsILoadInfo* loadInfo = aSubresourceChannel->LoadInfo();
14     if (loadInfo->HttpsOnlyMode() != HTTPS_ONLY_EXEMPT) {
15       return false;
16     }
17   }
18   // evaluate if subresource is active or passive content
19   return true;
20 }
```

Listing 2: Interaction of *HTTPS-Only* with the Mixed Content Blocker.

For every subresource load within Firefox, the browser consults the function `BlockMixedContent()`. As illustrated within Listing 2, if a the top-level document load is not `https`, then a browser's *Mixed Content Blocker* has nothing to evaluate and can return at this point (see Line 3). Further, if the subresource load is not `http` (which is the case when loading `data:` [9] or also `blob:` [38]), then the *Mixed Content Blocker* also has nothing to evaluate and can return (see Line 8). Generally, the actual work for the mixed content algorithm starts after Line 10, when we know the top-level load is `https` and the subresource load is `http`, indicating the load is actually mixed.

On Line 12 we have a check for whether the preference for *HTTPS-Only* is enabled. If the preference for *HTTPS-Only* is not set to true, then the *Mixed Content Blocker* implementation works as for every other subresource load despite having a branch for the presented *HTTPS-Only* implementation. If the preference is true, then we have to check the actual mode using HttpsOnlyMode() stored in the `nsILoadInfo` (Line 14). This flag ensures the load is not exempt from upgrading; more details on Exemptions are given in Section IV-C. If the load is not exempt from upgrading, then we return at Line 15, not blocking the subresource load as mixed content with the knowledge that the subresource request will be upgraded to `https` later in Necko before loading any data over the network.

b) Interaction with CORS: Cross-Origin Resource Sharing (CORS) [35] is a mechanism that uses additional headers to tell browsers to give a web application running at one origin, access to selected resources from a different origin. A web application executes a cross-origin `http` request when it requests a resource that has a different origin (scheme, host or port) [12] from its own.

Before performing any kind of CORS check, the browser first evaluates whether the request is same-origin with the encompassing security context. To illustrate, lets assume a top-level document of `https://www.example.com` performs an XMLHttpRequest (XHR) [41] to `http://www.example.com/foo`. In such a case, the browser has to issue a CORS request because the schemes of `http` and `https` differ, meaning the request is cross origin and hence requires CORS to succeed. But since our proposed approach will upgrade the XHR request to `https://www.example.com/foo` it will also render the CORS request obsolete and hence we need to discard it.

```
bool CheckHTTPSOnlyPreventsCORS(
  nsIURI aTopLevelDocURI, nsIChannel* aSubresourceChannel) {

  nsIURI* channelURI = aSubresourceChannel->GetURI();
  if (!channelURI->SchemeIs("http")) {
    return false;
  }

  nsString topLevelDocHost = aTopLevelDocURI->GetHost();
  nsString subresourceHost = channelURI->GetHost();

  if (topLevelDocHost.Equals(subresourceHost)) {
    return true;
  }
  return false;
}
```

Listing 3: Interaction of *HTTPS-Only* with CORS.

Once Firefox's CORS implementation detects that a request is cross-origin, it will normally enforce CORS (note that CORS only applies to `http(s):` requests and is discarded for all other schemes). Since our approach potentially upgrades requests from `http` to `https`, we have to add a carve-out to account for that scenario by consulting the function `CheckHTTPSOnlyPreventsCORS()`.

As illustrated in Listing 3, the newly added helper function, named `CheckHTTPSOnlyPreventsCORS()`, first checks if a request is `http` (Line 5), as otherwise our approach would not influence the result of the load. If the load is in fact `http`, meaning that it will be upgraded to `https` later in the loading cycle, the helper function simply needs to verify that the host of the top-level document (Line 9) and the host of the subresource load (Line 10) are equal (Line 12). If they are equal, meaning that only the scheme differs, then there is no need to issue a CORS request because our implementation makes the request to be same-origin by upgrading the subresource scheme from `http` to `https`. If that is not the case, and the hosts differ, then our approach has no influence on the result and CORS will be applied to the request, as it would without operating in *HTTPS-Only Mode*.

C. Upgrading Exemptions

Generally, and as previously mentioned, we designed *HTTPS-Only Mode* following the principle of *Secure by Default* which means that by default, our approach will upgrade all outgoing connections from `http` to `https`. Following this principle allows us to provide a future-proof product implementation where exceptions to the rule require explicit annotation, such as in the following two illustrative examples:

a) ***OCSP Requests:*** The Online Certificate Status Protocol (OCSP) [29] allows the browser to validate or determine the revocation status of an X. 509 certificate by sending an OCSP request to the OCSP server listed in the certificate. OCSP commonly works under the soft-fail principle, which means that if the server cannot be reached, then it is assumed that the certificate is still valid. Unsuccessfully upgrading such a request would carry a higher risk for users than allowing it to be sent over `http`. Internally, when creating the meta object named `nsILoadInfo` [18] for an OCSP request, we annotate the request by setting the flag `HTTPS_ONLY_EXEMPT`, which instructs our algorithm to exempt that request from being upgraded to `https`. We are mindful that having to rely on `http` is not optimal for preserving the user's privacy. While Firefox still supports OCSP, this privacy drawback is one of the many reasons Firefox will soon switch to CRLite [20] to determine certificate revocation status.

b) ***Captive Portal Requests:*** Captive portals are special websites that users need to visit to access a public network, commonly at hotel lobbies, airports or coffee shops, before access to the network and internet is granted. A common method to implement such captive portals is to intercept all web traffic to a web server and return an `http` redirect to a captive portal. To determine whether a user has access to the internet, Firefox sends a network request in the background to a specific website. If the website responds as expected, then Firefox can assume the user is connected to the internet. Since `https` requests cannot be modified by the network to redirect to the captive portal, this background request needs to remain a plain `http` request. Hence, we explicitly annotate these requests by setting the flag `HTTPS_ONLY_EXEMPT` on the `nsILoadInfo`-object, so that our *HTTPS-Only* algorithm does not upgrade them.

V. Evaluation

We break down the evaluation of our approach into four segments. We start out by first providing statistics, gathered over recent years, showcasing the percentage increase of websites relying on `https` (Section V-A). Second, we lay out fundamentals about our data-gathering process including the time frame and participating users of our study (Section V-B). Third, we provide detailed numbers on the effectiveness of our approach by showing how many top-level (document) loads our mechanism is able to upgrade (Section V-C), and finally, we present similar details for subresource loads (Section V-D).

A. State of the Internet - Websites loaded using `https`

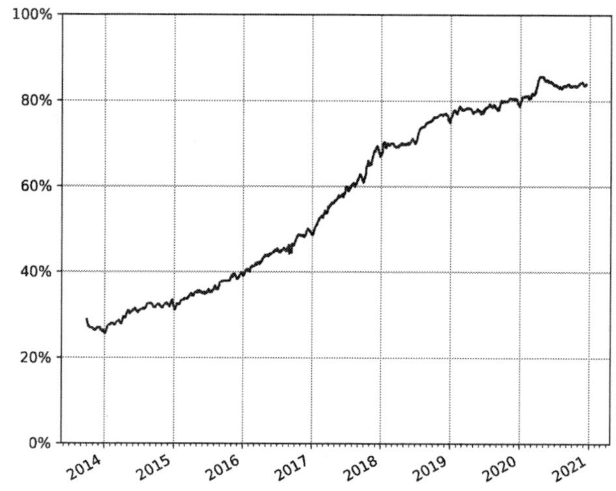

Fig. 2: Evolution of websites relying on `https` for the years 2014 to 2020. (Note: Mozilla also reports this evolvement of websites relying on `https` to *Let's Encrypt* [21]).

In 2015, a mere six years ago, not even 40% (Figure 2) of web pages were loaded using `https`, leaving more than half of the websites vulnerable to man-in-the-middle attacks, thereby jeopardising an end user's security and privacy.

In 2016, *Let's Encrypt* was launched, and likely had a large impact on increasing the number of websites relying on `https` by making it possible for website owners to automatically obtain a free browser-trusted certificate. As illustrated in Figure 2, the graph shows a doubling of `https` use between the years 2016 and 2019.

By 2020, around 84% (Figure 2) of web pages were loaded using `https`. While the exact usage rate varies by region, we note that in the United States, for example, the number of websites loading over `https` is as high as 92%. Taking a closer look at the development between the years 2019 and 2020, however, reveals that the increase of websites loading over `https` flattens. This flattening of the curve signals that we have entered a new phase. We hypothesize that new approaches, such as *HTTPS-Only Mode*, can help to close the gap and allow more websites to load using `https`, ultimately delivering a fully secure web with a 100% of connections being over `https`.

B. Background on Data-Gathering

We examine the capabilities and potential limitations of our approach by inspecting real world data from Firefox end users. *HTTPS-Only Mode* was launched as an opt-in security feature in Firefox 83, which was released on November 17th, 2020. Users can enable the feature by visiting `about:preferences#privacy` and flipping the radio button to enable *HTTPS-Only Mode*.

The *Mozilla Telemetry Portal* [26] allows us to present information which we gathered during one full Firefox release cycle, from **November 17th to December 17th, 2020**. Please note that our telemetry mechanisms measure and collect non-personal information, such as performance, usage and customisations and sends this information to Mozilla on a daily basis. All of the collected information used for analysis is subject to *Mozilla's Data Privacy Principles* which are covered in the Firefox Data Documentation [25].

During our collection period of one month we were able to **collect real world data of 103,431 Firefox users** who participated in our study and agreed to report information back to Mozilla. Evaluating real-world browsing behaviour of Firefox release users allows us to quantitatively examine *HTTPS-Only*, as presented in the following two subsections.

C. Upgrading Top-Level (HTML Document) Loads

To give a detailed picture of the potential of *HTTPS-Only* on top-level (document) loads, we report the results of four measurements: (1) the fraction of successful upgrades to `https` from legacy addresses, where browsers would traditionally connect using the outdated and insecure `http` protocol, (2) the fraction of secure page loads in general, (3) the rate at which users see an *HTTPS-Only* exception page due to the fact that the navigated site does not currently support `https`, and (4) the time required to establish a secure `https` (TLS) connection with a remote website.

*1) **Success rate of top-level (document) upgrades of legacy addresses:*** Our approach specifically aims to ensure connections use the secure `https` protocol, where browsers traditionally would connect using the `http` protocol. To target this data set, our telemetry logs a success when our mechanism is able to upgrade a connection by rewriting the scheme of a URL from `http` to `https` and a load succeeds.

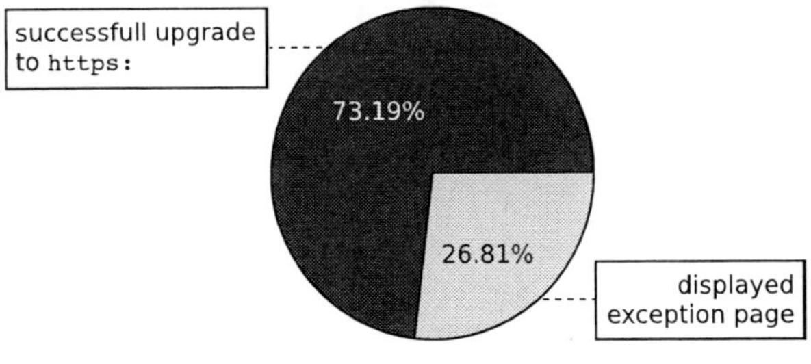

Fig. 3: Attempts to upgrade top-level (document) legacy addresses from `http` to `https` via *HTTPS-Only*.

As illustrated in Figure 3, the *HTTPS-Only* mechanism successfully upgrades top-level (document) loads from `http` to `https` for more than 73% of legacy address. These 73% of successful upgrades originate from the user clicking legacy `http` links, or entering `http` (or even scheme-less) URLs in the address-bar, where the target website, fortunately, supports `https`.

Our observation that *HTTPS-Only* can successfully upgrade seven out of ten of top-level loads from `http` to `https` reflects a general migration of websites supporting `https`. At the same time, this fraction of successful upgrades of legacy addresses also confirms that web pages still contain a multitude of `http`-based URLs where browsers would traditionally establish an insecure connection.

*2) **Rate of secure web page loads:*** In addition to measuring the upgrade ratio of our approach, we further examine the impact of *HTTPS-Only* on a browser's security by measuring the overall fraction of pages that load using `https`. Our telemetry allows us to compute and report the fraction of `http` to `https` connections for all top-level (document) loads.

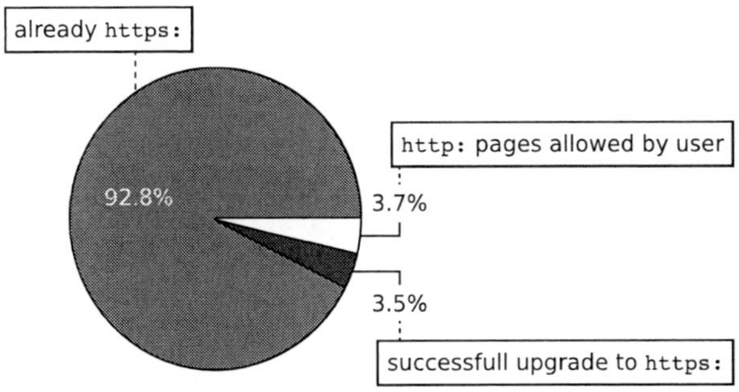

Fig. 4: Use of `https` for top-level (document) loads when *HTTPS-Only* is enabled.

As illustrated in Figure 4, telemetry from participating users in our study reports that in 92.8% of cases the top-level URL is already `https` without any need to upgrade. This rate is higher than the reported 84% of websites relying on `https` which we described in Section *State of the Internet* (see Section 2). We attribute the higher intrinsic `https` rate to the browsing behaviour of participating users. If a secure connection cannot be established, *HTTPS-Only Mode* shows an exception page, where users are then free to choose to abandon the connection attempt and not to visit a site that doesn't support `https`.

We further see that *HTTPS-Only* users experienced a successful upgrade from `http` to `https` in 3.5% of the loads, such that, overall, 96.3% of page loads are secure.

The remaining 3.7% of page loads are insecure, on websites for which the user has explicitly opted to allow insecure connections. Note that the total number of insecure top-level loads observed depends on how many pages a user visited on the website or websites they had exempted from *HTTPS-Only*.

*3) **Rate at which users see an exception page:*** We think that users are likely to perceive frequent exception pages as a degradation of their browsing experience. Hence we believe that the biggest impact to a user's experience when browsing the web using *HTTPS-Only* is the rate at which they will see an exception page. Our recording mechanism allows us to observe how often the user encounters an exception page as a result of *HTTPS-Only* trying to establish a secure `https` connection, but the remote website does not respond positively to the `https` request.

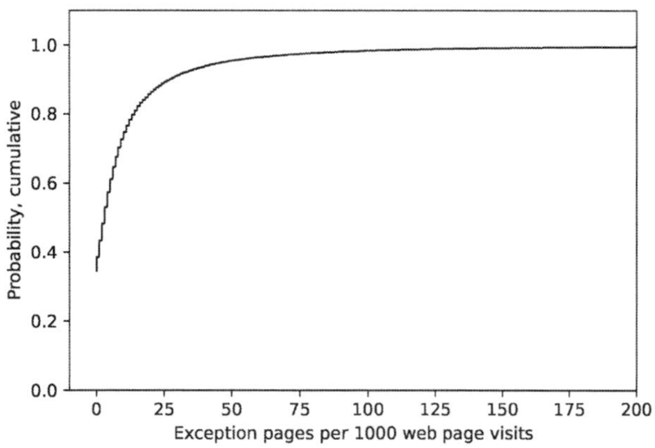

Fig. 5: Cumulative probability distribution of the rate at which users see exception pages as they browse.

We compute the frequency of exception pages seen by users per 1,000 web page visits. When users browse the web using *HTTPS-Only* they experience a range of error page frequencies, depending on the locale of the visited pages and their browsing preferences, hence we audit and examine the distribution.

In summary, the error page distribution, as illustrated in Figure 5, shows:

- The median user experienced 4.3 exception pages per 1,000 page visits
- 34% of users saw no exception pages at all when visiting 1,000 pages, and
- 95% of users saw fewer than 48 exception pages per 1,000 visits.

Our measurements show that across the population, the vast majority of attempts to visit a page securely succeed, and only a small minority of visit attempts result in an error page.

*4) **Time to successfully establish an `https` connection:*** We further record the time it takes the browser to successfully establish an `https` connection to a website. This information allows us to empirically determine after how many milliseconds it is unlikely to be able to connect securely to a website. As explained in Section III, and in particular in Listing 1, we use this information to mitigate connection timeouts and in turn improve the user experience of *HTTPS-Only*.

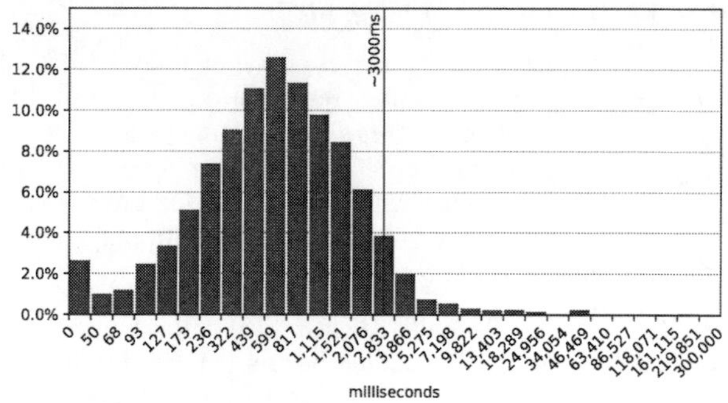

Fig. 6: Time in milliseconds for establishing a top-level (document) `https` connection.

As illustrated in Figure 6, we observe that in more than 96% of cases we are able to establish a secure `https` connection to a top-level page in less than 3,000 milliseconds. Therefore, after 3,000 milliseconds, we launch a background `http` request. If the server-client round-trip time of the background `http` request still manages to establish an `http` connection faster than the upgraded top-level request, then our algorithm cancels the top-level `https` request and shows the user an exception page giving them the option to connect using `http`.

Our approach aims to change the default connection mechanism within a browser and first tries to connect using `https`. Any feasible implementation of *HTTPS-Only*, however, needs to provide some kind of fallback to `http`, even if only as an interim solution. Again, our approach aims to upgrade as many connections to rely on `https` as possible but does not try to eliminate the reachability of legacy websites which do not (yet) support `https`.

D. Upgrading Subresource (Image, Stylesheet, Script) Loads

Similar to what is reported in Figure 4, showing that 93% of top-level loads already rely on `https`, the vast majority of subresource loads also already rely on `https`.

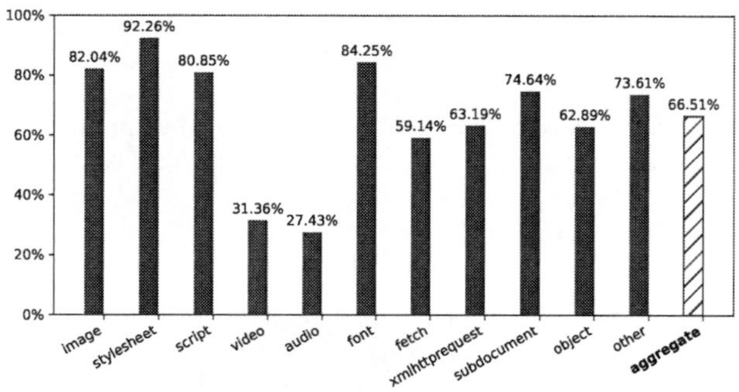

Fig. 7: Successful subresource upgrades of legacy addresses from `http` to `https` via *HTTPS-Only*.

Here, however, we focus on the success rate of *HTTPS-Only* for the minority of links using legacy `http` URLs, where browsers traditionally would carry out the subresource load using the insecure `http` protocol. Our recording logs a successful upgrade when *HTTPS-Only* is able to rewrite the scheme of a legacy URL from `http` to `https` and the subresource load succeeds.

Image, Stylesheet, Script: As illustrated in Figure 7 our approach is able to upgrade the majority of the three fundamental subresources for legacy addresses, namely resources of type image in 82% of cases, stylesheet in 92% of cases, and script in 80% of cases. In practice, website maintainers sometimes focus on securing the top-level document by making it available over `https` but do not update hyperlinks for subresources correspondingly. We believe that the high success rate reported is due to the fact that legacy image, style and script tags are mostly same-origin with the top-level document and therefore mostly have a secure version available.

Audio, Video, Font: Insecurely linked subresources of type video, audio or font appear much less often on websites than images, stylesheets or scripts. Our logging shows that on an average day we record 3,906 insecure video requests, 2,073 insecure audio requests and 3,079 insecure font-face requests. In contrast, on an average day we record 1,189,977 insecure image requests. As illustrated, we record successful upgrades for insecure video in 31% of cases, insecure audio in 27% of cases and insecure font-face in 84% of cases. We think that respective tags for audio and video gained popularity only recently - during the same time websites increasingly started to rely on `https` - in practice most video is streamed from services like `youtube.com` which all rely on `https` to begin with, meaning that our upgrading mechanism does not kick in.

Fetch and XMLHttprequest: Although fetch and XMLHttpRequest provide similar functionality, our recording shows that users encounter insecure XMLHttpRequests more than three times as often as insecure fetch requests. Most likely because the fetch specification gained popularity recently and developers were already aware of the security drawbacks of not using `https`. We see that both perform similarly in terms of upgrade success - almost 60% of fetch upgrades and more than 63% of XMLHttpRequests upgrades succeed.

Subdocument and Object: Loading a subdocument is in fact very similar to loading a top-level document, with the important difference being that the subdocument load appears in a frame or iframe. Hence the success ratio mirrors what we report in Figure 3: our approach is able to upgrade 74% of insecure subdocument loads from `http` to `https`.

Other: Firefox internally distinguishes between over 50 different content types for loading resources. We explicitly list the success ratio of the the most popular types above, and label the remaining types, such as download or web-manifest, as "other." Our measurements indicate a success rate of around 73% for all the types assigned to this bucket.

Summary of upgrades in aggregate: As mentioned above, we observe that the majority of subresources within an `https` document are already `https` in the first place. For the remaining legacy-linked subresources, which would load using `http` in a traditional browser setting, our approach is able to upgrade 66% in aggregate. Again, these 66% of successful upgrades originate from our approach being able to upgrade legacy `http` URLs, where browsers traditionally would carry out the subresource load using the insecure `http` protocol.

VI. Related Work

Relying on `https` is key to providing protection for any traffic between a web browser and the server. Studies conducted by Sivakorn et al. [30], [31], Drakonakis et al. [3] and Englehardt et al. [5] confirm the problematic situation of websites not properly deploying `https`. These studies conclude that websites which do not, or only partially, deploy `https` expose private information to attackers. Our approach mitigates the risk of exposing private user information by always encrypting and delivering content using `https`.

In 2008, Jackson and Barth proposed a mechanism [17] that allows web servers to force browsers to interact with a website only using secure `https` connections. This mechanism built the foundation for the HSTS specification [14] which, if properly deployed [19], allows websites to protect themselves against protocol downgrade attacks. However, the initial request remains unprotected from active attacks. To mitigate this risk, all major browsers deploy HSTS Preload lists which contain known websites supporting HSTS, thereby allowing a browser to perform the initial request over `https`. Unfortunately, HSTS Preload lists do not scale to the size of the internet and therefore leave the majority of websites unprotected against downgrade attacks. Further, HSTS has the downside that it opens up an additional tracking vector [28], [33]. Our proposed *HTTPS-Only* mechanism overcomes these limitations and automatically updates all requests so that websites can rely on `https`, starting with the initial request.

Statistics gathered by Porter Felt et al. [6] show that by 2017 over 50% of web browsing took place over `https`. In 2020, *Let's Encrypt* reported that their free, automated, and open Certificate Authority issued more than 1.5 million certificates daily. These numbers confirm that `https` is on the rise, and hence different approaches are being launched to try to deliver more content over `https`. For example, the Content-Security-Policy [32] (CSP) hosts the directive `upgrade-insecure-requests` [37], which provides a mechanism for websites to upgrade all of their requests from `http` to `https`. While this opt-in directive provides a mechanism for sites to upgrade legacy content within their own host range, it requires active deployment by the website maintainer.

The famous browser extension *HTTPS Everywhere* [4], and related mechanisms *Smart HTTPS* [15] and *HTTPZ* [2] allow browsers to fully encrypt communications with many major websites. The downside of any extension approach is that browsers typically block active mixed content before the extension gets the opportunity to upgrade a request.

Finally, the World Wide Web Consortium (W3C) is working on a specification for auto-upgrading mixed content [39] and the *Chrome* browser recently announced that it would ship this behaviour [7]. Ultimately, all upgrading mechanisms have to acknowledge that web architecture permits resource requests to return different content when queried using `http` or `https`. As discussed by Paracha et al. [27] the number of sites that exhibit such behaviour is small and we argue that this problem will vanish over time once `https` becomes the norm. While auto-upgrading mixed content only upgrades subresources of type image and media, our *HTTPS-Only* approach upgrades all subresources, and additionally attempts to upgrade top-level (document) connections to rely on `https`.

VII. Discussion

Currently, all major browsers (Chrome, Firefox, Edge, Safari) default to using `http` when the user enters a scheme-less URL into the address-bar. Similarly, all web browsers, by default, do not try to upgrade the scheme of the URL to `https` when the user clicks an outdated legacy `http` link or enters an `http` URL into the address-bar. We attribute this industry-wide behaviour of relying on the insecure `http` protocol rather than its secure successor to the desire of browser vendors to avoid downgrading a user's experience. Unfortunately, relying on a processing model which sends the initial request to a website in cleartext jeopardises the security and privacy of end users because it allows attackers to prevent subsequent upgrades to a secure connection.

Currently, it seems that browsers rely in on websites following best practice and redirecting an initial request to `https`. To illustrate the severity of this security shortcoming we note that the web application security community has been focussing on exactly this problem by introducing new mechanisms including HSTS and CSP's `upgrade-insecure-requests`. Both of these approaches require considerable effort from the website, however. For example, it is almost impossible for the developer of a website that uses HSTS to tell whether a given browser accessing the website has received HSTS information for the website. Getting a domain on a browser's HSTS Preload list, so that the browser only uses secure connections to interact with a website, presents an additional burden for website developers. Given the billions of websites, it is questionable whether HSTS Preload lists can ever scale to accommodate most of the web.

We argue that a better approach for user agents is to first try to establish a secure connection. This approach reduces the burden for website authors, and puts the security back under the control of user agents, operating in the best interests of the user. Requiring an explicit user opt-in to insecure `http` connections provides further protection against active downgrade attacks. Thus we believe that browser vendors should consider integrating some kind of native support similar to our proposed *HTTPS-Only Mode*, which first tries to establish a secure connection to a website and only falls back to an insecure connection in the case where the website is not reachable using the `https` protocol.

To summarize: a large majority of web connections already support `https`. Because the percentage of web pages loaded using `https` currently exceeds 84%, as reported by *Let's Encrypt* [21], we believe that we are entering a final phase of securing the web, where we anticipate that, ultimately, almost every website will be available over `https`. We think that the time has come for browser vendors to reconsider the default protocol used for establishing a connection to a website. Additionally, the presented upgrading mechanism has the ability to compensate for legacy `http` links, incorrectly entered URLs in the address-bar or incorrectly linked resources in websites, and therefore provides a mechanism to silently fix security compatibility issues. We think that the extra protection provided by explicitly prompting users to opt-in before they connect insecurely to a website is becoming more feasible now that such prompts need be shown only occasionally.

VIII. Conclusion

We have presented *HTTPS-Only*, a new browser connection model which first tries to establish a secure connection to a website using `https` and only allows a fall back to `http` if a secure connection cannot be established. Additionally, our approach silently upgrades all insecure `http` subresources (image, stylesheet, script) within a secure website to use `https`.

Evaluating real-world browsing behaviour of over 100,000 Firefox release users shows that our approach is capable of upgrading over 70% of top-level (document) loads to rely on `https`, where browsers traditionally would connect using the insecure and outdated `http` protocol. The success of *HTTPS-Only* in upgrading legacy links, together with our observation that the median user can successfully connect to a website using `https` 995 times when visiting 1,000 sites, suggests that our approach is useful and practical. We believe that *HTTPS-Only* highlights the path to achieving a fully secure web, and that now is a good time for browser vendors to begin re-evaluating their current connection model.

Acknowledgments

We would like to thank everyone in Security Engineering at Mozilla for their feedback, reviews, and insightful comments. In particular we are grateful to following Mozillians for making *HTTPS-Only Mode* possible: Meridel Walkington, Eric Pang, Martin Thomson, Steven Englehardt, Alice Fleischmann, Angela Lazar, Mikal Lewis, Wennie Leung, Frederik Braun, Tom Ritter, June Wilde, Sebastian Streich, Leli Schiestl, Daniel Veditz, Prangya Basu, Dragana Damjanovic, Valentin Gosu, Chris Lonnen, Andrew Overholt, and Selena Deckelmann.

References

[1] Chromium Project. Check HSTS preload status and eligibility. https://hstspreload.org/, 2012. (checked: January, 2021).

[2] claustromaniac. HTTPZ. https://github.com/claustromaniac/httpz, 2020. (checked: January, 2021).

[3] K. Drakonakis, S. Ioannidis, and J. Polakis. The cookie hunter: Automated black-box auditing for web authentication and authorization flaws. In *Proceedings of the Conference on Computer and Communications Security*, 2020.

[4] EFF. HTTPS:// Everywhere. https://www.eff.org/https-everywhere, 2014. (checked: January, 2021).

[5] S. Englehardt, D. Reisman, C. Eubank, P. Zimmerman, J. Mayer, A. Narayanan, and E. W. Felten. Cookies that give you away: The surveillance implications of web tracking. In *Proceedings of the International Conference on World Wide Web*, 2015.

[6] A. P. Felt, R. Barnes, A. King, C. Palmer, C. Bentzel, and P. Tabriz. Measuring HTTPS Adoption on the Web. In *USENIX Security Symposium*, 2017.

[7] Google. No More Mixed Messages About HTTPS. https://blog.chromium.org/2019/10/no-more-mixed-messages-about-https.html, 2020. (checked: January, 2021).

[8] IETF. Uniform Resource Locators (URL)). https://tools.ietf.org/html/rfc1738, 1994. (checked: January, 2021).

[9] IETF. The "data" URL scheme. https://tools.ietf.org/html/rfc2397, 1998. (checked: January, 2021).

[10] IETF. Hypertext Transfer Protocol – HTTP/1.1). https://tools.ietf.org/html/rfc2616, 1999. (checked: January, 2021).

[11] IETF. HTTP Over TLS. https://tools.ietf.org/html/rfc2818, 2000. (checked: January, 2021).

[12] IETF. The Web Origin Concept. https://tools.ietf.org/html/rfc6454, 2011. (checked: January, 2021).

[13] IETF. The WebSocket Protocol. https://tools.ietf.org/html/rfc6455, 2011. (checked: January, 2021).

[14] IETF. HTTP Strict Transport Security (HSTS). https://tools.ietf.org/html/rfc6797, 2012. (checked: January, 2021).

[15] ilGur. Smart HTTPS. https://mybrowseraddon.com/smart-https.html, 2020. (checked: January, 2021).

[16] Internet Live Stats. Total number of Websites. http://www.internetlivestats.com/total-number-of-websites/, 2014. (checked: January, 2021).

[17] C. Jackson and A. Barth. Forcehttps: protecting high-security web sites from network attacks. In *Proceedings of the International Conference on World Wide Web*, 2008.

[18] C. Kerschbaumer. Enforcing Content Security by default within Web Browsers. In *Proceedings of Cybersecurity Development Conference*, 2016.

[19] M. Kranch and J. Bonneau. Upgrading https in mid-air: An empirical study of strict transport security and key pinning. In *NDSS*, 2015.

[20] J. Larisch, D. Choffnes, D. Levin, B. M. Maggs, A. Mislove, and C. Wilson. Crlite: A scalable system for pushing all tls revocations to all browsers. In *Symposium on Security and Privacy*, 2017.

[21] Let's Encrypt. Let's Encrypt Stats. https://letsencrypt.org/stats/, 2020. (checked: January, 2021).

[22] Moxie Marlinspike. New Tricks For Defeating SSL In Practice. https://www.blackhat.com/presentations/bh-dc-09/Marlinspike/BlackHat-DC-09-Marlinspike-Defeating-SSL.pdf, 2009. (checked: January, 2021).

[23] Mozilla. Preloading HSTS. https://blog.mozilla.org/security/2012/11/01/preloading-hsts/, 2012. (checked: January, 2021).

[24] Mozilla. Insecure password warning in Firefox. https://support.mozilla.org/en-US/kb/insecure-password-warning-firefox, 2017. (checked: January, 2021).

[25] Mozilla. Mozilla Data Documentation. https://docs.telemetry.mozilla.org/, 2020. (checked: January, 2021).

[26] Mozilla. Telemetry Portal. https://telemetry.mozilla.org/, 2020. (checked: January, 2021).

[27] M. T. Paracha, B. Chandrasekaran, D. R. Choffnes, and D. Levin. A Deeper Look at Web Content Availability and Consistency over HTTP/S. 2020.

[28] Paul Syverson and Matthew Traudt. HSTS supports targeted surveillance. In *USENIX Security Symposium*, 2018.

[29] B. Santesson, M. Myers, R. Ankney, A. Malpani, S. Galperin, and C. Adams. X.509 Internet Public Key Infrastructure - Online Certificate Status Protocol - OCSP. https://tools.ietf.org/html/rfc6960, 2013. (checked: January, 2021).

[30] S. Sivakorn, A. D. Keromytis, and J. Polakis. That's the way the cookie crumbles: Evaluating https enforcing mechanisms. In *Proceedings of the Workshop on Privacy in the Electronic Society*, 2016.

[31] S. Sivakorn, I. Polakis, and A. D. Keromytis. The cracked cookie jar: HTTP cookie hijacking and the exposure of private information. In *Symposium on Security and Privacy*, 2016.

[32] S. Stamm, B. Sterne, and G. Markham. Reining in the Web with Content Security Policy. In *World Wide Web*, 2010.

[33] M. Traudt and P. Syverson. Does Pushing Security on Clients Make Them Safer? https://petsymposium.org/2019/files/hotpets/proposals/pushing-insecurity-hotpets19.pdf, 2019.

[34] W3C. Document Object Model (DOM). http://www.w3.org/TR/2004/REC-DOM-Level-3-Core-20040407/DOM3-Core.pdf, 2004. (checked: January, 2021).

[35] W3C. Cross-Origin Resource Sharing (CORS). http://www.w3.org/TR/cors, 2010. (checked: January, 2021).

[36] W3C. Mixed Content. https://www.w3.org/TR/mixed-content/, 2014. (checked: January, 2021).

[37] W3C. Upgrade Insecure Requests. https://www.w3.org/TR/upgrade-insecure-requests/, 2015. (checked: January, 2021).

[38] W3C. File API - The Blob Interface and Binary Data. https://w3c.github.io/FileAPI/#blob-section, 2020. (checked: January, 2021).

[39] W3C. Mixed Content Level 2. https://w3c.github.io/webappsec-mixed-content/, 2020. (checked: January, 2021).

[40] WHATWG. HTML. https://html.spec.whatwg.org/, 2020. (checked: January, 2021).

[41] WHATWG. XMLHttpRequest - Living Standard. https://xhr.spec.whatwg.org/, 2020. (checked: January, 2021).

CROW: Code Diversification for WebAssembly

Javier Cabrera Arteaga
KTH Royal Institute of Technology
javierca@kth.se

Orestis Floros
KTH Royal Institute of Technology
forestis@kth.se

Oscar Vera Perez
Univ Rennes, Inria, CNRS, IRISA
oscar.vera-perez@inria.fr

Benoit Baudry
KTH Royal Institute of Technology
baudry@kth.se

Martin Monperrus
KTH Royal Institute of Technology
martin.monperrus@csc.kth.se

***Abstract*—The adoption of WebAssembly increases rapidly, as it provides a fast and safe model for program execution in the browser. However, WebAssembly is not exempt from vulnerabilities that can be exploited by malicious observers. Code diversification can mitigate some of these attacks. In this paper, we present the first fully automated workflow for the diversification of WebAssembly binaries. We present CROW, an open-source tool implementing this workflow through enumerative synthesis of diverse code snippets expressed in the LLVM intermediate representation. We evaluate CROW's capabilities on 303 C programs and study its use on a real-life security-sensitive program: libsodium, a modern cryptographic library. Overall, CROW is able to generate diverse variants for 239 out of 303 (79%) small programs. Furthermore, our experiments show that our approach and tool is able to successfully diversify off-the-shelf cryptographic software (libsodium).**

I. Introduction

WebAssembly is the fourth official language of the Web [36]. The language provides low-level constructs enabling efficient execution times, much closer to native code than JavaScript. It constitutes a fast and safe platform to execute programs in the browser and embedded environments [21]. Consequently, the adoption of WebAssembly has been rapidly growing since its introduction in 2015. Nowadays, languages such as Rust and C/C++ can be compiled to WebAssembly using mature toolchains and can be executed in all notable browsers.

The WebAssembly execution model is designed to be secure and to prevent many memory and control flow attacks. Still, as its official documentation admits [11], WebAssembly is not exempt from vulnerabilities that could be exploited [30]. Code diversification [5], [28] is one additional protection that can harden the WebAssembly stack. This consists in synthesizing different variants of an original program that provide the same functionalities but exhibit different execution traces. In this paper, we investigate the feasibility of diversifying WebAssembly code, which is, to the best of our knowledge, an unresearched area.

Our contribution is a workflow and a tool, called CROW, for automatic diversification of WebAssembly programs. It takes as input a C/C++ program and produces a set of diverse WebAssembly binaries as output. The workflow is based on enumerative code synthesis. First, CROW lists blocks that are potentially relevant for diversification, second, CROW enumerates alternative instruction sequences, and third, CROW checks that the new instruction sequences are functionally equivalent to the original block. CROW builds on the idea of superdiversification [25] and extends the concept to the enumeration of a set of variants instead of synthesizing only one solution. We also take into account the specificities of WebAssembly and the details of its execution.

Workshop on Measurements, Attacks, and Defenses for the Web (MADWeb) 2021
25 February 2021, Virtual

https://dx.doi.org/10.14722/madweb.2021.23004
www.ndss-symposium.org

We evaluate the diversification capabilities of CROW in two ways. First, we diversify 303 small C programs compiled to WebAssembly. Second, we run CROW to diversify a real-life cryptographic library that natively supports WebAssembly. In both cases, we measure the diversity among binary code variants, as well as the diversity of execution traces. When measuring the diversity in binary code, we compare the WebAssembly and the machine code variants. This way we assess the ability of CROW at synthesizing variations in WebAssembly, as well as the extent to which these variations are preserved when compiling WebAssembly to machine code. Our original experiments demonstrate the feasibility of diversifying WebAssembly code. CROW generates diverse variants for 239/303 (79%) C programs. TurboFan, the optimizing compiler used in the V8 engine, preserves 99.48% of these variants. CROW successfully synthesizes variants for the cryptographic library. The variants indeed yield either different execution traces. This is promising milestone in getting a more secure Web environment through diversification.

To sum up, our contributions are:

- CROW: the first automated workflow and tool to diversify WebAssembly programs, it generates many diverse WebAssembly binaries from a single input program.
- A quantitative evaluation over 303 programs showing the capability of CROW to diversify WebAssembly binaries and measuring the impact of diversification on execution traces.
- A feasibility study of the diversification on a real-world WebAssembly program, demonstrating that CROW can handle libsodium, a state-of-the-art cryptographic library.

II. Background

A. WebAssembly

WebAssembly is a binary instruction format for a stack-based virtual machine. It is designed to address the problem of safe, fast, portable and compact low-level code on the Web. The language was first publicly announced in 2015 and since then, most major web browsers have implemented support for the standard. Besides the Web, WebAssembly is independent of any specific hardware or languages and can run in a standalone Virtual Machine (VM) or in other environments such as Arduino [20]. A paper by Haas et al. [21] formalizes the language and its type system, and explains the design rationale.

Listing 1 and 2 illustrate WebAssembly. Listing 1 presents the C code of two functions and Listing 2 shows the result of compiling these two functions into a WebAssembly module. The `type` directives at the top of the module declare the function: the types of its parameters and the type of the result. Then, the definitions for the function follow. These definitions are sequences of stack machine instructions. At the end, the `main` function is exported so that it can be called from outside this WebAssembly module, typically from JavaScript. WebAssembly has four primitive types: integers (`i32` and `i64`) and floats (`f32` and `f64`) and it includes structured instructions such as `block`, `loop` and `if`.

Listing 1: C function that calculates the quantity $2x + x$

```
int f(int x) { return 2 * x + x; }

int main(void) { return f(10); }
```

Listing 2: WebAssembly code for Listing 1.

```
(module
  (type (;0;) (func (param i32) (result i32)))
  (type (;1;) (func (result i32)))
  (func (;0;) (type 0) (param i32) (result i32)
    local.get 0
    local.get 0
    i32.const 2
    i32.mul
    i32.add)
  (func (;1;) (type 1) (result i32)
    i32.const 10
    call 0)
  (export "main" (func 1)))
```

WebAssembly is characterized by an extensive security model [11] founded on a sandboxed execution environment that provides protection against common security issues such as data corruption, code injection and return oriented programming (ROP). However, WebAssembly is no silver bullet and is vulnerable under certain conditions [30]. This motivates our work on software diversification as one possible mitigation among the wide range of security counter-measures.

B. Motivation for Moving Target Defense in the Web

The distribution model for web computing is as follows: build one binary and distribute millions of copies, all over the world, which run on browsers. In this model an attacker has two key advantages over the developers: she has a runtime environment that she fully controls and observes in any possible way. Consequently, when she finds a flaw in this virtually transparent environment, knowing that this flaw is present in the millions of copies that have been distributed over the world, she can exploit the flaw at scale.

The developers can never assume that they can control the web browser. Yet, they can challenge the second advantage of the attacker, known as the break-once-break-everywhere advantage. The developers can stop distributing clones of the binary and distribute diverse versions instead, as suggested by the pioneering software diversification works of Cohen [12] and Forrest et al. [19].

In the context of diversification, moving target defense [40] means distributing diverse variants constantly. In the context of the web, it means distributing a different variant at each HTTP request. Moving target defense is appropriate for mitigating yet unknown vulnerabilities. The diversification technique does not always remove the potential flaws, yet the vulnerabilities in the diversified binaries can be located in different places. With moving target defense, a successful attack on one browser cannot be performed on another browser with the same effectiveness. The diversified binaries that CROW outputs can be used interchangeably over the network, in a moving target defence choreographed over the web.

To sum up, by combining moving target defense deployment to diversification, we reduce the information asymmetry between the Web attacker and the defender, increasing the uncertainty and complexity of successful attacks over all client browsers [16], [42].

III. CROW's Diversification Technique

In this section we describe the workflow of CROW for diversifying WebAssembly programs. First we introduce the main concepts behind CROW. Then, we describe each stage of the workflow and we discuss the key implementation details.

A. Definitions

In this subsection we define the key concepts for CROW.

Definition 1: Block (based on Aho et al. [2]): Let P be a program. A block B is a grouping of declarations and statements in P inside a function F.

Definition 2: Program state (based on Mangpo et al. [35]): At any point in time, the program state S is defined as the collection of local and global variables, and, the program counter pointing to the next instruction.

Definition 3: Pure block: A block B is said to be pure if and only if, given the program state S_i, every execution of B produces the same state S_o.

Definition 4: Functional equivalence modulo program state (based on Le et al. [29]): Let B_1 and B_2 be two blocks. We consider the program state before the execution of the block, S_i, as the input and the program state after the execution of the block, S_o, as the output. B_1 and B_2 are functionally equivalent if given the same input S_i both codes produce the same output S_o.

Definition 5: Code replacement: Let P be a program and T a pair of blocks (B_1, B_2). T is a candidate code replacement if B_1 and B_2 are both pure as defined in Definition 3 and functionally equivalent as defined in Definition 4. Applying T to P means replacing B_1 by B_2. The application of T to P produces a program variant P' which consequently is functionally equivalent to P.

CROW generates new program variants by finding and applying code replacements as defined in Definition 5. A program variant could be produced by applying more than one candidate code replacement. For example, the tuple, composed by the code blocks in Listing 3 and Listing 4, is a code replacement for Listing 2.

Listing 3: WebAssembly pure code block from Listing 2.

```
local.get 0
i32.const 2
i32.mul ; 2 * x ;
```

Listing 4: Code block that is functionally equivalent to Listing 3

```
local.get 0
i32.const 1
i32.shl ; x << 1 ;
```

B. Overview

CROW synthesizes variants for WebAssembly programs. We assume that the programs are generated through the LLVM compilation pipeline. This assumption is motivated as follows: first, LLVM-based compilers are the most popular compilers to build WebAssembly programs [30]; second, the availability of source code (typically C/C++ for WebAssembly) provides a structure to perform code analysis and produce code replacements that is richer than the binary code.

CROW takes as input a C/C++ program and produces a set of unique, diversified WebAssembly binaries. Figure 1 shows the stages of this workflow. The workflow starts with compiling the input program into LLVM bitcode using clang. Then, CROW analyzes the bitcode to identify all pure blocks and to synthesize a set of candidate replacements for each pure block. This is what we call the *exploration* stage. In the *generation* stage, CROW combines the candidate code replacements to generate different LLVM bitcode variants. Finally, those bitcode variants are compiled to WebAssembly binaries that can be sent to web browsers.

Challenges. The concept of diversifying WebAssembly programs is novel and it is arguably hard for the following reasons. First, WebAssembly is a structured binary format, without goto-like instructions. This prevents the direct application of a wide range of diversification operators based on goto [41]. Second, the existing transformation and diversification tools target instruction sets larger than the one of WebAssembly [39]. This limits the efficiency of diversification, and the possibility of searching for a large number of equivalent code replacements. We address the former challenge using the LLVM intermediate representation as the target for diversification. We address the latter challenge by tailoring a superoptimizer for LLVM, using its subset of the LLVM intermediate representation. In particular, we prevent the superoptimizer from synthesizing instructions that have no correspondence in WebAssembly (for example, `freeze` instructions), which is an essential step to get executable diversified WebAssembly code.

C. Exploration stage

Given a program P for which we want to generate WebAssembly variants, the exploration stage of CROW identifies all pure blocks in the LLVM bitcode of P. CROW considers every directed acyclic graph contained in one function as a pure block. Then, CROW searches for code replacements for each one of them.

The generation of a code replacement consists of two steps. First, the synthesis of the new block, and, second, equivalence checking. Every variant block that passes the equivalence check is stored for use in diversification. The synthesis of block variants consists of enumerating all possible blocks that can be built as a combination of a given number of instructions, bounded by a maximum value to keep a tractable synthesis space.

There are two parameters to control the size of the search space and hence the time required to traverse it. On one hand, one can limit the size of the variants. In our experiments we limit the block variants to a maximum of 50 instructions. On the other hand, one can limit the set of instructions that are used for the synthesis. In our experiments, we use between 1 instruction (only additions) and 60 instructions (all supported instructions in the synthesizer). This configuration allows the user to find a trade-off between the amount of variants that are synthesized and the time taken to produce them.

Listing 5: Listing 1 in LLVM's intermediate representation.

```
define i32 @f(i32) {
 %2 = mul nsw i32 %0,2
 %3 = add nsw i32 %0,%2

 ret i32 %3
}

define i32 @main() {
 %1 = tail call i32 @f(i32 10)
 ret i32 %1
}
```

Block A

```
%2 = mul nsw i32 %0,2
```

Block B

```
%2 = mul nsw i32 %0,2
%3 = add nsw i32 %0,%2
```

In Listing 5 we illustrate the LLVM bitcode representation of Listing 1. In this bitcode, CROW identifies two pure blocks in function `f()`, which are displayed on the right part of the listing, in gray and green. The first pure block is composed of one single instruction (line 2) that performs the `2*x` multiplication. The second block has two instructions, one multiplication and one addition.

Using CROW, it is possible to diversify both blocks. For example, using a maximum of 1 instruction per replacement and searching over the complete bitcode instruction set, a potential replacement for Block A is: `%2 = shl nsw i32 %0,1 %`. This replacement calculates the same expression `2*x`, using a shift left operation.

To determine the equivalence between a pure block and a candidate replacement, we use an equivalence checker based on SMT [17]. In our example, the checker would prove that there cannot be a value of x such that $2 * x \neq x \ll 1$. In general, if no such counter-example exists, then the functional equivalence is assumed. On the other hand, if there exists an input resulting in different outputs for a block and a variant, then they are proven not equivalent and the variant is discarded.

D. Generation stage

In this stage, we select and combine code replacements that have been synthesized during the exploration stage, in order to generate WebAssembly binary variants. We apply each code replacement to the original program to produce a LLVM IR variant. Then, this IR is compiled into a WebAssembly binary. CROW generates WebAssembly binaries from all possible combinations of code replacements as the power set over all code replacements.

After the exploration phase, it is possible that two subsets of code replacements overlap, *i.e.*, they produce the same WebAssembly binary. The overlap between blocks is explained as follows: Let $S = \{(B_1, R_1), (B_1, R_2), \cdots, (B_n, R_m)\}$ be a set of candidate replacements over a program P. If two blocks from the original program B_i, B_j, $j \neq i$, overlap, *i.e.*, the intersection of CFG(B_i)[1] and CFG(B_j) is not empty,

[1]CFG(A) refers to backward Control Flow Graph starting at inst. A.

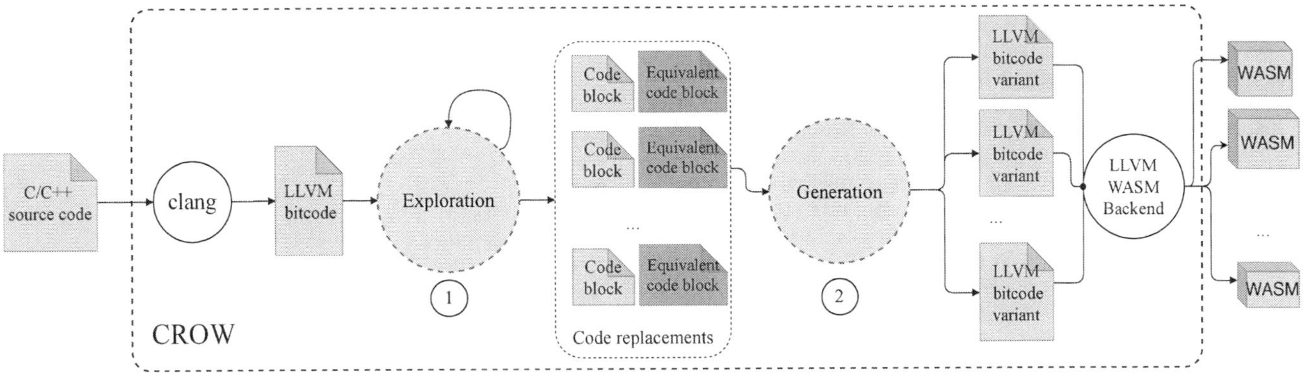

Fig. 1: CROW's workflow for diversifying WebAssembly programs.

then only the replacements of the largest original block are preserved when combining blocks.

In this example, the exploration stage synthesizes $6 + 1$ bitcode variants for the considered blocks respectively, which results in 14 module variants (the power set combination size). Yet, the generation stage would eventually generate 7 variants from the original WebAssembly binary. This gap between the number of potential and the actual number of variants is a consequence of the redundancy among the bitcode variants when composing several variants into one.

E. *Implementation*

The majority of the WebAssembly applications are built from C/C++ source code using the LLVM toolchain. Consequently, the implementation of CROW is based on LVVM/ Furthermore, CROW extends Souper [38], a superoptimizer for LLVM that aims to reduce the size of binary code. Souper has its own intermediate representation, which is a subset of the LLVM IR.

To extract code blocks, we scan LLVM modules, looking for instructions that return integer-typed values. Each such instruction is considered as the exit of a code block. Souper's representation of a code block is built as a backward traversal process through the dependencies of the detected instruction. If memory loads or function calls are found, the backward traversal process is stopped and the current instruction is considered as an input variable for the code block. Notice that, by construction, Souper's translation is oblivious to the memory model, thus, it cannot infer string data types or other abstract data types. The translation from Souper IR to a BitVector SMT theory is done on the fly. Souper uses the z3[2] solver to check the equivalence between a code block original and a potential replacement for it.

We now summarize the main changes that we implement in Souper and in the LLVM backend in order to support diversification. Souper, as a superoptimizer, aims at generating a single variant that is smaller than the original, yet we want to obtain as many blocks as possible. To achieve automatic diversification, we modify Souper to disable the key cost restriction functions, data-flow pruning and peephole optimizations, all being detrimental for diversification. In order to increase the number of variants that CROW can generate, CROW parallelizes the process of replacement synthesis.

[2]https://github.com/Z3Prover/z3

In addition, CROW orchestrates a series of Souper executions with various configurations (in particular the size of the replaced expression). Finally, we carefully fine-tune a set of 19 Souper options to ensure that the search is effective for diversification in feasible time.

In the generation stage of CROW, we also modify Souper to amplify the generation of WebAssembly binary diversity. Initially, Souper generates a single bitcode variant, inserting all replacements at once. We modify it so that we can obtain a combination of code replacements. Finally, on the LLVM side, we disable all peephole optimizations in the WebAssembly backend, in particular instructions merging and constant folding. This aims to preserve the variations introduced in the LLVM bitcode during the generation of binaries.

The implementation of CROW is publicly available for sake of open science and can be reviewed at https://github.com/KTH/slumps/tree/master/crow.

IV. Evaluation Protocol

To evaluate the capabilities of CROW to diversify WebAssembly programs, we formulate the following research questions:

RQ1: **To what extent are the program variants generated by CROW statically different?** We check whether the WebAssembly binary variants produced by CROW are different from the original WebAssembly binary. Then, we assess whether the generation of x86 machine code performed by V8's WebAssembly engine preserves CROW's transformations.

RQ2: **To what extent are the program variants generated by CROW dynamically different?** It is known that not all diversified programs produce distinguishable executions [15], sometimes it is impossible to observe different behaviors between variants. We check for the presence of different behaviors with a custom WebAssembly interpreter, characterizing the behavior of a WebAssembly program by its stack operation trace.

RQ3: **To what extent can CROW be applied to diversify real-world security-sensitive software?** We assess the ability of CROW to diversify a state-of-the-art cryptographic library for WebAssembly, libsodium [18].

A. *Corpus*

We answer RQ1 and RQ2 with a corpus of programs appropriate for our experiments. We take programs from the Rosetta

Code project[3]. This website hosts a curated set of solutions for specific programming tasks in various programming languages. It contains a wide range of tasks, from simple ones, such as adding two numbers, to complex algorithms like a compiler lexer. We first collect all C programs from Rosetta Code, which represents 989 programs as of 01/26/2020. Next, we apply a number of filters. We discard 1) all programs that do not compile with `clang`, 2) all interactive programs requiring input from users *i.e.,* invoking functions like `scanf`, 3) all programs that contain more than 100 blocks, 4) all programs without termination, 5) all programs with non-deterministic operations, for example, programs working with time or random functions. This filter produces a final set of 303 programs.

The result is a corpus of 303 C programs. These programs range from 7 to 150 lines of code and solve a variety of problems, from the *Babbage* problem to *Convex Hull* calculation.

B. Protocol for RQ1

With RQ1, we assess the ability of CROW to generate WebAssembly binaries that are different from the original program. For this, we compute a distance metric between the original WebAssembly binary and each binary generated by CROW. Since WebAssembly binaries are further transformed into machine code before they execute, we also check that this additional transformation preserves the difference introduces by CROW in the WebAssembly binary. We use the Turbofan ahead-of-time compiler of V8, with all its possible optimizations, to generate a x86 binary for each WebAssembly binary. Then, we compare the x86 version of each variant against the x86 binary corresponding to the original WebAssembly binary.

We compare the WebAssembly and machine code of each program and its variant using Dynamic Time Warping (DTW) [31]. DTW computes the global alignment between two sequences. It returns a value capturing the cost of this alignment, which is actually a distance metric, called DTW. The larger the DTW distance, the more different the two sequences are. In our case, we compare the sequence of instructions of each variant with the initial program and the other variants. We obtain two DTW distance values for each program-variant pair: one at the level of WebAssembly code and the another one at the level of x86 code. Metric 1 below defines these metrics.

Metric 1: dt_static: Given two programs P_X and V_X written in X code, $dt\_static(P_X, V_X)$, computes the DTW distance between the corresponding program instructions for representation X ($X \in \{Wasm, x86\}$). A $dt\_static(P_X, V_X)$ of 0 means that the code of both the original program and the variant is the same, i.e., they are statically identical in the representation X. The higher the value of dt_static, the more different the programs are in representation X.

We run CROW on our corpus of 303 programs. We configure CROW to run with a diversification timeout of 6 hours per program. For each program, we collect the set of generated variants. For all pairs program, variant that are different, we compute both dt_static for WebAssembly and x86 representations.

The key property we consider is as follows: if $dt\_static(P_{Wasm}, P'_{Wasm}) > 0$ and $dt\_static(P_{x86}, P'_{x86}) > 0$, this means that both programs are still different when compiled to machine code, and we conclude that V8's compiler does not remove the transformations made by CROW. Notice that, this property only makes sense between variants of the same program (including the original).

C. Protocol for RQ2

For RQ2, we compare the executions of a program and its variants for a given input. In this experiment, we characterize the execution of a WebAssembly binary according to its trace of stack operations.

This method of tracing allows us to evaluate CROW's effect on program execution according to the WebAssembly specification, independently of any specific engine.

For each execution of a WebAssembly program, we collect a trace of stack operations. These traces are composed of stack-type instructions: `push <value>` and `pop <value>`. All traces are ordered with respect to the timestamp of the events. We compare the traces of the original program against those of the variants with DTW. DTW computes the global alignment between two traces and provides a value for the cost of this alignment.

Metric 2: dt_dyn: Given a program P and a CROW generated variant P', dt_dyn(P,P'), computes the DTW distance between the corresponding stack operation traces collected during their execution. A dt_dyn of 0 means that both traces are identical. The higher the value, the more different the stack operation traces.

To answer RQ2 we compute Metric 2 for a study subject program and all the unique program variants generated by CROW in a pairwise comparison. The pairwise comparison allows us to compare the diversity between variants as well. We use SWAM[4] to collect the stack operation traces. SWAM is a WebAssembly interpreter that provides functionalities to capture the dynamic information of WebAssembly program executions including the stack operations. We compute the DTW distances with STRAC [10].

The builtin WebAssembly API for JavaScript is usually mutable, thus, the same model for traces collection can be implemented on top of V8. In other words, a custom interpreter can be implemented in order to collect the traces in the browser or standalone JavaScript engines. This validates the usage of SWAM to study the traces diversity.

D. Protocol for RQ3

In RQ3, we assess the ability of CROW to diversify a mature and complex software library related to security. We choose the libsodium [18] cryptographic library, which natively compiles to WebAssembly. With 3752 commits contributed by 96 developers, its API provides the basic blocks for encryption, decryption, signatures and password hashing. We experiment with code revision 2b5f8f2b, which contains 45232 lines of C code. Libsodium has 102 separate WebAssembly modules that we use as input for CROW. Each module corresponds to one C file that encompasses a set of related functions.

To answer RQ3, we run CROW on the libsodium bitcodes, generating a set of WebAssembly variants. Then, we assess both binary code diversity and behavioural diversity between the variants and the original libsodium, using the same techniques as in RQ1 and RQ2.

[3]http://www.rosettacode.org/wiki/Rosetta_Code

[4]https://github.com/satabin/swam

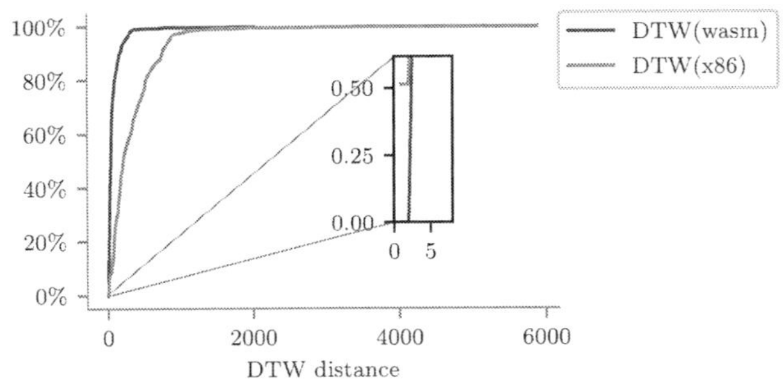

Fig. 2: Cumulative distribution for all pairwise comparisons between a program and its variants. Each line corresponds to a different program representation.

Collecting traces The libsodium repository includes an extensive test suite of 77 tests, where one test is one usage scenario. We use this test suite to measure the trace diversity among program variants. Since some test traces are larger than 1 GB each, we focus on reasonably sized tests: we select the $41/77$ test cases that produce a trace containing less than 50 million events each.

To measure the relative trace diversification for each test, we normalize the *dt_dyn* used in RQ2 by dividing it with the length of the original trace. This allows us to compare the relative success of CROW's diversification technique across different tests.

Since libsodium uses a pseudo-number generator, we set a static seed when executing libsodium, so that the diversity observed in traces is only due to CROW's diversification. In WebAssembly, libsodium generates random numbers using the ChaCha20 [8] cipher through the `arc4random` API. To quantify the effectiveness of our diversification technique, we compare the trace distance produced by our technique with the trace distance that occurs when the seed is changed (baseline).

V. Experimental Results

In this section we present the results for the research questions formulated in section IV.

A. To what extent are the program variants generated by CROW statically different?

We run CROW on 303 C programs compiled to WebAssembly. CROW produces at least one unique program variant for $239/303$ programs. For the rest of the programs ($64/303$), the timeout is reached before CROW can find any valid variant.

We subsequently perform a manual analysis of the programs that yield more than 100 unique WebAssembly variants. This reveals one key reason that favors a large number of unique WebAssembly variants: the programs include bounded loops. In these cases CROW synthesizes variants for the loops by unrolling them. Every time a loop is unrolled, the loop body is copied and moved as part of the outer scope of the loop. This creates a new, statically different, program. The number of programs grows exponentially with nested loops.

A second key factor for the synthesis of many variants relates to the presence of arithmetic. Souper, the synthesis engine used by CROW, is effective in replacing arithmetic instructions by equivalent instructions that lead to the same result. For example, CROW generates unique variants by replacing multiplications with additions or shift left instructions (Listing 8). Also, logical comparisons are replaced, inverting the operation and the operands (Listing 9).

Listing 8: Diversification through arithmetic expression replacement.

```
local.get 0      local.get 0
i32.const 2      i32.const 1
i32.mul          i32.shl
```

Listing 9: Diversification through inversion of comparison operations.

```
local.get 0      i32.const 11
i32.const 10     local.get 0
i32.gt_s         i32.le_s
```

Listing 10: Excerpt of WebAssembly program p74: CROW replaces a loop by a constant.

```
local.set 1
loop ;; label = @1                local.get 0
  ...                             i32.const 25264
end
...
i32.store                         i32.store
```

We now discuss the prevalence of the transformations made by CROW when the WebAssembly binaries are transformed to machine code, specifically with the V8's engine. In Figure 2 we plot the cumulative distribution of *dt_static*, comparing WebAssembly binaries (in blue) and x86 binaries (in orange). The figure plots a total of 103003 *dt_static* values for each representation, two values for each variant pair comparison (including original) for the 239 program. The value on the y-axis shows which percentage of the total comparisons lie below the corresponding *dt_static* value on the x-axis. Since we measure the distances between original programs and WebAssembly variants, then 100% of these binaries have *dt_static* > 0. Let us consider the x86 variants: *dt_static* is strictly positive for 99.48% of variants. In all these cases, the V8 compilation phase does not undo the CROW diversification transformations. Also, we see that there is a gap between both distributions, the main reason is the natural inflation of machine code. For example, two variants that differ by one single instruction in WebAssembly, can be translated to machine code where the difference is increased by more than one machine code instruction.

The zoomed subplot focuses on the beginning of the distribution, it shows that the *dt_static* is zero for 0.52% of the x86 binaries. In these cases the V8 TurboFan compiler from WebAssembly to x86 reverts the CROW transformations. We find that CROW produces at least one of these reversible transformations for $34/239$ programs. Listing 11 shows one of the most common transformations that is reversed by TurboFan, according to our experiments.

Listing 11: Replacement in WebAssembly that is translated to the same x86 code by V8-TurboFan.

```
i32.const -<n>        i32.const <n>
i32.sub               i32.add
```

We look at the cases that yield a small number of variants. There is no direct correlation between the number of identified blocks and the number of unique variants. We manually analyze programs that include a significant number of pure blocks, for which CROW generates few variants. We identify two main challenges for diversification.

1) Constant computation We have observed that Souper searches for a constant replacement for more than 45% of the blocks of each program while constant values cannot be inferred. For instance, constant values cannot be inferred for memory load operations because CROW is oblivious to a memory model.

2) Combination computation The overlap between code replacements, discussed in subsection III-D, is a second factor that limits the number of unique variants. CROW can generate a high number of variants, but not all replacement combinations are necessarily unique.

Regarding the potential size overhead of the generated variants, we have compared the WebAssembly binary size of the 239 programs with their variants. The ratio of size change between the original program and the variants ranges from 82% (variants are smaller) to 125% (variants are larger) for all Rosetta programs. This limited impact on the binary size of the variants is good news because they are meant to be distributed to browsers over the network.

Answer to RQ1

CROW is able to generate diverse variants of WebAssembly programs for 239/303 (79%) programs in our corpus. We observe that programs that include bounded loops and arithmetic expressions are highly prone to diversification. V8's TurboFan compilation to x86 code preserves 99.48% of the transformations performed by CROW. To our knowledge, this is the first ever realization of automated diversification for WebAssembly.

B. To what extent are the program variants generated by CROW dynamically different?

Now, we focus on the 41 programs that have at least 9 unique WebAssembly variants in order to study the diversity of execution traces. We apply the protocol described in subsection IV-C by executing the WebAssembly programs and their unique variants in order to collect the stack operation traces. Then, we compare the traces of each pair of original program and a variant. We run 1906 program executions and we perform 98774 trace pair comparisons.

Table I summarizes the observed trace diversity, as captured by dt_dyn (Metric 2), among each program and their variants. The table is structured as follows: the first, second and third columns contain the program id, the number of unique variants and the overall sum of all blocks replacements respectively. The table summarizes the distribution of distances between stack operation trace pairs: the minimum value, the maximum value, the median value, the percentage of values equal to zero and the percentage of values greater than zero. The programs are sorted with respect to the number of unique variants. The green highlight color in $>0\%$ columns represents more than 50% of non-zero comparisons, *i.e.,* high diversification. For instance, the first row shows the trace diversity for `p96`, where 99.70% of the pairwise comparisons between all collected traces have a different dt_dyn.

Listing 12: Statically different WebAssembly replacements with the same behavior, gray for the original code, green for the replacement.

```
(1) i32.lt_u  i32.lt_s      (3) i32.ne         i32.lt_u
(2) i32.le_s  i32.lt_u      (4) local.get 6    local.get 4
```

For the stack operation traces, all programs have at least one variant that produces a trace different from the original. All but one (`p81`) programs have the majority of variants producing a different stack operation trace. This shows the real effectiveness of CROW for diversifying stack operation traces.

We manually analyze variants with high and low trace diversity. We observe that constant inferring is effective at changing the stack operation trace. For instance, for program `p74` shown in Listing 10, CROW removes a loop by replacing it with a constant assignment. The execution of this variant produces traces that are different because the loop pattern is not visible anymore in the trace, and consequently, the distance between the original and the variant traces is large.

We note that there is no relation between the trace distance and the number of block replacements. A high trace distance does not necessarily imply a high number of replacements. For instance, program `p135` has only 4 possible replacements overall its 5 identified blocks yet a median dt_dyn of 20163.

We subsequently analyze the cases where diversification is not reflected in stack operation traces. For example, more than 40% of the pairwise dt_dyn distances for `p166`, `p91` and `p81` are equal to zero. This indicates a lower diversity among the population of variants, than for all the other programs. This happens because some variants have two different bitcode instructions (original and replacement) that trigger the same stack operations. The instructions in Listing 12 are concrete cases of such kind of replacements. The four cases in Listing 12 leave the same value in the stack operation trace. For each case, the original instruction and the replacement are semantically equal in the program domain. The fourth case is a local variable index reallocation, this replacement only changes the index of the local variable but not the event in the stack operation trace. These replacements are sound, produce statically diverse code, but they are not useful to dynamically diversify the original program. This confirms the complementary of using static and dynamic metrics to assess diversification.

The effectiveness of CROW on diversifying stack operation traces is significant. In a security context, such diverse stack operation traces are likely to mitigate potential side-channel attacks [30]. Notably, the attacks based on code profiling are affected when the executed opcodes and the corresponding profiles are different [37].

Answer to RQ2

CROW is successful at generating diverse WebAssembly variant programs, for which we are able to observe different stack operation traces. In other words, CROW generates dynamically different binaries, and ensures that variants of a given program yield different stack operation traces.

	NAME	#var	Σ	Min	Max	Median	0 %	> 0 %
1	**p96**	220	15	0	24062	820	0.30	99.70
2	p56	192	36	0	45420	1416	1.84	98.16
3	p78	159	35	0	20501	759	1.52	98.48
4	p111	144	45	0	2114	520	3.74	96.26
5	**p166**	101	152	0	44538	66	45.80	54.20
6	p122	91	34	0	46026	6434	0.24	99.76
7	p67	89	77	0	94036	85692	0.29	99.71
8	p68	85	10	0	10554	260	3.64	96.36
9	p80	78	9	0	17238	618	3.92	96.08
10	p204	77	42	0	36428	3356	0.33	99.67
11	p183	76	9	0	90628	84402	0.57	99.43
12	p136	62	70	0	62953	58028	0.60	99.40
13	p167	46	232	8	888	724	0.00	100.00
14	p226	42	13	0	90736	74476	8.26	91.74
15	p99	38	74	16	9936	5037	0.00	100.00
16	p18	36	7	0	15620	145	1.10	98.90
17	**p140**	29	17	0	13280	172	6.59	93.41
18	p59	27	6	0	85390	40	1.43	98.57
19	p199	21	87	0	27482	728	4.68	95.32
20	**p91**	21	21	0	50002	228	43.81	56.19
21	p223	21	115	16	40911	632	0.00	100.00
22	p168	20	6	0	22200	18896	2.20	97.80
23	p174	18	40	6	6566	6395	0.00	100.00
24	**p81**	17	86	0	4419	0	84.62	15.38
25	p141	17	6	8	2894	132	0.00	100.00
26	p108	16	6	0	85168	79903	8.97	91.03
27	p98	15	4	0	33	25	6.06	93.94
28	p89	14	45	10	15952	89	0.00	100.00
29	p36	14	52	312	33266	30298	0.00	100.00
30	**p135**	13	5	0	20288	20163	3.57	96.43
31	p161	12	91	240	9792	1056	0.00	100.00
32	p147	12	32	0	54071	21274	7.14	92.86
33	p11	10	38	29798	51846	35119	0.00	100.00
34	p125	10	51	0	4399	4368	7.14	92.86
35	p131	9	4	140	1454	685	0.00	100.00
36	p69	9	48	28	29243	28956	0.00	100.00
37	p134	9	20	4	514	186	0.00	100.00
38	**p74**	9	19	126	8332	6727	0.00	100.00
39	p79	9	97	4	29	16	0.00	100.00
40	p33	9	52	4	2342	15	0.00	100.00
41	p157	9	64	36	242	166	0.00	100.00

TABLE I: Dynamic diversity for 41 diversified WASM programs. The dynamic diversity is captured by dt_dyn between traces. The rows are sorted by the number of unique variants per program. The table is structured as follows: the first, second and third columns contain the program id, the number of unique variants and the overall sum of all blocks replacements respectively. Following, the stats for the dt_dyn metric. The colorized cells in the $> 0\%$ column represent high diversification.

C. To what extent can CROW be applied to diversify real-world security-sensitive software?

We run CROW on each of the 102 modules of libsodium with a 6-hour timeout. We find $45/102$ modules that do not contain any pure block, so they are not amenable to our diversification technique. CROW produces at least one valid WebAssembly module variant for 15 of the remaining 57 modules.

Table II presents the key results for these 15 successfully diversified modules. The first two columns contain the name and description of the diversified module, and, the number of unique static variants. The other columns show the total number of functions inside the module, the names of the diversified functions and the number of calls to each function in the considered tests.

Generation of WebAssembly library variants from WebAssembly module variants. The successfully diversified modules can be combined to obtain a large pool of different versions of the packaged libsodium WebAssembly library. The Cartesian product of all module variants produces in theory 1.66E+15 unique libsodium variants. Yet, it is unpractical to store and execute this large number of variants. Thus, we sample the pool of possible variants to evaluate our generated variants. First, for each of the 256 modules, we rank each module variant with respect to the number of lines changed in the final WebAssembly textual format. Then, to produce the i-th library variant, we combine the i-th variant for each module of libsodium, in order to produce maximally diversified library variants first. If a module has less than i variants, we use the original, non-diversified module. According to Table II, the maximum number of unique variants for a single module is 79 (`codecs` module). Thus, we sample 79 unique libsodium variants, ordered by the amount of diversification (the first variant contains the most changes, and so on). For each variant we execute the complete test suite to validate its correctness. All test cases successfully pass for all diversified library binaries.

Dynamic evaluation of libsodium variants. We compare the dynamic behaviour of the original libsodium and the 79 library variants. Figure 3 illustrates the distribution of dt_dyn of all collected traces for each libsodium test. The dt_dyn distance is calculated between each diversified trace and the corresponding original trace for the same test. Each horizontal bar gives the distribution of dt_dyn over the 79 diversified libraries per test. The black triangles show the dt_dyn distance between two different executions of the same test with different random seeds. They serve as a baseline to compare the artificial diversity introduced by CROW, against the natural trace diversity that appears because of random number generation.

For $18/19$ tests, we observe that CROW's diversified modules produce a different trace than the original. The wider violin plots that reach the right-hand side of the figure include variants that significantly diversify the test execution. We observe that $4/18$ tests stand out as they include variants with at least 0.8 normalized dt_dyn distance. For $6/18$ tests, there is a medium trace diversity as their dt_dyn distributions lie in the mid/left side of the plot. For the rest $8/18$ tests we observe a significantly smaller dt_dyn distance.

This means that, in the context of this cryptographic library, CROW is able to find variants that have a huge impact on the dynamic stack behaviour of the program. Meanwhile, some other replacements can have only a marginal impact during the operation of the program. One factor that can affect this is the

Module & Description	#var	#func	Diversified Functions	#calls
argon2-core Core functions for the implementation of the Argon2 key derivation (hash) function [9].	17	6	argon2_finalize	0
			argon2_free_instance	0
			argon2_initialize	0
argon2-encoding Functions for encoding and decoding (including salting) Argon2 [9] hash strings.	11	2	argon2_decode_string	0
			argon2_encode_string	0
blake2b-ref Reference implementation for the BLAKE2 [4] hash function.	7	11	blake2b	0
			blake2b_salt_personal	1.46E+04
			blake2b_update	2.04E+04
chacha20_ref Reference implementation of the ChaCha20 stream cipher [6].	7	5	chacha20_encrypt_bytes	3.51E+06
			stream_ietf_ext_ref_xor_ic	7.62E+03
			stream_ref	1.14E+04
			stream_ref_xor_ic	1.14E+05
codecs Implementations of commonly used codecs for conversions between binary formats like Base64 [26].	79	5	sodium_base642bin	0
			sodium_base64_encoded_len	0
			sodium_bin2base64	0
			sodium_bin2hex	2.57E+05
			sodium_hex2bin	0
core_ed25519 Implementation of the Edwards-curve Digital Signature Algorithm [8].	2	19	crypto_core_ed25519_is_valid_point	0
crypto_scrypt-common Utility and low-level API functions for the scrypt key derivation (hash) function [34].	5	5	escrypt_gensalt_r	0
pbkdf2-sha256 Implementation of the Password-Based Key Derivation Function 2 (PBKDF2) [27].	14	1	escrypt_PBKDF2_SHA256	0
pwhash_scryptsalsa208sha256 High-level API for the scrypt key derivation function [34].	8	19	crypto_pwhash_scryptsalsa208sha256	0
pwhash_scryptsalsa208sha256_nosse Same as above, but does not use Streaming SIMD Extensions (SSE).	32	3	escrypt_kdf_nosse	0
			salsa20_8	0
randombytes Pseudorandom number generators.	1	11	randombytes_uniform	5.61E+02
salsa20_ref Contains a reference implementation of the Salsa20 stream cipher [7].	12	2	stream_ref	1.14E+04
			stream_ref_xor_ic	1.14E+05
scalarmult_ristretto255_ref10 Implementation of the Ristretto255 prime order elliptic curve group [22].	29	4	scalarmult_ristretto255	0
			scalarmult_ristretto255_base	0
			scalarmult_ristretto255_scalarbytes	0
stream_chacha20 High-level API for the ChaCha20 stream cipher [8].	2	15	crypto_stream_chacha20	6.65E+02
			crypto_stream_chacha20_ietf	3.19E+03
			crypto_stream_chacha20_ietf_ext	2.66E+03
			crypto_stream_chacha20_ietf_ext_xor_ic	1.68E+02
			crypto_stream_chacha20_ietf_xor	1.68E+02
			crypto_stream_chacha20_ietf_xor_ic	2.32E+03
			crypto_stream_chacha20_xor	0
			crypto_stream_chacha20_xor_ic	1.68E+02
verify Functions used to compare secrets in constant time to avoid timing attacks.	7	6	crypto_verify_16	2.69E+05
			crypto_verify_32	3.40E+03
			crypto_verify_64	0
Total	**256**	**114**	**40 functions**	

TABLE II: Libsodium modules with at least one variant generated by CROW. The columns on the left include the facts about each module. The first column contains the name and the functional description of the modules. The second column, *#var* (highlighted) gives the number of unique variants generated by CROW. The third column, *#func*, lists the total amount of functions in each module. The remaining columns include a list of functions that CROW has successfully diversified and the number of calls per function in the test suite.

"centrality" of the code that is being replaced. Diversified code that is called often, potentially inside loops, will have a greater impact on the stack trace of a program compared to code that is only called, for example, only during the initialization of the program.

When we compare the trace diversity against the diversity due to pseudo-number generation (black triangles in Figure 3), we observe that: for $2/18$ tests CROW trace diversification is always larger than the one due to random number generation, for $11/18$ tests there exist some variants that exhibit larger trace diversification than random number generation and for $5/18$ tests CROW trace diversification is always smaller than the one due to random number generation.

Answer to RQ3

We have successfully applied CROW to libsodium, one of the leading WebAssembly cryptography libraries. We have shown that CROW is able to create statically different variants of this real-world library, all of which being distributable to users. Our original experiments to measure the trace diversity of libsodium have proven that the generated variants exhibit significantly different execution traces compared to the original non-diversified libsodium binary. The take-away of this experiment is that CROW works on complex code.

VI. Threats to Validity

Internal: The timeout in the exploration stage is a determinant factor to generate unique variants. It is required to bound the experimental time. If the timeout is increased, the number of variants and unique variants might increase.

External: The 303 programs in our Rosetta corpus may not reflect the constructs used in the WebAssembly programs in the wild. Yet our experiment on libsodium shows that the results on the Rosetta corpus hold on real code. To increase external

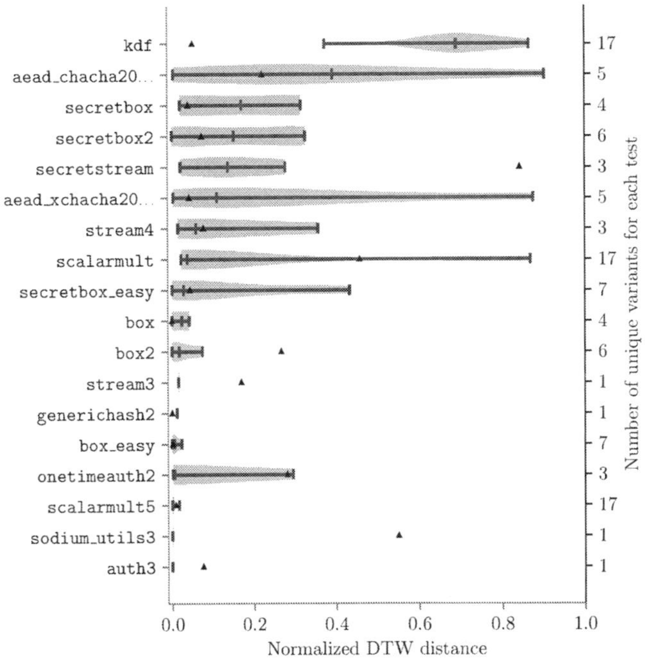

Fig. 3: Distribution of normalized *dt_dyn* distances over the set of libsodium variants covered by each test. The left Y axis lists the name of each test. The number of unique variants used per test is listed on the right Y axis. The black triangles point to the *dt_dyn* distance between two different stack operation traces of the original test with different random seeds.

validity, we hope to see more benchmarks of WebAssembly programs published by the research community.

Scale: We measure behavioral diversity with DTW. We are aware that this behavioral diversity metric does not scale infinitely. To make comparisons between large execution traces, it may be necessary to use a more scalable metric. To mitigate this scale problem in future work, one option is to compare software traces using entropy analysis, as proposed by Miranskyy et al. [33].

VII. Related Work

Program diversification approaches can be applied at different stages of the development pipeline.

Static diversification: This kind of diversification consists in synthesizing, building and distributing different, functionally equivalent, binaries to end users. This aims at increasing the complexity and applicability of an attack against a large population of users [12]. Jackson et al. [24] argue that the compiler can be placed at the heart of the solution for software diversification; they propose the use of multiple semantic-preserving transformations to implement massive-scale software diversity in which each user gets their own diversified variant. Dealing with code-reuse attacks, Homescu et al. [23] propose inserting NOP instruction directly in LLVM IR to generate a variant with different code layout at each compilation. In this area, Coppens et al. [13] use compiler transformations to iteratively diversify software. The aim of their work is to prevent reverse engineering of security patches for attackers targeting vulnerable programs. Their approach, continuously applies a random selection of predefined transformations using a binary diffing tool as feedback. A downside of their method is that attackers are, in theory, able to identify the type of transformations applied and find a way to ignore or reverse them. Our work can be extended to address this issue, providing a synthesizing solution which is more general than specific transformations.

The work closest to ours is that by Jacob et al. [25]. These authors propose the use of a "superdiversification" technique, inspired by superoptimization [32], to synthesize individualized versions of programs. In the work of Massalin, a superoptimizer aims to synthesize the shortest instruction sequence that is equivalent to the original given sequence. On the contrary, the tool developed by Jacob et al. does not output only the shortest instruction sequence, but any sequences that implement the input function. This work focuses on a specific subset of X86 instructions. Meanwhile, our approach works directly with LLVM IR, enabling it to generalize to more languages and CPU architectures. Specifically, we apply our tool on WebAssembly, something not possible with the X86-specific approach of that paper.

Runtime diversification: Previous works have attempted to generate diversified variants that are alternated during execution. It has been shown to drastically increase the number of execution traces that a side-channel attack requires to succeed. Amarilli et al. [3] are the first to propose generation of code variants against side-channel attacks. Agosta et al. [1] and Crane et al. [15] modify the LLVM toolchain to compile multiple functionally equivalent variants to randomize the control flow of software, while Couroussé et al. [14] implement an assembly-like DSL to generate equivalent code at runtime in order to increase protection against side-channel attacks. CROW focuses on static diversification of software. However, because of the specificities of code execution in the browser, this is not far from being a dynamic approach. Since WebAssembly is served at each page refreshment, every time a user asks for a WebAssembly binary, she can be served a different variant provided by CROW.

VIII. Conclusion

Security has been a major driver for the design of WebAssembly. Diversification is one additional protection mechanism that has been not yet realized for it. In this paper, we have presented CROW, the first code diversification approach for WebAssembly. We have shown that CROW is able to generate variants for a large variety of programs, including a real-world cryptographic library. Our original experiments have comprehensively assessed the generated diversity: we have shown that CROW generates diversity both among the binary code variants as well as in the execution traces collected when executing the variants. Also, we have successfully observed diverse execution traces for the considered cryptographic library, which can protect it against a range of side channel attacks.

Future work includes increasing the number of unique variants that are generated, by working on block replacement overlapping detection. Also, the exploration stage and the identification of code replacements is a highly parallelizable process, this would increase diversification performance in order to meet the demands of the internet scale.

Acknowledgement

This work has been partially supported by the WASP program, and by the TrustFull project financed by the Swedish Foundation for Strategic Research. We would like to thank John Regehr, the Souper's team, and the Fastly team for their support.

References

[1] G. Agosta, A. Barenghi, G. Pelosi, and M. Scandale, "The MEET approach: Securing cryptographic embedded software against side channel attacks," *IEEE Transactions on Computer-Aided Design of Integrated Circuits and Systems*, vol. 34, no. 8, pp. 1320–1333, 2015.

[2] A. V. Aho, R. Sethi, and J. D. Ullman, *Compilers: Principles, Techniques, and Tools*. USA: Addison-Wesley Longman Publishing Co., Inc., 1986, ch. 1, pp. 28–31.

[3] A. Amarilli, S. Müller, D. Naccache, D. Page, P. Rauzy, and M. Tunstall, "Can code polymorphism limit information leakage?" in *IFIP International Workshop on Information Security Theory and Practices*. Springer, 2011, pp. 1–21.

[4] J.-P. Aumasson, S. Neves, Z. Wilcox-O'Hearn, and C. Winnerlein, "BLAKE2: simpler, smaller, fast as MD5," in *International Conference on Applied Cryptography and Network Security*. Springer, 2013, pp. 119–135.

[5] B. Baudry and M. Monperrus, "The multiple facets of software diversity: Recent developments in year 2000 and beyond," *ACM Computing Surveys (CSUR)*, vol. 48, no. 1, pp. 1–26, 2015.

[6] D. J. Bernstein, "The ChaCha family of stream ciphers," 2008. [Online]. Available: http://cr.yp.to/chacha.html

[7] ——, "The Salsa20 family of stream ciphers," in *New stream cipher designs*. Springer, 2008, pp. 84–97.

[8] D. J. Bernstein, N. Duif, T. Lange, P. Schwabe, and B.-Y. Yang, "High-speed high-security signatures," *Journal of cryptographic engineering*, vol. 2, no. 2, pp. 77–89, 2012.

[9] A. Biryukov, D. Dinu, and D. Khovratovich, "Argon2: new generation of memory-hard functions for password hashing and other applications," in *2016 IEEE European Symposium on Security and Privacy (EuroS&P)*. IEEE, 2016, pp. 292–302.

[10] J. Cabrera Arteaga, M. Monperrus, and B. Baudry, "Scalable comparison of javascript V8 bytecode traces," in *Proceedings of the 11th ACM SIGPLAN International Workshop on Virtual Machines and Intermediate Languages*. New York, NY, USA: Association for Computing Machinery, 2019, p. 22–31.

[11] D. Chen and W3C group, "WebAssembly documentation: Security," W3C, Accessed: 18 June 2020. [Online]. Available: https://webassembly.org/docs/security/

[12] F. B. Cohen, "Operating system protection through program evolution." *Computers & Security*, vol. 12, no. 6, pp. 565–584, 1993.

[13] B. Coppens, B. De Sutter, and J. Maebe, "Feedback-driven binary code diversification," *ACM Transactions on Architecture and Code Optimization (TACO)*, vol. 9, no. 4, pp. 1–26, 2013.

[14] D. Couroussé, T. Barry, B. Robisson, P. Jaillon, O. Potin, and J.-L. Lanet, "Runtime code polymorphism as a protection against side channel attacks," in *IFIP International Conference on Information Security Theory and Practice*. Springer, 2016, pp. 136–152.

[15] S. Crane, A. Homescu, S. Brunthaler, P. Larsen, and M. Franz, "Thwarting cache side-channel attacks through dynamic software diversity." in *NDSS*, 2015, pp. 8–11.

[16] A. Cui and S. J. Stolfo, "Symbiotes and defensive mutualism: Moving target defense," in *Moving target defense*. Springer, 2011, pp. 99–108.

[17] L. de Moura and N. Bjørner, "Z3: An efficient smt solver," in *Tools and Algorithms for the Construction and Analysis of Systems*, C. R. Ramakrishnan and J. Rehof, Eds. Berlin, Heidelberg: Springer Berlin Heidelberg, 2008, pp. 337–340.

[18] F. Denis, "The Sodium cryptography library," Jun 2013. [Online]. Available: https://download.libsodium.org/doc/

[19] S. Forrest, A. Somayaji, and D. H. Ackley, "Building diverse computer systems," in *Proceedings. The Sixth Workshop on Hot Topics in Operating Systems (Cat. No. 97TB100133)*. IEEE, 1997, pp. 67–72.

[20] R. Gurdeep Singh and C. Scholliers, "WARDuino: A dynamic WebAssembly virtual machine for programming microcontrollers," in *Proceedings of the 16th ACM SIGPLAN International Conference on Managed Programming Languages and Runtimes*, ser. MPLR 2019, 2019, pp. 27–36.

[21] A. Haas, A. Rossberg, D. L. Schuff, B. L. Titzer, M. Holman, D. Gohman, L. Wagner, A. Zakai, and J. Bastien, "Bringing the web up to speed with WebAssembly," in *Proceedings of the 38th ACM SIGPLAN Conference on Programming Language Design and Implementation*, 2017, pp. 185–200.

[22] M. Hamburg, H. de Valance, I. Lovecruft, and T. Arcieri, "The ristretto group," 2017.

[23] A. Homescu, S. Neisius, P. Larsen, S. Brunthaler, and M. Franz, "Profile-guided automated software diversity," in *Proceedings of the 2013 IEEE/ACM International Symposium on Code Generation and Optimization (CGO)*. IEEE, 2013, pp. 1–11.

[24] T. Jackson, B. Salamat, A. Homescu, K. Manivannan, G. Wagner, A. Gal, S. Brunthaler, C. Wimmer, and M. Franz, "Compiler-generated software diversity," in *Moving Target Defense*. Springer, 2011, pp. 77–98.

[25] M. Jacob, M. H. Jakubowski, P. Naldurg, C. W. N. Saw, and R. Venkatesan, "The superdiversifier: Peephole individualization for software protection," in *International Workshop on Security*. Springer, 2008, pp. 100–120.

[26] S. Josefsson, "The Base16, Base32, and Base64 data encodings," Internet Requests for Comments, RFC Editor, RFC 4648, October 2006, http://www.rfc-editor.org/rfc/rfc4648.txt. [Online]. Available: http://www.rfc-editor.org/rfc/rfc4648.txt

[27] B. Kaliski, "PKCS #5: Password-based cryptography specification version 2.0," Internet Requests for Comments, RFC Editor, RFC 2898, September 2000, http://www.rfc-editor.org/rfc/rfc2898.txt. [Online]. Available: http://www.rfc-editor.org/rfc/rfc2898.txt

[28] P. Larsen, A. Homescu, S. Brunthaler, and M. Franz, "Sok: Automated software diversity," in *2014 IEEE Symposium on Security and Privacy*, 2014, pp. 276–291.

[29] V. Le, M. Afshari, and Z. Su, "Compiler validation via equivalence modulo inputs," in *Proceedings of the 35th ACM SIGPLAN Conference on Programming Language Design and Implementation*, ser. PLDI '14, 2014, p. 216–226.

[30] D. Lehmann, J. Kinder, and M. Pradel, "Everything old is new again: Binary security of WebAssembly," in *29th USENIX Security Symposium (USENIX Security 20)*. USENIX Association, Aug. 2020.

[31] M. D. A. Maia, V. Sobreira, K. R. Paixão, R. A. D. Amo, and I. R. Silva, "Using a sequence alignment algorithm to identify specific and common code from execution traces," in *Proceedings of the 4th International Workshop on Program Comprehension through Dynamic Analysis (PCODA*, 2008, pp. 6–10.

[32] H. Massalin, "Superoptimizer— A Look at the Smallest Program," *ACM SIGPLAN Notices*, vol. 22, no. 10, pp. 122–126, 10 1987.

[33] A. V. Miranskyy, M. Davison, R. M. Reesor, and S. S. Murtaza, "Using entropy measures for comparison of software traces," *Information Sciences*, vol. 203, pp. 59–72, oct 2012.

[34] C. Percival, "Stronger key derivation via sequential memory-hard functions," 2009.

[35] P. M. Phothilimthana, A. Thakur, R. Bodik, and D. Dhurjati, "Scaling up superoptimization," *SIGARCH Comput. Archit. News*, vol. 44, no. 2, p. 297–310, Mar. 2016.

[36] A. Rossberg, "WebAssembly Core Specification," W3C, Tech. Rep., Dec. 2019. [Online]. Available: https://www.w3.org/TR/wasm-core-1/

[37] R. Rudd, R. Skowyra, D. Bigelow, V. Dedhia, T. Hobson, S. Crane, C. Liebchen, P. Larsen, L. Davi, M. Franz, A.-R. Sadeghi, and H. Okhravi, "Address oblivious code reuse: On the effectiveness of leakage resilient diversity," in *NDSS*, 2017.

[38] R. Sasnauskas, Y. Chen, P. Collingbourne, J. Ketema, G. Lup, J. Taneja, and J. Regehr, "Souper: A Synthesizing Superoptimizer," *arXiv preprint 1711.04422*, 2017.

[39] J. Seibert, H. Okhravi, and E. Söderström, "Information leaks without memory disclosures: Remote side channel attacks on diversified code," in *Proceedings of the 2014 ACM SIGSAC Conference on Computer and Communications Security*, 2014, pp. 54–65.

[40] M. Taguinod, A. Doupé, Z. Zhao, and G.-J. Ahn, "Toward a moving target defense for web applications," in *2015 IEEE International Conference on Information Reuse and Integration*. IEEE, 2015, pp. 510–517.

[41] C. Wang, J. Davidson, J. Hill, and J. Knight, "Protection of software-based survivability mechanisms," in *Proc. of the Int. Conf. on Dependable Systems and Networks (DSN)*. IEEE, 2001, pp. 193–202.

[42] R. Zhuang, S. A. DeLoach, and X. Ou, "Towards a theory of moving target defense," in *Proceedings of the First ACM Workshop on Moving Target Defense*, 2014, pp. 31–40.

Comparative Analysis of DoT and HTTPS Certificate Ecosystems

Ali Sadeghi Jahromi
Carleton University
alisadeghijahromi@cmail.carleton.ca

AbdelRahman Abdou
Carleton University
abdou@scs.carleton.ca

Abstract—**The Internet's Public Key Infrastructure (PKI) has been used to provide security to HTTPS and other protocols over the Internet. Such infrastructure began to be increasingly relied upon for DNS security. DNS-over-TLS (DoT) is one recent rising and prominent example, whereby DNS traffic between stub and recursive resolver gets transmitted over a TLS-secured session. The security research community has studied and improved security shortcomings in the web certificate ecosystem. DoT's certificates, on the other hand, have not been investigated comprehensively. It is also unclear if DoT client-side tools (*e.g.,* stub resolvers) enforce security properly as modern-day browsers and mail clients do for HTTPS and secure email. In this research, we compare the DoT and HTTPS certificate ecosystems. Preliminary results are so far promising, as they show that DoT appears to have benefited from the PKI security advancements that were mostly tailored to HTTPS.**

I. Introduction

The Domain Name System (DNS) is critical to the Internet; every communication that uses a domain name starts with a name resolution to discover the associated IP address. Due to the lack of security in DNS, a large number of privacy and security problems, such as large-scale monitoring [31], world-wide DNS manipulation, and censorship [22], [8], [36] arose. The proliferation of numerous IoT devices exacerbates these problems; 25 billion IoT devices are expected to be Internet-connected by 2025 [28]. Such devices resolve domain names to communicate with their cloud backends. The lack of privacy in DNS enables intermediate entities, such as Internet Service Providers (ISPs) and other Autonomous Systems (ASes), to identify the type of IoT devices that a user owns [7].

DNS-over-TLS (DoT) was standardized in 2016 to protect DNS messages between the stub- and recursive- resolver from manipulation, eavesdropping, and privacy leaks [42], [12]. When configured with persistent connections, DoT adds negligible overhead to vanilla DNS [27]. Page load times with DoT are faster than other alternatives, *e.g.,* DNS-over-HTTPS (DoH) [23]. DoT has been adopted by large public DNS resolvers such as Cloudflare, Google, and Comcast [15]. Popular platforms, such as Android *"Pie"* and Linux *"Systemd-resolved"*, among others, have implemented DoT stub-resolvers [16]. As a result, DoT queries have increased over the Internet since 2018 [27]. Similar to securing web (HTTPS) and email (S/MIME), DoT in the Internet relies on the Internet's Public Key Infrastructure (PKI) and associated Certification Authorities (CAs) for signing and delivering resolvers' standard X.509 certificates.

On security, we investigate whether DoT would be susceptible to classic (or historic) PKI shortcomings, such as invalid/self-signed certificates, weak cryptographic parameters, or fraudulent certificates issued by compromised CAs. Over time, browsers enhanced HTTPS security by stringent certificate validation and indispensable demand of security features, like the placement of certificates in Certificate Transparency (CT) logs [38], [6]; CAs have accordingly been stepping-up their issuance standards. It is unclear how many of the browser-implemented reinforcements for HTTPS are adopted in DoT, and how the relatively lax security in DoT affects issued certificates. For example, successful authentication [4] and encryption are unnecessary in DoT depending on the client's configured usage profile (see opportunistic mode in RFC 7858 [42]).

We present results upon comparing a random sample of DoT and HTTPS certificates collected from Rapid7 [32]. Particularly, this paper contributes results upon comparing DoT and HTTPS certificates for the following aspects:

- Distribution and characteristics of certificate issuers (Sec. IV).
- Certificate parameters, including validity windows and cipher-suites (Sec. V).
- Proportion and distribution of certificates in CT-logs (Sec. VI).

Our results highlight non-major differences between both ecosystems, including differences in: the dominant CA, certificate validity, and cryptographic properties. The proportion of invalid certificates appears almost similar in both ecosystems, likewise the expiry windows and cryptographic functions. We also found almost equivalent rates of CT-log inclusion in both ecosystems. These results suggest that so far, the deployment and usage of DoT certificates in practice appears promising, and not significantly affected by the lack of strict security checks in sub-resolvers.

Workshop on Measurements, Attacks, and Defenses for the Web (MADWeb) 2021
25 February 2021, Virtual

https://dx.doi.org/10.14722/madweb.2021.23027
www.ndss-symposium.org

II. Related Work

Numerous previous literature analyzed HTTPS certificates. In 2012, Durmuric *et al.* [19] actively collected HTTPS certificates in the wild, and found approximately 12.8% invalid certificates. Chung *et al.* [14] used Rapid7's dataset, plus active collections of certificates, and found that 65% of web certificates were invalid. More recently, Tehrani *et al.* [39] studied the security and HTTPS certificates of alerting authorities in USA and found 15% are not-existing or invalid certificates.

DoT was standardized 16 years after HTTPS. In 2019, Lu *et al.* [27] discovered 1.5K open DoT resolvers over the Internet, and 25% of the used certificates by these resolvers were invalid. Others studied security and overhead of DoT [41], and DoT's resistance to traffic analysis attacks [35], [24].

III. Data Collection and Analysis Methodology

We employ a passive measurement methodology, where we used two certificate datasets gathered by Rapid7's Project Sonar [33] in March 2020: one for HTTPS, the other DoT. Project Sonar actively scans the Internet for different services, similar to Censys [18]. Project sonar scans for a specific service port over the IPv4 address space using Zmap [32]. Further information and protocol metadata are then extracted by communicating with the IP addresses over the open ports, analogous to banner grabs [18]. The gathered data then gets released on the Open Data web page [32].

The DoT and HTTPS datasets that we used were gathered by Rapid7 on the 4th and 23rd of March 2020, respectively. They consist of X.509 certificates and their fingerprints collected from scanning DoT resolvers (port 853) and HTTPS webservers (port 443), respectively [32]. The DoT dataset consists of ~10K certificates, the HTTPS ~9.3M. However, ~54% of the DoT certificates (collected over ports 853) were also found in the HTTP certificate dataset (collected over port 443). The overlapping certificates belonged to less than a quarter of the DoT certificate owners (942 of 4632 unique subjects); these owners apparently chose to use the same certificate for both DoT and HTTPS.

We used the OpenSSL toolkit, `SCTcheck`, and the `Pyopenssl` library to parse and process certificates in both datasets. For certificate validity, we used OpenSSL's *verify* utility. Validating a certificate also involves chain validation [11]. For that, we relied on Mozilla's intermediate CA certificate lists released on April 2020 [29],[1] and the certificate root store of Ubuntu 18.04. OpenSSL's *verify* utility stops validating certificates when the first invalidity reason is encountered. For example, if the certificate is self-signed and expired, the tool would report only one of those two invalidity reasons and quit. As such, for every certificate in our dataset, we had to write our own scripts to list all reasons of invalidity.

Finally, we noticed that many certificates had an IP address placed as a string in the *Subject* and *Issuer* fields. Those were mostly self-signed certificates. We used MaxMind's IP/Country database to geolocate these addresses.[2]

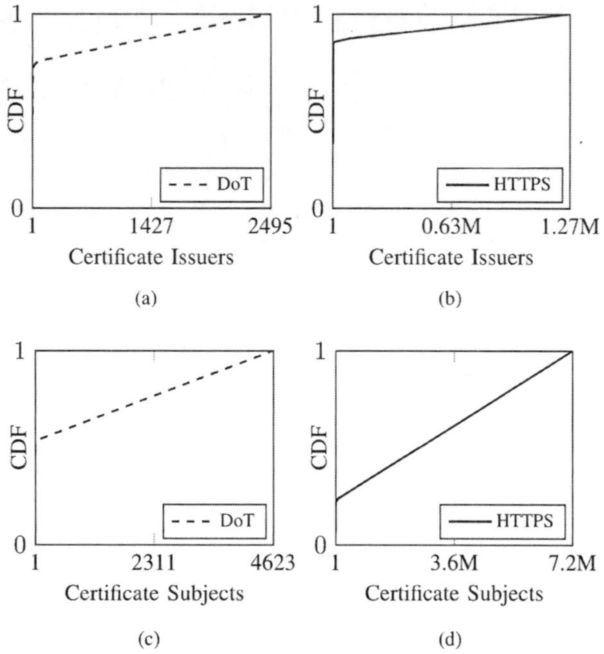

Fig. 1. Distribution of Certificate Issuers and Subjects in DoT and HTTPS.

IV. Certificate Issuers

In this section, we investigate the distribution of certificate issuers and subjects among DoT and HTTPS certificates.

Figures 1(a) and 1(b) show CDFs of certificate issuers. For DoT, 105 of 2495 issuers were responsible for ~76% of DoT certificates. In HTTPS, ~91K of ~1.27M issuers were responsible for 87% of HTTPS certificates. Although many issuers were untrusted, about two-thirds of the certificates in both ecosystems were issued by trusted issuers. The long tails in Figures 1(a) and 1(b) represent issuers that issued very few certificates. The majority of those (> 90% for both ecosystems) were either non-existent issuers or untrusted CAs, and they mostly issued one certificate. Collectively, these have issued < 37% of certificates in both ecosystems.

Figures 1(c) and 1(d) show a CDF of the *Subject* field, which identifies the certificate owner (the entity that owns the public key). Many (~50%) DoT certificates in our dataset are owned by a single entity. This organization is *incapsula.com.* Imperva Incapsula is an American cybersecurity company, which provides cloud-based security solutions to its customers. We assume that as a part of their security solutions, they deployed these DoT resolvers for their clients. The distribution was less skewed in HTTPS, with *Technicolor* network devices owning ~7% of HTTPS certificates in our dataset.

Figure 2 shows the top five DoT issuers and the proportion of HTTPS certificates that they have issued. *GlobalSign* is

[1] The difference between the scanning time and the intermediate certificates release time might lead to a negligible inaccuracy as Mozilla releases the list of intermediate certificates daily [29].

[2] Securely geolocating these addresses [3] is out of the scope of the current paper.

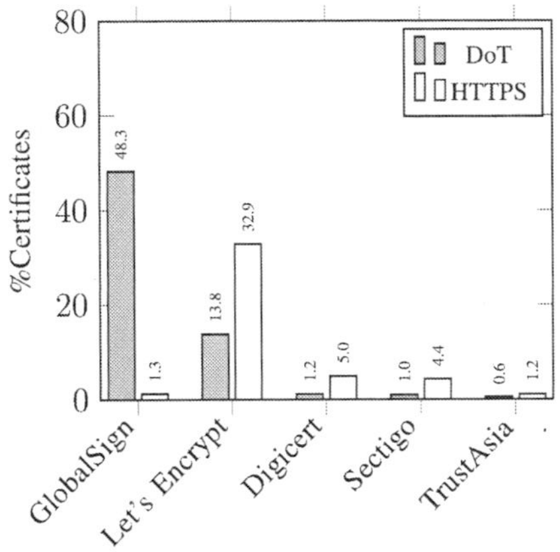

Fig. 2. The proportion of certificates issued by the 5-most popular CAs in DoT, and the proportion of HTTPS certificates issued by these CAs.

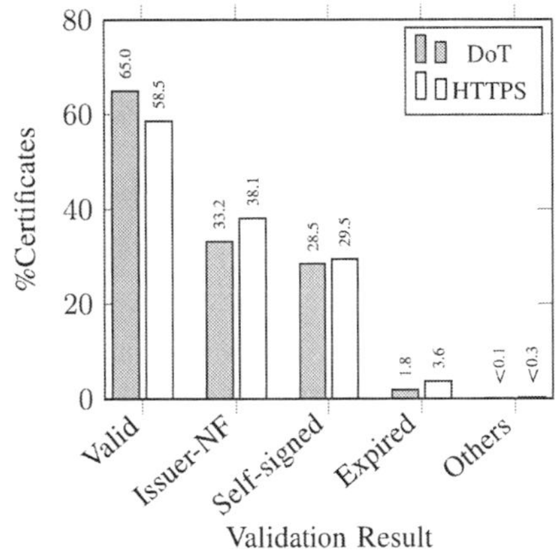

Fig. 3. Proportion of valid and invalid certificates in our datasets, and the reasons of invalidity.

the dominant CA in DoT. However, the majority of the certificates *GlobalSign* has issued belong to a single owner (*incapsula.com*), rather than being distributed amongst many DoT services. The ~10K DoT certificates in our dataset belong to ~4.6K unique owners; the numerous DoT certificates that *GlobalSign* has issued belong to only 31 of the 4.6K owners. In contrast, the 13.8% of DoT certificates issued by *Let's Encrypt* belong to 1348 owners. So *Let's Encrypt* can be considered equally popular in the DoT ecosystem, despite issuing significantly fewer DoT certificates (13.8%). For HTTPS, *Let's Encrypt* remains the dominant certificate issuer, which aligns with previous literature [34], [2], whereas *GlobalSign* has only issued 1.3% of the HTTPS certificates in our dataset.

Summary. *GlobalSign* and *Let's Encrypt* are the two most popular CAs in the DoT ecosystem. The former was founded in 1996 [20], and the latter has established a strong security reputation worldwide. Both CAs employ the Automatic Certificate Management Environment (ACME) protocol [10], which automates certificate renewal. Together they are responsible for almost two-thirds of the DoT certificates in our dataset. Our analysis on certificate issuers, thus, shows no outstanding signs of security concerns in the DoT ecosystem.

V. Certificate Parameters and Characteristics

We now move to certificate parameters, specifically focusing on the characteristics of invalid certificates (Sec. V-C to Sec. V-A), expiry windows (Sec. V-D), and cryptographic properties (Sec. V-E).

Figure 3 shows the proportion of valid and invalid certificates in both ecosystems, with invalid certificates clustered by reasons of invalidity. As a certificate can be invalid for multiple reasons (*e.g.,* expired and has an untrusted issuer), the sum of the proportions exceeds 100% on the vertical axis. As shown, 65% of the DoT certificates in our dataset were valid, compared to 58% for HTTPS. We now analyze and compare the top three invalidity reasons across both ecosystems.

A. *Issuer-not-Found*

The most common invalidity reason is Issuer Not Found *"Issuer-NF"*, meaning the leaf certificate issuer could not be found in the list of trusted (intermediate) issuers or root certificates. The majority of the DoT issuer-NF certificates were issued by *Fortinet* network devices, which also constitute a considerable proportion of issuer-NF certificates in our HTTPS certificate dataset. But the most popular issuer of issuer-NF HTTPS certificates was *Technicolor.* These certificates had long expiry-windows (⩾5 years), which raises further concerns about their security. Chung *et al.* [14] explained that many client-side network devices regularly generate invalid certificates that increase the proportion of invalid certificates in an ecosystem. Overall, issuer-NF certificates in both ecosystems were mostly issued by network devices rather than CAs, and had relatively long expiry windows.

B. *Self-Signed Certificates*

A self-signed certificate is one where the Common Name (CN) field under *Issuer* is the same as the CN field under *Subject.* Self-signed certificates not present in a trust root store expose users to several attacks, including MitM, resolver impersonation, and pharming attacks. From Figure 3, the proportion of self-signed certificates in our data set was almost equal in both ecosystems: 28.5% of DoT certificates and 29.5% of HTTPS.

There were ~2.4K unique issuers responsible for issuing the 2.85K self-signed DoT certificates (the 28.5% in Fig. 3)—no significant dominant of self-signed certificates in DoT. The two most popular CN strings in self-signed DoT certificates were "Server" and "localhost," respectively constituting 8% and 5% of the self-signed DoT certificates. In contrast, ~1M unique issuers have issued the 2.7M self-signed HTTPS certificates (29.5% in Fig. 3), suggesting that the distribution of issuers among self-signed HTTPS certificates is more skewed than in DoT. The most popular two self-signed HTTPS certificate issuers were "Vigor Router" (5%) and "192.168.1.1" (4%).

Of the self-signed certificates, 61% (DoT) and 15% (HTTPS) had a string that mimics an IP address structure in the CN fields. Table I shows that using IPv4 addresses as the subject field is only present in self-signed certificates. From Table II, public IP addresses form $> 80\%$, and $> 99\%$ of the found IP addresses in HTTPS and DoT self-signed certificates, respectively.

Upon geolocating the public IP addresses, we found that DoT's addresses map to 17 countries and HTTPS' to 201, which expectedly illustrates the size and distribution difference between both ecosystems. Half the HTTPS self-signed certificates with an IP address in the CN fields are located in the DoT's 17 countries. Therefore, despite minor differences between DoT and HTTPS self-signed certificates in our dataset, their proportion, distribution, and characteristics generally appear comparable.

TABLE I
SUBJECT FIELDS CONTAINING IP ADDRESSES, AND THEIR COUNT AMONG SELF-SIGNED AND NON-SELF-SIGNED CERTIFICATES.

Data Set	*Subject Field*	*Self-Signed*	*Not Self-Signed*
DoT	IP address	1,736	0
	Non IP address	1,100	7,119
HTTPS	IP address	404,231	0
	Non IP address	2,344,244	6,573,467

TABLE II
DISTRIBUTION OF PUBLIC AND PRIVATE IP ADDRESSES.

IP address	*HTTPS(%)*	*DoT(%)*
Public	324,571 (80.4)	1,724 (99.3)
Private	79,160 (19.6)	12 (0.7)

C. Expired Certificates

A certificate has a *Not-After* field indicating the date and time when the certificate validity ends. We analyze the proportion of expired certificates in both datasets. We classify a certificate as expired if the *Not-After* field is before the time that Rapid7 has collected said certificates.

From Figure 3, although the portion of expired certificates in HTTPS is double that in DoT, they generally constitute a small proportion in both ecosystems. This can be attributed to CAs increasingly employing the ACME protocol. Investigating the top trusted CAs in both DoT and HTTPS, we observed from our dataset that all of these CAs except GoDaddy (as of this writing) are supporting ACME based certificate issuance and auto-renewal mechanisms to avoid unexpected expiration of certificates.[3]

We observe that the majority of expired certificates in both ecosystems are issued by Let's Encrypt: ~78% for DoT, ~60% for HTTPS. Despite being more popular among HTTPS certificates, the proportion of the expired certificates issued by

[3]GoDaddy provides independent mechanisms for automatic certificate renewal [26], [21].

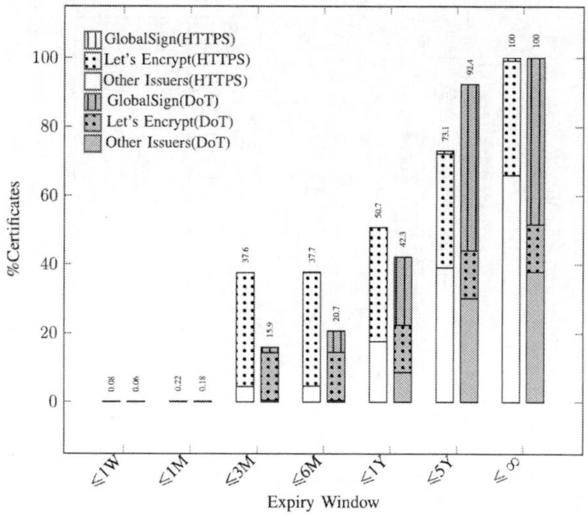

Fig. 4. Distribution of expiry windows in DoT and HTTPS certificates. White bars represent HTTPS, gray DoT. The proportion issued by each of the two most popular issuers (namely, GlobalSign and Let's Encrypt) is illustrated.

Let's Encrypt in HTTPS is smaller compared to DoT. As such, there appears no positive correlation between Let's Encrypt-issued certificates and expired ones. Let's Encrypt enforces an expiry window of $\leqslant$ 90 days, which suggests that Let's Encrypt DoT certificates may not have been configured for auto-renewal. Next, we shed light on the certificate expiry windows in both ecosystems.

D. Expiry Windows

Shorter certificate lifespan is a healthier security practice [40], but might lead to functional and security problems as, *e.g.,* management and operational costs increase [13]. Over the past several years, the security community has been advocating for shorter certificate expiry windows for the web. For example, before 2018, browsers required certificates to have an expiry window of 39 months or shorter, and later (from March 2018) agreed on accepting certificates with a maximum lifetime of 825 days (~2 years) [1], [30]. Google then announced the maximum accepted certificate lifespan by the Chrome browser would be 397 days (~1 year) [37]. On September 2020, Apple followed suit, accepting a maximum certificate life span of 398 days (~1 year) [5].

Figure 4 shows a cumulative histogram of various expiry windows for the certificates in our dataset. A negligible number of certificates were issued with a lifespan of less than a month in both DoT and HTTPS certificates. Unexpectedly, a few number of (invalid) certificates had a negative expiry window—their *not-after* date was before their *not-before*. Very few certificates had less than one month expiry window. For HTTPS, 50% of certificates in the $\leqslant$1M bin have been issued by trusted CAs, such as GTS, Sectigo, and Digicert. In contrast, all DoT certificates in that bin were issued by untrusted issuers. That is a minor plus point for HTTPS, but is potentially negligible due to the significantly small proportion of certificates in that bin for both ecosystems. For the $\leqslant$3M bin, the HTTPS proportion is more than double the DoT, which can be attributed to the larger proportion of Let's Encrypt-issued certificates in HTTPS (see Sec. IV); the proportion of certificates the CA has issued in this bin is almost equal across both ecosystems—∼88% for HTTPS, ∼87% for DoT. Analogous patterns can be observed for the remaining bins.

Overall, certificates with less than one-year lifespan are common in HTTPS, which can be attributed to (1) browsers (including Chrome and Safari) enforcing such shorter lifespans, and (2) the popular CA in HTTPS, Let's Encrypt, only issues certificates with $\leqslant$ 90 days lifespan. This appears to have not been carried over to the DoT ecosystem—over 60% of the certificates in DoT were issued with a lifespan of $\leqslant$ 2 years, and Let's Encrypt has only issued ∼14% of DoT certificates in our dataset (*cf.* Figure 2). A corollary of the above two points, although there is no short certificate lifespan enforcement in DoT client-side tools, we observe that the majority of the DoT certificates were issued with relatively short expiry windows. The majority of certificates issued by the dominant DoT CA, GlobalSign, had an expiry window between one and two years. As such, DoT certificate life spans appear to not suffer severe security weaknesses.

We also noticed that a large portion of invalid certificates in HTTPS had a lifespan of more than five years; however, the portion of these enormous lifespan certificates in DoT is roughly three times smaller.

E. Public-key and Hash Function

In this section, we investigate public keys and hash function algorithms used in the DoT and HTTPS certificates as a part of their cryptographic properties. We rely on NIST recommendations for key management [9]. For asymmetric-key algorithms, $\leqslant$ 80 bits, such as RSA-1024 and ECC (160-223), is considered weak. For hash functions, SHA-1 is also considered weak, and was formally deprecated in 2011 [9].

Figure 5 shows the asymmetric key algorithms used in both certificates in our datasets. RSA-2048, which has sufficient strength of 112 bits, is used by the majority of certificates in both ecosystems, with ∼87% in HTTPS and ∼75% in DoT. The weaker variant, RSA-1024, is five-times more popular in DoT. The HTTPS ecosystem thus appears to have a slight advantage over DoT.

TABLE III
MAIN HASH FUNCTIONS

Hash Algorithm	*DoT*	*HTTPS*
SHA-256	∼98%	∼96%
SHA-1	∼2%	∼4%

Regarding hash functions, Table III shows that $>$ 95% of certificates in both ecosystems used SHA-256, which has a security strength of 125 bits and is considered secure [9]. Only 2% of DoT certificates used SHA-1, but the proportion was double in HTTPS. Therefore, regarding the used hash functions, DoT certificates appear in a slightly better position. We note that there was a negligible proportion of $\leqslant$ 0.1% of other deprecated and non-deprecated hash functions, such as MD5 and SHA-384, in both ecosystems.

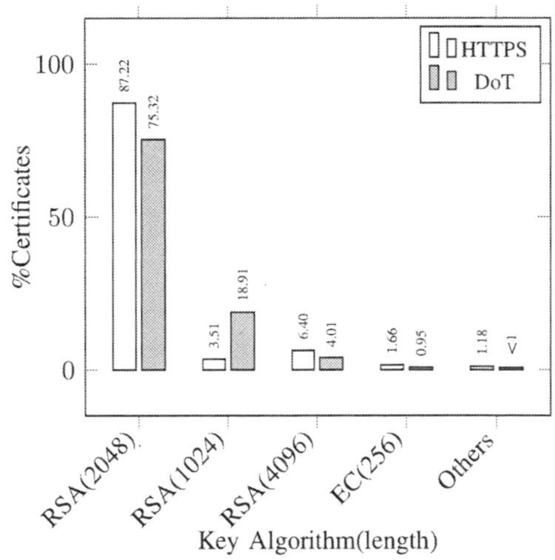

Fig. 5. Asymmetric key algorithms (length) in DoT and HTTPS certificates.

Summary. The characteristics of the DoT certificates appear to be comparable to HTTPS, especially in hash functions, certificate validity periods, and invalidity reasons. Minor exceptions exist in used public keys and expiry windows. However, similar to the previous section, we find no concerning evidence of lack of security in DoT certificates.

VI. Inclusion in Certificate Transparency Logs

CT-logs are append-only and publicly auditable databases of certificates [25]. Certificate issuers append their issued certificates to CT-logs. Upon the receipt of a certificate, CT-logs return a Signed Certificate Timestamp (SCT). The included certificate becomes publicly accessible, and the SCT is signed by the CT-log's private key to verify that the certificate has been included. Domain owners thus become aware of certificates issued for their domain, allowing them to detect bogus activity. We now compare two aspects: the proportion of certificates included in CT-logs, and the distribution of certificates among different CT-logs.

From our dataset, ∼61.4% and ∼66.8% of HTTPS and DoT certificates respectively had SCTs. Approximately 62% of the DoT certificates that contained SCTS were issued by either GlobalSign or Let's Encrypt. The top issuers adopted automatic inclusion of certificates in the CT-logs, and DoT certificates also benefited from this advancement.

Figure 6 shows a CDF of the distribution of certificates with SCTs among CT-logs. Both ecosystems exhibit a similar pattern. One notable point is that Digicert's CT2 log had been deactivated on May 2020 due to possible private key leakage [17]. In Figure 6, the line between points a and b, and points c and d illustrates the proportion of DoT and HTTPS certificates logged into Digicert CT2 log. As the proportion in Digicert CT2 log is greater in DoT, deactivation of this CT-log would negatively affect the DoT ecosystem. Regarding popularity, Google *Xenon2020* is the top CT-log among HTTPS certificates, whereas Sectigo *Mammoth* is the top among in DoT. Overall, the top three Google's CT-logs in HTTPS included more portion of certificates compared to the top three Google's CT-logs in DoT.

Summary. As browsers, like Chrome and Safari, enforced the inclusion of web certificates in CT-logs, CAs increasingly implemented CT-log inclusion policies [38], [6]. Therefore, approximately all of the valid certificates in both ecosystems have been logged. The forced CT-log inclusion in the HTTPS ecosystem appears to have boosted the inclusion of DoT certificates.

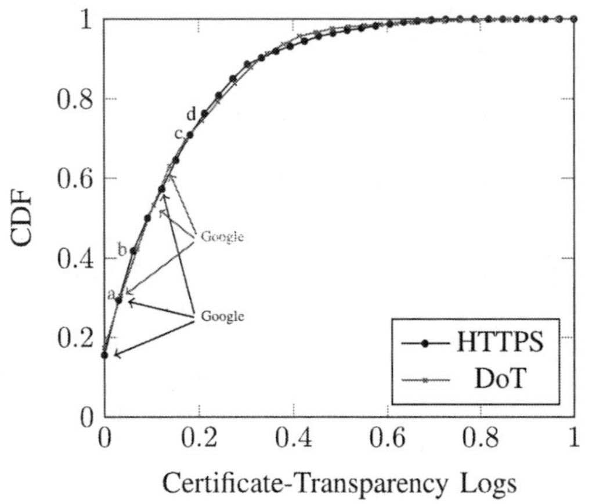

Fig. 6. Embedded SCTs in DoT and HTTPS certificates. The distance between red marked points with a, b, and the black points marked with c, d are representing the portion of certificates in DoT and HTTPS that were logged to the Digicert CT-2 log.

VII. Conclusion

The security of the HTTPS ecosystem has improved over time, with browser vendors, industry standards, CAs, and researchers coordinating efforts to advance aspects like CT-log inclusion, short certificate expiry windows, and improved cryptographic properties. Our analysis herein shows that the DoT ecosystem appears to have seized the momentum, reaping the benefits of the advancements made in HTTPS. We observed some differences between the invalid certificates of both ecosystems. Valid certificates, on the other hand, exhibit almost similar characteristics. Some certificates existed in both the DoT and HTTPS datasets. Those overlapping certificates are presumably stronger than ones present only in the DoT dataset because they (the overlapping) should satisfy the strict constraints of the HTTPS ecosystem. It would be unfair to judge the security of the DoT ecosystem with the DoT-only (non-overlapping) certificates because the overlapping ones are still used to establish DoT sessions in practice. As such, we took the conscious decision of conducting our analysis in both datasets as-is, without removing the overlapping certificates from the DoT dataset. A notable concern is that client-side DoT tools in the *opportunistic* mode can undermine the observed security strength of the DoT ecosystem. Client-side DoT tools must thus mimic the tenacity of modern browsers. Our research herein constitutes a work-in-progress, reflecting part of our journey towards a comprehensive evaluation of DoT security. Next, we will focus on evaluating client-side DoT tools, including a comparative assessment involving DoT stub-resolvers, web browsers, and mail clients, and their security features.

VIII. Acknowledgments

The second author acknowledges support from the Natural Sciences and Engineering Research Council of Canada (NSERC) through a Discovery Grant.

References

[1] "Baseline requirements for the issuance and management of publicly-trusted certificates, v.1.2.3," in *CA/Browser Forum*, 2014.

[2] J. Aas, R. Barnes, B. Case, Z. Durumeric, P. Eckersley, A. Flores-López, J. A. Halderman, J. Hoffman-Andrews, J. Kasten, E. Rescorla, S. Schoen, and B. Warren, "Let's Encrypt: An Automated Certificate Authority to Encrypt the Entire Web," in *ACM CCS*, 2019.

[3] A. Abdou, A. Matrawy, and P. C. van Oorschot, "Location verification on the Internet: Towards enforcing location-aware access policies over Internet clients," in *IEEE Conference on Communications and Network Security (CNS)*, 2014.

[4] F. Alaca, A. Abdou, and P. C. van Oorschot, "Comparative Analysis and Framework Evaluating Mimicry-Resistant and Invisible Web Authentication Schemes," *IEEE Trans. Dependable and Secure Computing (TDSC)*, vol. 18, no. 2, pp. 534–549, 2021.

[5] Apple, "About upcoming limits on trusted certificates," 03/03/2020. [Online]. Available: https://support.apple.com/en-ca/HT211025

[6] ——, "Apple's certificate transparency policy," 2019. [Online]. Available: https://support.apple.com/en-ca/HT205280

[7] N. Apthorpe, D. Reisman, and N. Feamster, "Closing the blinds: Four strategies for protecting smart home privacy from network observers," *arXiv preprint arXiv:1705.06809*, 2017.

[8] S. Aryan, H. Aryan, and J. A. Halderman, "Internet censorship in Iran: A first look," in *USENIX Workshop on Free and Open Communications on the Internet (FOCI)*, 2013.

[9] E. Barker, "Recommendation for key management: Part 1 – general," National Institute of Standards and Technology, 2020.

[10] R. Barnes, J. Hoffman-Andrews, D. McCarney, and J. Kasten, "Automatic Certificate Management Environment (ACME)," RFC 8555, 2019.

[11] S. Boeyen, S. Santesson, T. Polk, R. Housley, S. Farrell, and D. Cooper, "Internet X.509 Public Key Infrastructure Certificate and Certificate Revocation List (CRL) Profile," RFC 5280, 2008.

[12] S. Bortzmeyer, "DNS Privacy Considerations," RFC 7626, Aug. 2015.

[13] L. Chuat, A. Abdou, R. Sasse, C. Sprenger, D. Basin, and A. Perrig, "SoK: Delegation and Revocation, the Missing Links in the Web's Chain of Trust," in *IEEE European Symposium on Security and Privacy (EuroSP)*, 2020.

[14] T. Chung, Y. Liu, D. Choffnes, D. Levin, B. M. Maggs, A. Mislove, and C. Wilson, "Measuring and applying invalid SSL certificates: The silent majority," in *ACM IMC*, 2016.

[15] S. Dickinson, "DNS Privacy Public Resolvers," Nov 2019. [Online]. Available: https://dnsprivacy.org/wiki/display/DP/DNS+Privacy+Public+Resolvers

[16] ——, "DNS Privacy Clients," Dec 2020. [Online]. Available: https://dnsprivacy.org/wiki/display/DP/DNS+Privacy+Clients#DNSPrivacyClients-DOT

[17] Digicert, "Moving forward: What DigiCert's CT2 log retirement means for you," May 2020. [Online]. Available: https://www.digicert.com/dc/blog/digicert-statement-on-ct2-log/

[18] Z. Durumeric, D. Adrian, A. Mirian, M. Bailey, and J. A. Halderman, "A search engine backed by Internet-wide scanning," in *ACM CCS*, 2015.

[19] Z. Durumeric, J. Kasten, M. Bailey, and J. A. Halderman, "Analysis of the HTTPS certificate ecosystem," in *ACM IMC*, 2013.

[20] GlobalSign, "GlobalSign, About Us," 2001. [Online]. Available: https://web.archive.org/web/20010205010600/http://globalsign.net/company/index.cfm

[21] GoDaddy, "Renewing my SSL Certificate." [Online]. Available: https://ca.godaddy.com/help/renewing-my-ssl-certificate-864

[22] C. Grothoff, M. Wachs, and M. Ermert, "NSA's MORECOWBELL: Knell for DNS," 2015.

[23] A. Hounsel, K. Borgolte, P. Schmitt, J. Holland, and N. Feamster, "Analyzing the costs (and benefits) of DNS, DoT, and DoH for the modern web," in *ACM Applied Networking Research Workshop*, 2019.

[24] R. Houser, Z. Li, C. Cotton, and H. Wang, "An investigation on information leakage of dns over tls," in *ACM International Conference on Emerging Networking Experiments And Technologies (CoNEXT)*, 2019.

[25] B. Laurie, A. Langley, and E. Kasper, "Certificate Transparency," RFC 6962, 2013.

[26] Let's Encrypt, "Let's Encrypt Certificates on GoDaddy Hosting." [Online]. Available: https://letsencrypt.org/docs/godaddy/

[27] C. Lu, B. Liu, Z. Li, S. Hao, H. Duan, M. Zhang, C. Leng, Y. Liu, Z. Zhang, and J. Wu, "An End-to-End, Large-Scale Measurement of DNS-over-Encryption: How Far Have We Come?" in *ACM IMC*, 2019.

[28] A. Mourad, R. Yang, P. H. Lehne, and A. De La Oliva, "A baseline roadmap for advanced wireless research beyond 5G," *Electronics*, vol. 9, no. 2, p. 351, 2020.

[29] Mozilla, "CA/Intermediate Certificates," Apr 2020. [Online]. Available: https://wiki.mozilla.org/CA/Intermediate_Certificates

[30] M. Špaček, "Maximum HTTPS certificate lifetime to be 1 year soon," 2020. [Online]. Available: https://www.michalspacek.com/maximum-https-certificate-lifetime-to-be-1-year-soon

[31] P. Pearce, B. Jones, F. Li, R. Ensafi, N. Feamster, N. Weaver, and V. Paxson, "Global measurement of DNS manipulation," in *USENIX Security Symposium*, 2017.

[32] Rapid7, "About Open Data." [Online]. Available: https://opendata.rapid7.com/about/

[33] ——, "An Introduction to Project Sonar." [Online]. Available: https://www.rapid7.com/research/project-sonar/

[34] Q. Scheitle, O. Gasser, T. Nolte, J. Amann, L. Brent, G. Carle, R. Holz, T. C. Schmidt, and M. Wählisch, "The rise of certificate transparency and its implications on the Internet ecosystem," in *ACM IMC*, 2018.

[35] S. Siby, M. Juarez, C. Diaz, N. Vallina-Rodriguez, and C. Troncoso, "Encrypted DNS→Privacy? A Traffic Analysis Perspective," *arXiv preprint arXiv:1906.09682*, 2019.

[36] K. Singh, G. Grover, and V. Bansal, "How India Censors the Web," in *ACM Conference on Web Science (WebSci)*, 2020.

[37] R. Sleevi, "Ballot SC22: Reduce Certificate Lifetimes," 2019. [Online]. Available: https://github.com/cabforum/documents/pull/138/commits/2b06f7839daa45f685e37c51d74e255ef4ff9d75#diff-7f6d14a20e7f3beb696b45e1bf8196f2R1454

[38] E. Stark, R. Sleevi, R. Muminovic, D. O'Brien, E. Messeri, A. P. Felt, B. McMillion, and P. Tabriz, "Does certificate transparency break the web? measuring adoption and error rate," in *IEEE Symposium on Security and Privacy (SP)*, 2019.

[39] P. F. Tehrani, E. Osterweil, J. H. Schiller, T. C. Schmidt, and M. Wählisch, "Who ya gonna call? (Alerting Authorities): Measuring Namespaces, Web Certificates, and DNSSEC," *arXiv preprint arXiv:2008.10497*, 2020.

[40] E. Topalovic, B. Saeta, L.-S. Huang, C. Jackson, and D. Boneh, "Towards short-lived certificates," *Web 2.0 Security and Privacy*, 2012.

[41] L. Zhu, Z. Hu, J. Heidemann, D. Wessels, A. Mankin, and N. Somaiya, "Connection-oriented DNS to improve privacy and security," in *IEEE Symposium on Security and Privacy (SP)*, 2015.

[42] L. Zhu, Z. Hu, J. Heidemann, A. Mankin, D. Wessels, and P. Hoffman, "Specification for DNS over Transport Layer Security (TLS)," RFC 7858, May 2016. [Online]. Available: https://tools.ietf.org/html/rfc7858

Empirical Scanning Analysis of Censys and Shodan

Christopher Bennett, AbdelRahman Abdou, and Paul C. van Oorschot
School of Computer Science, Carleton University, Canada

***Abstract*—Engines that scan Internet-connected devices allow for fast retrieval of useful information regarding said devices, and their running services. Examples of such engines include Censys and Shodan. We present a snapshot of our in-progress effort towards the characterization and systematic evaluation of such engines, herein focusing on results obtained from an empirical study that sheds light on several aspects. These include: the freshness of a result obtained from querying Censys and Shodan, the resources they consume from the scanned devices, and several interesting operational differences between engines observed from the network edge. Preliminary results confirm that the information retrieved from both engines can reflect updates within 24 hours, which aligns with implicit usage expectations in recent literature. The results also suggest that the consumed resources appear insignificant for common Internet applications, *e.g.*, one full application-layer connection (banner grab) per port, per day. Results so far highlight the value of such engines to the research community.**

I. Introduction

As the Internet evolves, and its usage morphs over time, the need for systemic search engines that help us understand more about its connected devices arose. Censys [1] and Shodan [2] are two prominent such engines, increasingly relied upon recently by researchers and practitioners alike. Censys was realized in 2015 [13], and is designed to increase the accessibility of Internet-wide scanning by providing an approximate real-time view of the Internet as an online, publicly available, service. Shodan was realized in 2009 as a commercial service, and was targeted to provide real-time "market intelligence" about Internet-connected devices [20].

Censys is built upon a suite of technologies (*e.g.,* ZMap [14], ZGrab [3]) that provide the means to efficiently enumerate the IPv4 address space and contact devices therein. It first scans the entire IPv4 address space for a single port (*i.e.,* horizontal scanning), then further collects *banners* (*i.e.,* metadata about a service, or the resources served by such a service) from responding ports. Shodan, on the other hand, is less transparent; how it conducts Internet-wide scans remains unclear to the public.

From the perspective of the scanned devices, both Censys and Shodan provide means to allow administrators to opt-out from scans, thus abiding by widely agreed-upon Internet citizenship habits [14]. This is analogous to the means available to website owners to signal to a web search engine (like Google and Bing) their lack of desire to have their website indexed (*e.g.,* using the `robots.txt` file). Both Censys and Shodan provide a search interface on their websites, where a user may enter a query and retrieve a list of matching IP addresses; and both return only a subset of the results for free, and require a payment for the full set.

Upon conducting a preliminary empirical analysis, we provide insights into the following questions:

- How fresh are the results obtained from searching Censys/Shodan (Sec. III)?
- How much resources can we expect to be consumed from the scanned devices by Censys/Shodan scans (Sec. IV)?
- From the network edge, how does the operation of Censys and Shodan differ (Sec. V)?

Approaching these question can help validate research relying on these engines. It can also provide insights to: aid practitioners in deciding whether to opt-out from scans, understand the context from which results to their search queries are returned, and spark longer-term discussions regarding the value (relative to the cost) of such large-scale scans.

We setup virtual machines (VMs) in five locations: San Jose (California), Tokyo, Montreal, Paris, and Sao Paulo, and ran four popular services on each VM to receive port scans and banner grabs. This allows us to receive traffic from Censys and Shodan, and analyze and compare scanning patterns, thus approach the above questions. We now detail our data collection methodology.

II. Data Collection and Analysis Methodology

We used Amazon Web Services (AWS) Elastic Compute Cloud (EC2) instances to host our VMs. Each EC2 instance ran Linux 2 Amazon Machine Images (AMI) on top of Linux kernel 4.14 64bit(x86). VMs were assigned a public IP address that remained unchanged for the duration of our experiment. Each VM ran four public-facing services: FTP (using `vsftpd`), SSH (using `Open SSH`), HTTP and HTTPS (using `Apache`), thus having four open ports, respectively 21, 22, 80, and 443. We chose these services as they are popular and both Censys and Shodan scan them. Firewalls were configured with no restrictions, allowing any traffic inbound and outbound. Data collection lasted 47 days, beginning on March 10, 2020. We used the `tcpdump` packet capture tool on each VM to collect all network traffic as `pcap` (packet capture) files, which were later searched for Censys and Shodan scans. We note a potential bias due to using only VMs hosted by AWS as the engines may put a special focus on big cloud service providers.

Workshop on Measurements, Attacks, and Defenses for the Web (MADWeb) 2021
25 February 2021, Virtual

https://dx.doi.org/10.14722/madweb.2021.23009
www.ndss-symposium.org

Identifying Censys' scans. Censys' IP address are publicly known; during our experiment, Censys was scanning from the subnet `198.108.66.0/23` [4]. We assume that any packet whose source IP address matches this subnet is from Censys. We saw 186 IP addresses from this subnet.

Identifying Shodan's scans. Unlike Censys, Shodan does not announce its source IP addresses. To identify them, we ran a DNS history search for the domain `*.shodan.io` using SecurityTrails [5]. The SeucrityTrails API allowed us to find the first time it became aware of a domain (*first seen*) and when it became aware of the domain changing (*last seen*). Any packet with source IP address belonging to one of Shodan's subdomains is assumed to be from Shodan if the timestamp on the first packet in the TCP session was after the *first seen* date and before *last seen*. If Shodan scans from an IP address that is not found with our methodology then our experiment would underestimate the results for Shodan.

Following this methodology, we saw 16 IP addresses with corresponding names matching `*.shodan.io`. To confirm that these belong to independent Shodan scanners, we compared their SHA1 hashes to Shodan's *crawler* field—a 40 character hexadecimal string returned upon querying Shodan. Each of the 16 hashes appeared in the *crawler* field at least once, suggesting that a single IP address likely correlates to a single scanner.

Classifying sessions into Port Scans and Banner Grabs. We analyze port scans and banner grabs independently. To do so, some processing needs to be made on the `pcap` files because, (1) `pcap` files are raw, containing one packet per line, so the representation of a "TCP session" is not directly available; (2) we need a consistent methodology to classify several possible cases of the received packets—cases such as receiving only a TCP SYN packet, only a RST packet, or a SYN followed by a SYN/ACK and RST; and (3) we configured four open ports on each VM, but we still received scans on other (closed) ports. We used the Python library `pcap-splitter` [6] to extract and group together packets that belong to the same TCP session. We then categorized each session (grouped packets) as follows:

- *S*: A session of a single packet having the SYN flag set.
- *SRE*: First packet has SYN flag, second has RST.
- *SR*: First packet has only SYN flag, second has RST.
- *SAR*: First packet has only SYN flag, second has only SYN and ACK flags, last has RST.
- *BG*: Any TCP session that reaches the TCP ESTABLISHED state [19], contains at least one packet with an ACK value >1, and ends with a TCP teardown or RST.
- *Dangling TCP Handshake*: Any TCP session that does not contain a packet with an ACK value >1, and contains no packets with RST or FIN flags.
- *Dangling TCP Session*: Any TCP session that contains a packet with an ACK value >1, and contains no packets with RST or FIN flags.

We now formally distinguish a *Closed Port Scan* from an *Open Port Scan* from a *Banner Grab* as follows:

– *Closed Port Scan* = *SR* ∪ *SRE*

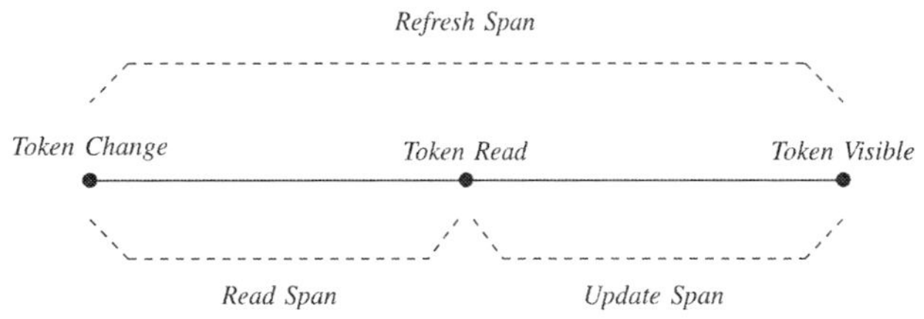

Fig. 1: Variables used to assess the freshness of search results.

– *Open Port Scan* = *SAR* ∪ *Dangling TCP Handshake*
– *Banner Grab* = *BG* ∪ *Dangling TCP Session*

III. Freshness of Search Results

We analyze the freshness of the results returned upon running a search query. For example, if a banner search returns 1.2.3.4:80, is this information stale? In other terms, if the banner is no longer served by this device, how long would it take Censys/Shodan to capture this? And how long would it take them to reflect the change in their search results?

Herein we only focus on the freshness of banner grabs on port 80 (HTTP). To analyze this, we generated a unique 64 character string (*token* henceforth) for each VM everyday, for the duration of our data collection phase (47 days). We updated the `index.html` page everyday at 10pm EST to serve the new token. We call this the *Token Change* instance. We then searched our `pcaps` for the moment when an HTTP GET response (with the new token) was returned to a banner grab from Censys/Shodan—the *Token Read* instance. Finally, everyday we used Censys' and Shodan's API search interfaces to find the new token. If found, we call this the *Token Visible* instance. We then analyze the time delays between the three instances, namely: *Read Span*, *Update Span*, and *Refresh Span* (Fig. 1). The *Refresh Span* chart is particularly helpful as it shows the delay between the changed event and the reflection of this change to the user. Note that because it is a function of the time when we queried both engines for the token, the *Token Visible* instance is an upper bound, *i.e.,* the token could have become visible sooner. Accordingly, this applies to the *Refresh Span* and *Update Span* delay variables.

By inspecting our `pcap` files, we found that many tokens were never captured (*i.e.,* banner grabbed) by Censys and Shodan. That is, our next token would replace the previous one before any banner grab occurs on the replaced token. In fact, we found that out of the 47 (days) × 5 (VMs) = 235 tokens we generated, only 25 were captured by Censys and 19 by Shodan. More surprising is the fact that for the duration of the 47 days, we received 46 HTTP banner grabs from Censys (*i.e.,* summing up all five VMs). From Shodan, we received 102 HTTP banner grabs. Neither Shodan nor Censys would have been able to capture all tokens, even if the banner grabs were spaced perfectly.

To analyze their efficiency in reflecting updates onto their search interfaces, we calculate how fast did the 25 Censys-captured and the 19 Shodan-captured tokens become visible after they were captured. Figure 2 shows CDFs of the three

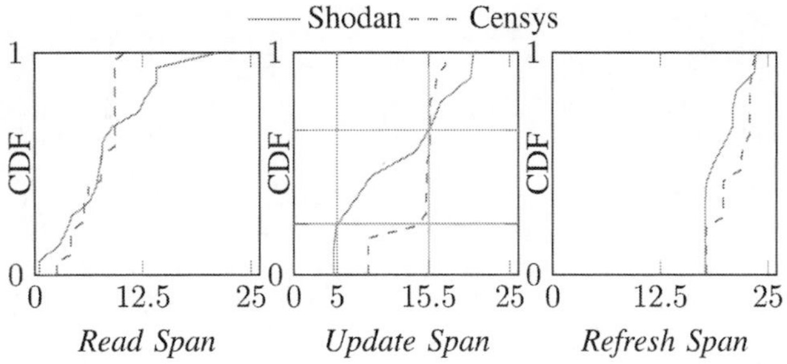

Fig. 2: CDFs of freshness results, in hours.

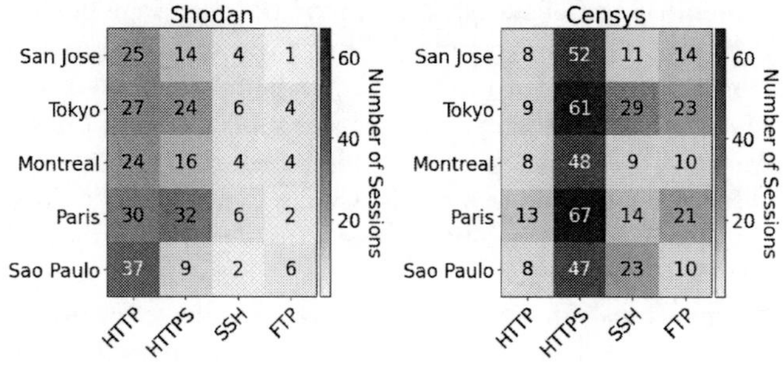

Fig. 3: Number of open port scans for each service per VM.

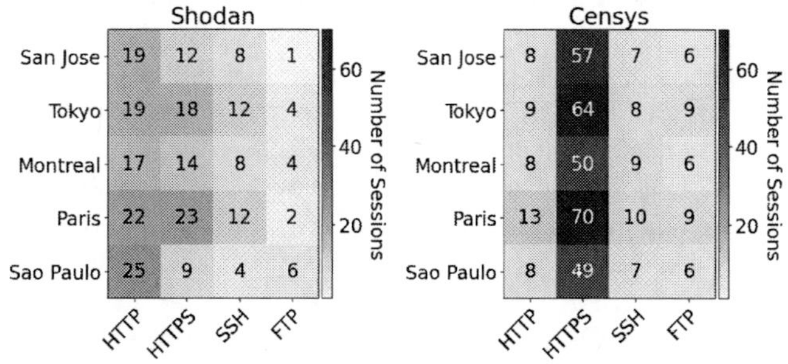

Fig. 4: Number of banner grabs for each service on each VM.

delay variables for the captured tokens. The results show that both engines are fast to refresh their query responses, with 65% of captured tokens becoming visible on their search interfaces (*Update Span*) within ~15 hours of capturing. Shodan was slightly faster; 20% of its captured tokens became visible within 5 hours of being captured (15 hours for Censys). For the *Refresh Span*, both engines made all captured tokens visible within 24 hours of generating these tokens.

IV. Scanning Resource Consumption

We now switch to resource consumption. In particular, using our collected `pcap` files, we measure the number of SYN scans and banner grabs per time window (Sec. IV-A), and the duration with which TCP sessions remain open (Sec. IV-B).

A. Number of Scans

Over the course of our data collection phase (47 days), each VM received ~27,614 SYN scans, or a little more than 587 scans per day (176 per day from Shodan, 411 from Censys). We focus on open port scans and banner grabs, as these generate more traffic than closed port scans. Figures 3 and 4 show heat maps of the number of open port scans and banner grabs for each service on each VM. For Censys, despite the darkness of the (vertical) HTTPS bar (*e.g.*, averaging more than five times that of HTTP), Censys has generated an average of ~97 open port scans on each VM, Shodan half that. According to our results, a server with only ports 443 and 80 open can expect to receive < 40 banner grabs per month from each engine. These results are relatively consistent across our five VMs, with the exception of Paris and Tokyo receiving 37% and 24% more HTTPS scans from Censys than other locations. Sao Paulo received the largest number of HTTP scans from Shodan.

B. Duration of Scans

A TCP session duration is the time difference between receiving the first TCP SYN packet (hence, resources allocated) and the event when the session was terminated (hence, resources released). The latter occurs when a TCP RST is received/sent, when the second TCP FIN packet is received/sent, or when a session times-out and gets terminated by the OS. This applies to closed/open port scans and banner grabs.

For closed ports, almost all scans finished in $<$ 1ms. For open port scans and banner grabs, Fig. 5 shows CDFs of the session duration. On average, open port scans lasted ~1s (139ms Censys and over 2s Shodan). This can be acceptable in many cases in practice, depending on the available resources and the number of open ports. Banner grab sessions took slightly longer, averaging $<$ 3s across all services and VMs. The longest session lasted ~248s, which was an HTTPS banner grab from Shodan running on the Montreal VM; the banner grab was completed in 42ms, but the final RST[1] packet was delayed over 248s. The fastest closed port scan was from Shodan on port 10554 (on the San Jose VM), which was terminated almost instantly.

V. Theory of Operation: Censys vs Shodan

We now present a preliminary comparison between Censys and Shodan, viewing their operation from the network edge. We again use information extracted from our five VMs and the `pcaps` collected. We focus our comparison on: the services both engines appear interested in (Sec. V-A), their available resources, particularly their pool of IP addresses (Sec. V-B), and their scanning configuration (Sec. V-C).

A. Interest in services

Table I shows the five most scanned ports on each VM, ordered from most (left) to least (right) scanned. Censys and Shodan were different in the most commonly scanned port: 443 for Censys and 80 for Shodan (with the exception of Paris, where Shodan scanned 443 a little more than 80). Port

[1]Most scans were terminated with a RST from Censys/Shodan, not a FIN.

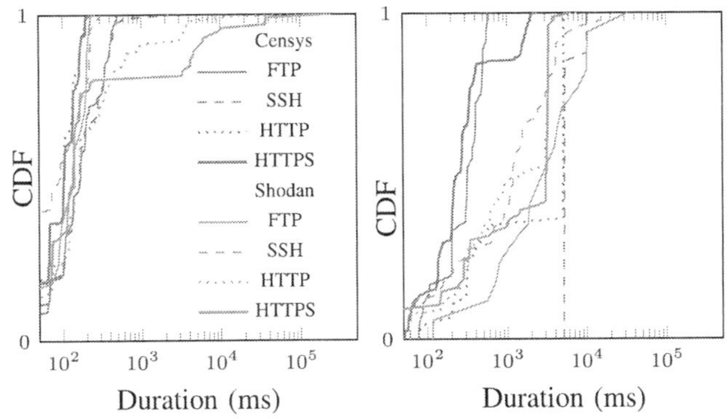

Fig. 5: Duration of open port scans (left) and banner grabs (right) received by all VMs on four services.

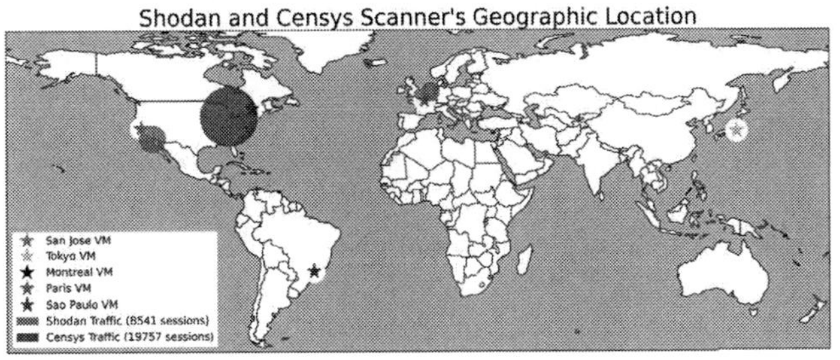

Fig. 6: Geographic locations of Censys (blue) and Shodan (red) scanners, and our VMs (stars). Marker size increases with the number of scans to our VMs. Map generated using Python Cartopy v0.18.0 [8].

443 came second for Shodan. In contrast, ports 21 (FTP) and 22 (SSH) came second (almost tied) for Censys, with the exception of Montreal where ports 9200, 2082, 8081, and 8088 were scanned more than ports 21 and 22. In a stark contrast between both engines, our logs show that Shodan's most scanned port (80) came in the ninth position for Censys. The complete set of ports and services that Censys and Shodan may have been scanning for, as well as the IANA-registered service for these ports can be found, respectively, in Tables V and VI in the appendix.

VM	TCP Port (P) Count (C) Most Common → Least Common									
	P	C	P	C	P	C	P	C	P	C
Top five Shodan-scanned ports										
San Jose	80	25	443	14	444	12	1177	11	81	10
Tokyo	80	27	443	24	1177	17	7443	14	53	14
Montreal	80	24	443	16	1177	13	81	11	4782	11
Paris	443	32	80	30	81	19	444	16	2086	15
Sao Paulo	80	37	443	9	3460	12	82	11	6666	11
Top five Censys-scanned ports										
San Jose	443	52	21	14	5900	14	9200	13	83	13
Tokyo	443	61	22	29	21	23	9200	19	5902	18
Montreal	443	48	9200	13	2082	12	8081	11	8088	11
Paris	443	67	21	21	9200	19	5902	19	8090	18
Sao Paulo	443	47	22	23	9200	13	2083	13	8081	13

TABLE I: Most scanned ports.

B. IP addresses: Pool and Configuration Characteristics

Figure 6 shows the geographic locations of Shodan's 16 and Censys' 186 IP addresses that we observed in our `pcaps` (Sec. II). WhoisXMLAPI [7] was used for location data.

Shodan's 16 IP addresses originate from four countries, whereas Censys' 186 addresses appear to be only in Michigan, USA. Figure 7(a) shows the number of TCP sessions initiated from these locations. In terms of the distribution of scanning effort on these locations, Fig. 7(b) shows that 40% of Shodan's 16 scanners contacted all of our five VMs, and about a third contacted only one VM. This is in contrast to Censys, where the majority of the 186 scanners contacted all of our VMs. This reflects what appears to be a fundamental difference between the configuration of both engines' scanners: Censys conducting more horizontal scans (each scanner potentially scanning the entire IPv4 space), whereas for Shodan the IPv4 space appears divided among its scanners. The latter arrangement can be more efficient, and can potentially reduce placement of such IP addresses in globally-coordinated blacklists. Additionally, Wan *et al.* [21] found that a single origin scan will miss 4% of HTTP(S) and 16% of SSH traffic. They found that scanning from two origins reduces this to 1.7% of HTTP(S) traffic missed and three origins further reduces the miss rate to 1%. This appears to provide a coverage advantage to Shodan over Censys. Nonetheless, Censys' scanners and activities are relatively more transparent.

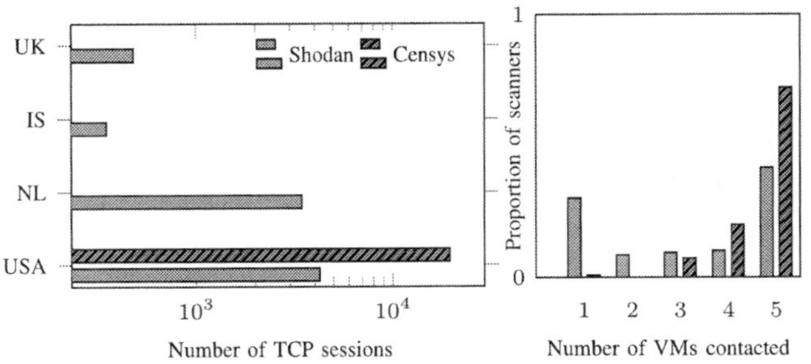

(a) Scanning origins. (b) Distinctly contacted VMs

Fig. 7: Geographic targets and origins of scanners.

To test whether Shodan configures its geographically-scattered scanners to scan nearby devices, we calculate the average of the actual distances between Shodan's scanners and our VMs, AD_v, and the average of the distances between the endpoints of observed TCP session, OD_v, as follows:

$$AD_v = \sum_{s \in S} \frac{distance(s, v)}{|S|}, \quad OD_v = \sum_{k \in K_v} \frac{distance(F(k), v)}{|K_v|}$$

where S is the set of Shodan scanners, K_v is the set of TCP sessions involving VM v, $F(k)$ is the scanner that initiated

TCP session k, and *distance*(x,y) is the big circle geographic distance between points x and y. A ratio of AD_v to OD_v close to 1 refutes the hypothesis that the geographic distance is a parameter in matching scanned devices with scanners. A ratio $\gg 1$ suggests that devices are contacted by nearby scanners, and $\ll 1$ suggests otherwise. Table II shows the results, which generally show no evidence of geographic bias, except for Montreal. Upon investigating further, we found that this is due a nearby scanner being responsible for generating more Shodan traffic to all VMs than other Shodan scanners (some scanners only scan a subset of ports; see Sec. V-C below).

VM	AD_{vm} (km)	OD_{vm} (km)	$\frac{AD_{vm}}{OD_{vm}}$
San Jose	4210	3645	1.15
Tokyo	9108	9950	0.9154
Montreal	4547	2009	2.2633
Paris	5304	5880	0.902
Sao Paulo	9769	8725	1.1197

TABLE II: Ratio of the average distance between Shodan scanners and each VM (AD_{vm}) to the average between the endpoints of observed TCP session (OD_{vm}).

C. *Scanning Configuration*

We shed light on several configuration parameters that we analyzed during our experiment. Specifically, analogous to the previous analysis regarding whether each scanner was responsible for scanning a dedicated subset of the IPv4 address space, we investigate whether every scanner has a dedicated set of port numbers (services) to scan on each target host. We also look at the means by which each engine is configured to request resources. Finally, we analyze and compare the timing consistency of the engines' scanning scripts.

Port distribution across scanners. We count the number of ports scanned by each scanner. For example, if a scanner made 1000 HTTP port scans, 1 HTTPS, and 10 SSH over the entire 47 days, then it has scanned three ports (namely, 443, 80, and 22). Figure 8 shows a histogram of the results. The majority of Censys scanners are focused on 20 or fewer ports, and very few scanners are assigned hundreds of ports to scan. Shodan appears to operate differently yet again, where each scanner is assigned a different number of ports, but generally in larger numbers than Censys. For example, only two of Shodan's scanners were assigned fewer than 200 ports; the rest were assigned between 200 and 1000 ports. For banner grabs, the chart on the right (Fig. 8) suggests that banner grabbing might be the responsibility of few Censys scanners—only 13 (out of 186) conducted banner grabbing. In contrast, most of Shodan's scanners conducted banner grabbing, with seven scanners (*i.e.,* half of Shodan's) banner-grabbed from all four open ports.

Configuration of requesting resources. We examine the HTTP GET requests in the banner grabs of Censys and Shodan to see what resources are being requested from our HTTP service, and how. Combing all five VMs, Censys used one user agent in all 46 HTTP banner grabs, and always requested

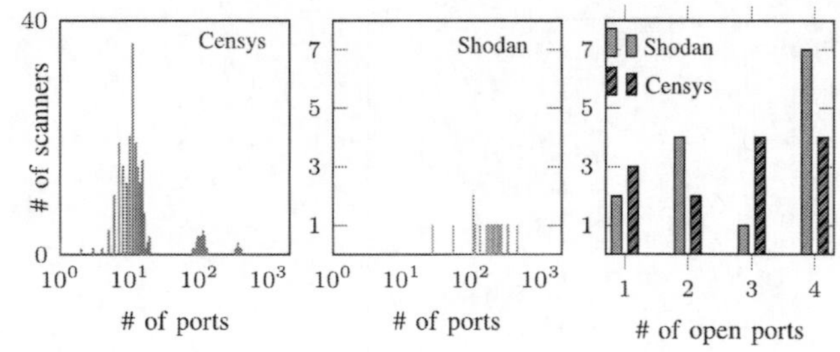

Fig. 8: Per scanner: number of ports scanned by Censys (left) and Shodan (middle), and the number of ports banner grabbed by both (right).

the root path. Shodan on the other hand used several user agents (see Table III in the appendix for a complete list) and requested multiple paths (Table IV in the appendix). Using different user agents can provide a higher likelihood of bypassing traffic filters on the application layer. Configuring the scans to look as if they are coming from a browser can further enhance the accessibility of content; *e.g.,* many sites require a browser to have javascript enabled. The browser of choice was different across both engines, with Censys using "Mozilla/5.0 zgrab/0.x", and Shodan claiming to be a Google Chrome running on a Windows machine.

Scanning consistency. We examine and compare the consistency, in terms of the time of day, across both engines. Figures 9 and 10 show the standard deviation of hours between the start of each SYN scan and banner grab respectively. We require at least two events to calculate the time between them (hence, the standard deviation). The empty cells in Fig. 9 and 10 are due to having a single corresponding event. Overall, Shodan appears slightly more consistent than Censys.

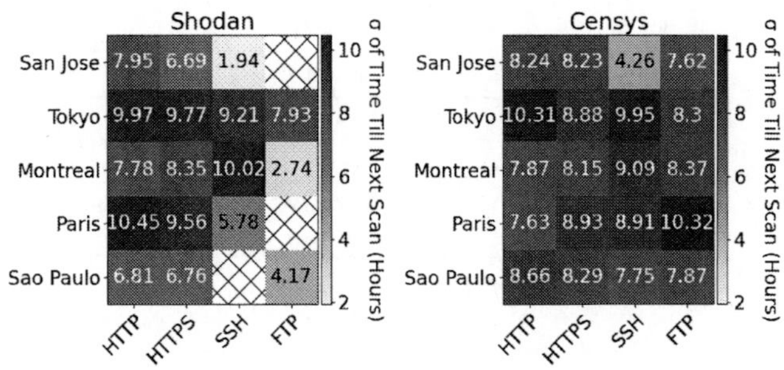

Fig. 9: The standard deviation (σ) of the number of hours between the start of each SYN scan.

VI. Related Work

Identifying Internet-wide scanners. Analogous to our methodology, Chen *et al.* [12] deployed six honeypots and collected three months worth of network traffic. They used machine learning on the scanning patterns, which found 16 scanners similar to Shodan but did not belong to Shodan. Upon analyzing patterns of other scanners (10 belong to Censys and 6 to PLCscan), and the services they most commonly

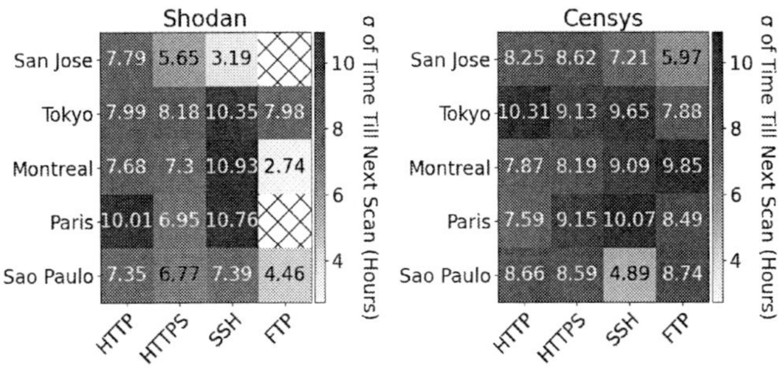

Fig. 10: The standard deviation (σ) of the number of hours between the start of each banner grab.

targeted, Durumeric *et al.* [18] found that many focus on services commonly associated with vulnerabilities. Heo *et al.* [17] study network scanning trends from a 31-day-long connection log they obtained from two firewalls of a campus network. They analyzed over 21 billion combined TCP and UDP connections to determine the characteristics of network scans targeting the campus. They created heuristics to identify scanners (scanners were identified by their IP addresses, as we do herein), and to classify the type of scanning as horizontal or vertical.

Evaluating search engine functionality. In 2014, Bodenheim *et al.* [11] investigated the functionality of Shodan. They deployed, in one subnet, four Internet-connected Allen-Bradley ControlLogix Programmable Logic Controllers (PLCs) with a static IP address publicly reachable via the Internet. Each PLC exposed two services: HTTP (port 80) and a common industrial control service (port 44818). Two PLCs were left with the default configuration, one had its banner obfuscated, and one had its banner changed to claim it was an Allen-Bradly ControlLogix. All four PLCs received at least one port scan from Shodan in fewer than 4 days. (Shodan does not index port 44818.) The HTTP banners were grabbed from all four PLCs within 14 days. Using keywords only, the authors [11] searched Shodan for the PLCs; each PLC was found within 19 days of the initial deployment. In 2020, Zhao *et al.* [22] evaluated five popular search engines, including Censys and Shodan, measuring their searching ability (how many devices each engine returns), raw data accuracy (ratio of valid data), response time (how long until a new device is indexed) and the scanning period (time difference between two contiguous scans). They found that Censys and Shodan had similar searching ability, and both are appropriate for users who wish to find newly exposed devices. The authors [22] recommended users who conduct research on recent data to use Shodan.

Search engines' output processing. Genge *et al.* [16] developed ShoVAT, a tool which processes the output of Shodan queries and compares it with the National Vulnerability Database [9] to detect vulnerable devices on the Internet. They found 3,922 known vulnerabilities across 1,501 services [16]. Ercolani *et al.* [15] used the data Shodan collects about devices to create visual models used to attempt to identify what the devices are.

VII. Discussion and Concluding Remarks

Our empirical analysis provides evidence that both Censys and Shodan have the technical capability of reflecting updates from their banner grabs onto their search interfaces in a timely manner. Our analysis on HTTP banner grabs shows that despite not capturing $\sim$90% of our daily-changed banners, remaining (captured) banners were made visible on Censys and Shodan search interfaces within a day of generating them. Shodan was slightly faster than Censys in grabbing new banners, and in making them visible through its search interface. Based on our experiment, both engines can benefit from an increased banner grabbing rate, which complement their efficiency in making new banners visible. Upon analyzing resource consumption, one can expect to receive < 40 banner grabs per month from each engine. Port scan sessions for open ports typically lasted less than a second, with Censys generally being faster than Shodan to close a session, especially for HTTP and HTTPS sessions. Banner grabs were slower, with many sessions lasting longer than 3 seconds. Finally, we noticed several differences in the operation of Censys and Shodan. For example, Shodan's scanners appear to be geographically scattered around the world, unlike Censys whose IP addresses are all in Michigan, USA; Censys appears more focused on HTTP/HTTPS than Shodan, and it appears to dedicate a specific port to certain scanners, and have other scanners probe many ports (*e.g.,* several hundred ports for a single scanner). Shodan's distribution of ports among scanners appears less skewed. Possibly a consequence of the previous point, the time of receiving Shodan's scanning traffic every day is slightly more consistent than Censys.

There are several avenues to expand upon the empirical work presented herein. For example, Censys/Shodan maybe scanning Amazon's AWS VMs different from non-Amazon devices. Additionally, our packet captures can be analyzed to understand how each engine addresses *diurnal effects*, *i.e.,* variations in scans to account for change in results based on the time of day [14]. Our HTTPS banner-grab freshness analysis can be extended to other services. In general, the data collection and analysis methodology used herein can also be applied to analyze non-TCP traffic from Censys and Shodan, like ICMP or UDP. Finally, we believe that more work is needed towards devising a systemic methodology for identifying traffic and source IP addresses of Internet-wide scanners that do not make this information publicly available.

Acknowledgements. The second author acknowledges funding from the Natural Sciences and Engineering Research Council of Canada (NSERC) through a Discovery Grant. The third author acknowledges funding from NSERC for both his Canada Research Chair and a Discovery Grant.

References

[1] Censys https://censys.io/.
[2] Shodan https://shodan.io/.
[3] The ZMap Project https://zmap.io/.

[4] Censys Contact Us https://web.archive.org/web/20190629110633/https://censys.io/contact Accessed June 2019.
[5] SecurityTrails https://securitytrails.com/.
[6] Pcap-splitter 1.0.0 https://pypi.org/project/pcap-splitter.
[7] WhoisXMLAPI https://ip-geolocation.whoisxmlapi.com/.
[8] Cartopy 0.18.0 https://pypi.org/project/Cartopy/.
[9] National Vulnerability Database (NIST) https://nvd.nist.gov/.
[10] Internet Assigned Numbers Authority https://www.iana.org/.
[11] R. Bodenheim, J. Butts, S. Dunlap, and B. Mullins, "Evaluation of the Ability of the Shodan Search Engine to Identify Internet-facing Industrial Control Devices," *International Journal of Critical Infrastructure Protection*, vol. 7, no. 2, pp. 114–123, 2014.
[12] Y. Chen, X. Lian, D. Yu, S. Lv, S. Hao, and Y. Ma, "Exploring Shodan From the Perspective of Industrial Control Systems," in *IEEE Access 8: 75359-75369*, 2020.
[13] Z. Durumeric, D. Adrian, A. Mirian, M. Bailey, and J. A. Halderman, "A Search Engine Backed by Internet-wide Scanning," in *ACM CCS*, 2015.
[14] Z. Durumeric, E. Wustrow, and J. A. Halderman, "ZMap: Fast Internet-wide Scanning and its Security Applications," in *USENIX Security Symposium*, 2013, pp. 605–620.
[15] V. J. Ercolani, M. W. Patton, and H. Chen, "Shodan Visualized," in *IEEE Conference on Intelligence and Security Informatics (ISI)*, 2016.
[16] B. Genge and C. Enăchescu, "ShoVAT: Shodan-based Vulnerability Assessment Tool for Internet-facing Services," *Security and Communication Networks*, vol. 9, no. 15, pp. 2696–2714, 2016.
[17] H. Heo and S. Shin, "Who is Knocking on the Telnet Port: A Large-Scale Empirical Study of Network Scanning," in *ACM AsiaCCS*, 2018.
[18] A. Mirian, Z. Ma, D. Adrian, M. Tischer, T. Chuenchujit, T. Yardley, R. Berthier, J. Mason, Z. Durumeric, J. A. Halderman, and M. Bailey, "An Internet-wide View of ICS Devices," in *IEEE PST*, 2016.
[19] J. Postel, "Transmission Control Protocol," IETF RFC 793, September 1981.
[20] S. Pritchard, "Shodan Founder John Matherly on IoT Security, Dual-Purpose Hacking Tools, and Information Overload," https://portswigger.net/daily-swig/shodan-founder-john-matherly-on-iot-security-dual-purpose-hacking-tools-and-information-overload Accessed Oct 2020.
[21] G. Wan, L. Izhikevich, D. Adrian, K. Yoshioka, R. Holz, C. Rossow, and Z. Durumeric, "On the Origin of Scanning: The Impact of Location on Internet-wide Scans," in *ACM IMC*, 2020.
[22] B. Zhao, S. Ji, W.-H. Lee, C. Lin, H. Weng, J. Wu, P. Zhou, L. Fang, and R. Beyah, "A Large-scale Empirical Study on the Vulnerability of Deployed IoT Devices," *IEEE Transactions on Dependable and Secure Computing (TDSC)*, 2020 (early access).

APPENDIX

In Sec. IV, we analyze HTTP GET requests (banner grabs) from Censys and Shodan. Table III shows the user agents used by Shodan scanners, and Table IV shows the paths Shodan scanners requested. Censys scanners always used user agent "Mozilla/5.0 zgrab/0.x" and the path "/".

Shodan User Agents	Count
No User Agent	58
Mozilla/5.0 (Windows NT 6.1) AppleWebKit/537.36 (KHTML, like Gecko) Chrome/41.0.2228.0 Safari/537.36	20
python-requests/2.23.0	2
python-requests/2.10.0	9
python-requests/2.11.1	1
python-requests/2.19.1	5
python-requests/2.22.0	2

TABLE III: Shodan user agents when requesting a resource from the HTTP service.

In Table I, Sec. V-A, we listed the ports most commonly scanned by Censys and Shodan. In Table V (Censys) and Table VI (Shodan) we list the IANA [10] registered service for these ports, as well as which service a search on the respective engine returns when queried for the given port.

Shodan Paths	Count
/	20
/robots.txt	20
/sitemap.xml	19
/.well-known/security.txt	19
/favicon.ico	19

TABLE IV: Shodan HTTP resources requested.

Port	IANA Registry	Censys Search Result
25	SMTP	SMTP
81	-	-
83	MIT ML Device	-
88	Kerberos	-
2082	HTTP	-
2083	HTTP	-
4567	TRAM	
5900	Remote Frame Buffer	VNC
5901	-	VNC
5902	-	VNC
8080	http-alt	HTTP
8081	sunproxyadmin	-
8088	radan-http	-
8090	opsmessaging	-
9200	wap-wsp	Elasticsearch
16993	Intel(R) AMT SOAP/HTTPS	HTTPS

TABLE V: List of Censys-scanned ports, and their IANA-associated services.

Port	IANA Registry	Shodan Search Result
25	SMTP	SMTP
53	DNS	-
81	-	HTTP
82	xfer	XtremeRAT
102	iso-tsap	multiple
444	Simple Network Paging Protocol	SonicWALL
1177	DKMessenger Protocol	FileZilla Server
1604	icabrowser	OpenSSH
1723	pptp	OpenSSH
2086	GNUnet	HTTP
2222	EtherNet-IP-1	HTTP
3460	EDM Manger	Unreal ircd
4782	-	OpenSSH
5555	Dual Stack MIPv6 NAT Traversal	OpenSSH
5800	-	RealVNC
6666	-	OpenSSH
7443	Oracle Application Server HTTPS	SonicWALL
51235	-	rippled

TABLE VI: List of Shodan-scanned ports, and their IANA-associated services.

Detecting Tor Bridge from Sampled Traffic in Backbone Networks

Hua Wu*†‡, Shuyi Guo*†, Guang Cheng*†, Xiaoyan Hu*†
*School of Cyber Science & Engineering, Southeast University, Nanjing, China
†Key Laboratory of Computer Network and Information Integration (Southeast University), Ministry of Education, Jiangsu Nanjing
‡Purple Mountain Laboratories for Network and Communication Security (Nanjing, Jiangsu)
Email: hwu@seu.edu.cn, shuyguo@seu.edu.cn, gcheng@njnet.edu.cn, xyhu@njnet.edu.cn

Abstract—**Due to the concealment of the dark web, many criminal activities choose to be conducted on it. The use of Tor bridges further obfuscates the traffic and enhances the concealment. Current researches on Tor bridge detection have used a small amount of complete traffic, which makes their methods not very practical in the backbone network. In this paper, we proposed a method for the detection of obfs4 bridge in backbone networks. To solve current limitations, we sample traffic to reduce the amount of data and put forward the Nested Count Bloom Filter structure to process the sampled network traffic. Besides, we extract features that can be used for bridge detection after traffic sampling. The experiment uses real backbone network traffic mixed with Tor traffic for verification. The experimental result shows that when Tor traffic accounts for only 0.15% and the sampling ratio is 64:1, the F1 score of the detection result is maintained at about 0.9.**

I. Introduction

In recent years, the expansion of the network scale has led to an increasing number of threats in the network. Network managers need to identify and deal with threats on time. Among the many cyber threats, the crimes that occur on the dark web undoubtedly cause great harm to the network and even society.

An important part of dark web crimes is illegal transactions. Criminals trade in guns, drugs, and other illegal goods on the dark web. According to the <The Chainalysis 2021 Crypto Crime Report> [1] published by Chainalysis, the total amount of transaction on the dark web in 2020 is already more than $900 million, and there were still 37 active darknet markets in November. Unlike commonly used networks, the dark web requires the use of anonymous communication tools to access. Therefore, it is more difficult for network managers to trace the criminals on the dark web.

As the most widely used and convenient anonymous communication system, Tor has more than 2.5 million daily active users as of November 2020[2]. To further enhance the anonymity of communications, Tor provides bridges and obfuscation protocols to disguise traffic accessing the dark web as normal traffic. The bridge is used in conjunction with the obfuscation protocol. Commonly used obfuscation protocols include meek and obfs4, so there are obfs4 bridge and meek bridge. When the user connects to the dark web through the bridge, the traffic is first processed by the obfuscation protocol and then enters the dark web via the bridge.

Although the bridges and obfuscation protocols are used only to enhance Tor's anonymity, such functions are also exploited by cybercriminals. In order to identify anomalous behavior in networks that use bridge to access, it is first necessary to detect the bridges to flag suspicious connections.

The biggest problem faced when performing detections in real networks is how to handle large-scale network traffic. In the field of network management such as intrusion detection and software-defined networks (SDN) measurement, traffic sampling has been widely used. Due to the large scale of traffic in the backbone network, we need to study how to detect Tor bridges after traffic sampling.

The current research on Tor traffic is mainly focused on traffic identification, and there is a small part of research on Tor bridge detection. However, these researches have used a small amount of complete traffic for experiments, which is collected in chronological order. They did not consider the large-scale traffic and the low proportion of Tor traffic in the actual network. These reasons make their method not very applicable in the real network.

Since the IP address of the meek bridge cannot be obtained directly from the traffic, we propose a method for the detection of obfs4 bridges in backbone networks in this paper. To handle large-scale traffic, we implement a sampling operation on the traffic to reduce the amount of data to be processed. To achieve efficient storing of packet statistics, we design the Nest Count Bloom Filter (NCBF) structure based on Count Bloom Filter (CBF). Besides, we extract features that can be obtained from the sampled traffic. Through experiments, we verify the usability of this method in backbone networks.

Our contributions here include the following three points:

(1) We design the NCBF structure to store the statistics of the sampled packets in the backbone network. This structure is based on CBF, which enables fast and efficient record of packet statistics in backbone networks.

(2) We extract 14 features that are still available in the post-sampling traffic that can be used for Tor bridge detection.

Workshop on Measurements, Attacks, and Defenses for the Web (MADWeb) 2021
25 February 2021, Virtual

https://dx.doi.org/10.14722/madweb.2021.23011
www.ndss-symposium.org

(3) We mix the Tor traffic with real backbone network traffic in different ratios in our experiments to validate the usability of our method.

The rest of this article is organized as follows. Section II describes the related work. In Section III, we introduce the background information, including information about Tor, the feasibility of Sampling, and Bloom Filter. Section IV describes the main parts of the method we use. Section V introduces the experiment and analyses the results. In Section VI, we compare our method with others' and express the limitations and future work. Finally, Section VII is the conclusion.

II. Related Work

This section presents three types of researches related to the background knowledge mentioned in this paper.

A. Tor

The widely used Tor [3] is the second-generation onion routing technology that can be used to anonymize TCP-based applications and has a large number of users worldwide. The use of bridge and obfuscation protocols makes the features of Tor traffic similar to normal traffic, such as the length of packet. It enhances the anonymity of communication.

B. Research on Tor traffic

Among the existing researches based on Tor traffic, the researchers mainly focus on traffic identification. Lashkari A H et al.[4] used up to 67834 packets for Tor traffic identification and extracted a total of 23 features such as the minimum flow inter arrival time. Kim M et al.[5] used the ISCXTor 2016 data set for their experiments, parsing the first 54 bytes of each packet as a feature. Lingyu J et al.[6] conducted experiments on an 18G backbone traffic data set with four features based on the length and time of packets, they also improved the decision tree algorithm. Rao Z et al. [7] extracted time-dependent features of the packets and used them on 23292 mixed flows to validate their improved clustering algorithm.

Since bridges and obfuscation protocols are used together, there have been some researches in the identification of these protocols. Soleimani M H M et al.[8] were able to achieve 99% accuracy for each obfuscation protocol with machine learning approach, but did not go further to detect bridges. He Y et al.[9] used a randomness detection algorithm to identify the Tor traffic hiding under obfs4 protocol.

Although the experiments of these researches prove that these identification methods for Tor traffic and obfuscation protocols can achieve high accuracy, they do not use backbone network traffic or do not take into account the low ratio of Tor traffic in the backbone network. Moreover, the experimental data sets they used are complete traffic and the extracted features are related to the continuity of the traffic. The volume of traffic in the backbone network is too large to perform complete traffic processing.

The above research is only for the identification of Tor traffic and traffic using obfuscation protocol. While M Yang et al.[10] conducted research on the detection of Tor bridges. They suggested that there existed high correlations among the subscribed tuple of three bridges, so it is possible to expand the bridge set to get all bridges. However, in the validation experiments, the online detection of this method can only get about 86% accuracy.

Similar to the shortcomings of Tor traffic identification researches, this method processed complete traffic when detecting a bridge. When dealing with large-scale traffic, this method consumed a lot of resources, which makes it difficult to apply to backbone networks.

Research [8][9] and [10] are partially related to our research, so we compare their methods with ours.

C. Traffic Sampling

With the growth of network size, sampling has been widely used in the field of network management. As early as 1993, research[11] has used packet sampling techniques in network traffic. In 1996, Cisco proposed that NetFlow[12] techniques could be used for anomaly traffic detection. In 2003, sFlow[13] was proposed by InMon. Both techniques can sample traffic and output flow information for network monitoring.

Traffic sampling is also widely used in the field of network measurement and network security. In the field of network security, traffic sampling is the technology that most intrusion detection systems are equipped with. Mahmood A N et al.[14] proposed a new two-stage sampling technique, which makes it possible to avoid wasting too much sampling resources on the elephant flows when the network is under large-scale traffic attacks. In the research [15], the focus of the research is to improve the efficiency of trust computation in a large-scale network, so the researchers only used systematic sampling and Random n-out-of-N Sampling techniques.

In the field of network measurement, SDN also uses traffic sampling technology due to its special architecture. In SDN, the controller is responsible for measuring traffic. Due to the limited memory of the controller, in research [16], L Huo et al. proposed a lightweight measurement architecture that can run in the controller. In this architecture, they used a pull-based sampling method to measure the flow rate, so that only a small amount of measurement values are stored in the controller to achieve coarse-grained measurement.

In addition, a new network measurement framework using sampling is proposed by R Jang[17]. He designed a new sampling scheme to handle the bad tradeoff caused by the standard simple random sampling. The sampling scheme chooses to sample each flow separately to obtain the most accurate information of each flow after sampling.

Although traffic sampling has been applied in many aspects of network management, it has not been studied to use it for Tor bridge detection in backbone networks. In fact, the detection of Tor bridges is helpful for network management, and it is a reasonable choice to sample traffic when conducting this research.

III. Background

In this section, we first introduce the basic architecture of the Tor network and the architecture after using bridges, followed by knowledge of probability theory to demonstrate the feasibility of sampling. Finally, Bloom Filter and Count Bloom

Filter structures are introduced to provide basic information for the design of NCBF.

A. Tor network

Compared with other anonymous communication systems, Tor[3] is the most widely used because of its long development time, good integration, and the ease with which even non-experts can use the Tor Browser to access the dark web. Figure 1 shows the basic architecture of the Tor network.

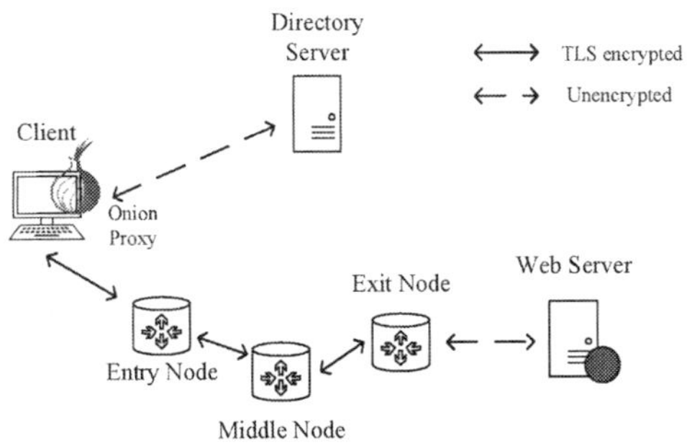

Fig. 1: Tor network

When a client needs network access via Tor, it first runs an onion proxy on the client side which makes a request to the directory server, then chooses three onion routers as relay nodes to establish a communication link in which the client-server communication is encrypted. Each onion router in the link can only get the information of the two routers before and after, and the client can only get the information of the onion router connected to it.

To further enhance the anonymity of communication, Tor was developed to include optional functions such as bridges and obfuscation protocols. A bridge serves a similar purpose as a relay node, except the address of the bridge is not store publicly in the directory server, but is obtained via https or email. Obfuscation protocols such as obfs4 and meek are used to encrypt or obfuscate Tor traffic so that it appears similar to normal traffic. Bridge and obfuscation protocols are often used simultaneously.

According to the official website[18], there are more than 6000 normal relay nodes and about 1500 bridges running in the Tor system every day, and the average number of bridge users is more than 40000 per day. At the same time, since any third-party user can configure his client as a bridge, the network manager can't get all the bridge addresses in advance. Therefore, using these functions can effectively improve the anonymity when accessing the network via Tor.

B. Tor bridge

Since the relay nodes used in building the basic architecture of the Tor network are public in the directory server, it is easy for network managers to obtain all these addresses. To avoid this, the use of bridges in conjunction with obfuscation protocols has the effect of enhancing the concealment of communication at multiple levels.

The two common obfuscation protocols used with the bridge are obfs4[19] and meek[20]. When obfs4 is used for traffic obfuscation, the client first obtains a bridge by either applying for it via https and email or by choosing a built-in bridge in Tor. Then the network traffic is sent to the obfs4 server after obfuscation.

Unlike the obfs4 protocol, which requires a bridge application, meek chooses to send Tor traffic to a cloud server first, and then forward it through the cloud server to a meek bridge to access the Tor network. By this obfuscation method, the Tor bridge is hidden under the cloud service provider's address, making it more difficult to detect. For network managers, under the premise that they monitor the traffic sent and received by the client, they cannot get the address of the meek bridge, and can only identify the Tor traffic that uses the bridge in the traffic interacting with the cloud server.

The Tor network structure is shown in Figure 2 when bridges are used.

Network managers typically analyze network traffic on the client side when user targeting is required. For Tor bridge detection, the address of the obfs4 bridge can be obtained visually in the traffic data as source/destination address, so we only need to detect the obfuscated Tor traffic using the obfs4 protocol to further obtain the bridge's address. While the address of the meek bridge is not directly available, and by analyzing the traffic, we can only identify the Tor traffic that uses the bridge among a large amount of traffic interacting with the cloud server.

Therefore, the bridge detection method presented in this paper is mainly for the obfs4 bridge, and the Tor traffic mentioned below represents the obfuscated Tor traffic using obfs4.

C. Sampling theory

The bandwidth of the backbone network is usually about 10Gbps, so the collection and analysis methods of complete traffic cannot handle such a large amount of data. In order to reduce the amount of data to be processed, traffic sampling technology is widely used in the management of the backbone network.

In actual networks, the volume of traffic is extremely large and there are mouse flows and elephant flows [21]. Mouse flows are small, containing few data packets but the amount is very large. On the contrary, the amount of elephant flows is small but each flow contains much more packets.

Tor traffic accounts for only a small portion of the network and consists mainly of mouse flows. When using Tor for a long time, the number of the packets of the same quintuple increases, and some of the mouse flows will shift to elephant flows.

Probability theory has proved that the sampled traffic can be used for the detection. According to the central limit theorem, when we randomly sample n samples from a population with overall mean μ and standard deviation σ, the mean of the distribution of the sample mean equals to μ, and the standard

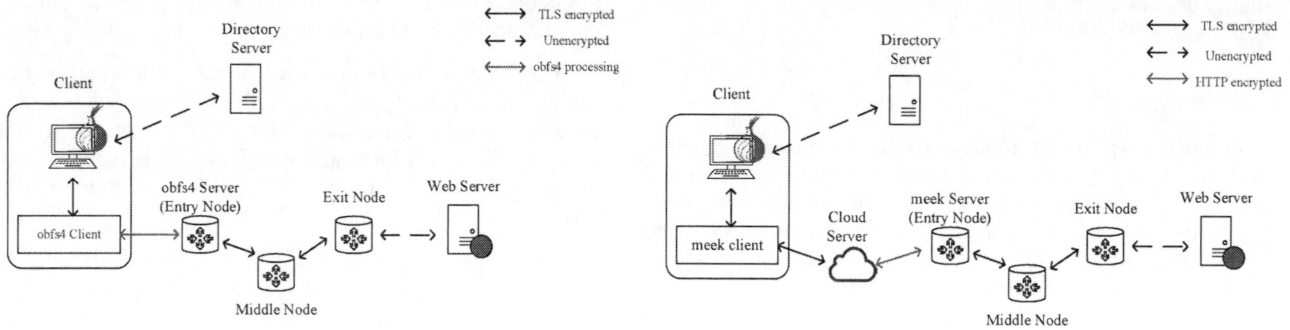

(a) Tor network with obfs4 (b) Tor network with meek

Fig. 2: Tor network architecture with bridge

deviation equals to $\frac{\sigma}{\sqrt{n}}$. As $n \to \infty$, the distribution is close to normal distribution.

In the case of a large sample size, the sampling distribution of the sample proportion $\hat{p}$ also approximately conforms to normal distribution. Assuming that the population proportion is p, then Formula 1 can be used to calculate the confidence interval for a population proportion.

$$\hat{p} - z\sqrt{\frac{\hat{p}(1-\hat{p})}{n}} \leq p \leq \hat{p} + z\sqrt{\frac{\hat{p}(1-\hat{p})}{n}} \quad (1)$$

Where n represents the sample size, z is the z-score for the confidence level α you want.

When we want the difference between the overall proportion and the sample proportion to be no more than $k\%$, we can use Formula 2 for calculation.

$$n \geq \left\lceil p(1-p)\frac{z^2}{(0.01 \times k \times p)^2} \right\rceil \quad (2)$$

In the actual network, the proportion of Tor traffic is very small, that means the value of p is small, and when the confidence level is set to 95% and the difference is limited to about 10%, the sample size n can be calculated. Sampling the traffic according to n ensures the sample proportion of Tor traffic.

Based on the theorems mentioned above, we can know that the sampled traffic can represent the overall traffic.

The packets obtained after sampling are mainly derived from elephant flows. Although the number of packets in the mouse flow is much smaller than that of the elephant flow, it is still possible to sample packets from the mouse flow by adjusting the sampling rate in the actual network.

Actually, the sampled packets are not directly used to calculate the eigenvalues. To ensure the consistency of the eigenvalue calculation, a threshold value needs to be specified, and when the number of packets with the same quintuple reaches the threshold, the stored statistics are then used for calculation.

Since the number of packets originating from the mouse flow in the sample is small, the packets of these quintuples may not reach the threshold to calculate the eigenvalue. The calculation of eigenvalues relies heavily on elephant flows.

D. Bloom Filter

To store the statistics of sampled traffic, we propose the NCBF structure based on Count Bloom Filter (CBF). And CBF was designed based on Bloom Filter (BF).

BF[22] is a stochastic storage structure that uses vector space to represent a set and this structure favors the efficiency of queries to quickly determine whether an element belongs to the set.

As shown in Figure 3, the BF structure requires the use of k hash functions $h_1, h_2, \ldots, h_k$ to perform insertion and query operations. In its initial state, BF is an m-bit array, and each bit is set to 0. Supposing the set $S = \{x_1, x_2, \ldots, x_r\}$ is inserted, k independent hash functions will map elements of the set to the $1, 2, \ldots, m$ bit. For any element x,k hash functions will map it to the $hash_i(x), i \in 1, 2, \ldots, k$ bit of the array and set the bit to 1. If one bit is mapped more than once, only the first mapping will result in a set to 1.

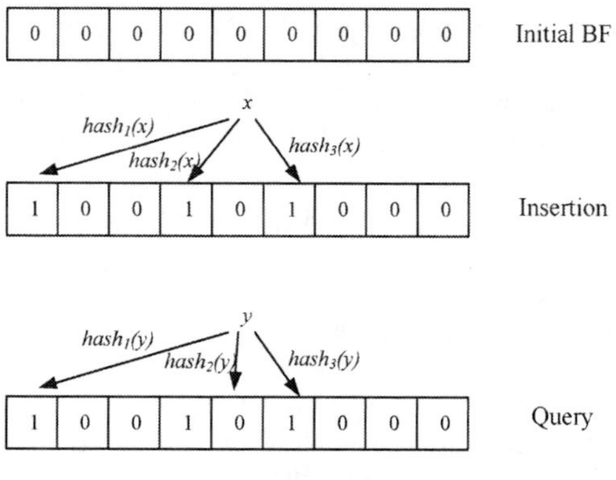

Fig. 3: Bloom Filter

When performing a query, the queried element is processed using hash functions to map it to the corresponding bits. If each bit mapped to has been set to 1, it is assumed that this element has been recorded in the BF. In the query operation shown in

Figure 3, the $hash_2(y)$ bit is not set to 1, which means y is not an element in the set.

BF also has shortcomings. It may misjudge elements that not in the set as elements in the set. In other words, the newly input element may be mapped to the bit of an existing element, causing a hash collision. The probability of misjudgment is called the false positive rate (FPR). This probability is shown in Formula 3.

$$\varepsilon = (1 - (1 - \frac{1}{m})^{kr})^k \approx (1 - e^{\frac{-kr}{m}})^k \qquad (3)$$

Where m indicates the number of bits. r indicates the number of elements. And k indicates the number of hash functions.

The classic BF is a simple storage structure that supports only insertion and query operations, but not deletion operations, and cannot record the existence of a changed set.

To address the shortcomings of the classic BF, Fan L et al.[23] proposed the concept of Count Bloom Filter (CBF). CBF expands every bit to a counting cell. During the insertion operation, when any element x of the set is mapped to the $hash_i(x), i \in 1, 2, \ldots, k$ cell, the counting value increases by 1. If other elements are mapped to the same cell, the counting value continues to increase, so that CBF can support the deletion of elements. When the element x is deleted from CBF, if the counting value in the cells to which it is mapped is greater than 0, all are reduced by 1. CBF can therefore implement the three operations of insertion, query, and deletion.

However, it is not appropriate to use only BF or CBF when storing traffic statistics. A data packet contains a variety of statistics. Using BF can only determine whether the data packet or specific statistic exists, and CBF can only store one statistic of data packets. If multiple CBFs are used for storing, then each CBF needs to perform hash functions. And this will increase the memory and time consumption of the calculation.

IV. Methodology

In this section, we introduce the detection method. The architecture of this method is shown in Figure 4.

First, we perform feature engineering to filter out the features that can be obtained in the sampled traffic that can be used for bridge detection. This is followed by the training of the machine learning model used for detection.

Next, we perform a traffic sampling operation on the backbone network and use NCBF to record the statistics of the sampled packets. Then we calculate the eigenvalues.

Finally, we use the training model to make the detection, get the list of bridge addresses, and complete the bridge detection.

A. Feature engineering

To implement Tor bridge detection in backbone networks, we sample the traffic to reduce the amount of data to be processed, as in large-scale network management. So we need to choose stable features that can be used for detection after traffic sampling. The detailed process of feature engineering is provided in Appendix A. Finally, we chose 14 features and 12 statistics that needed to be stored.

When traffic is sampled in backbone networks, a huge number of packets still exist after sampling. Although each packet only needs to record 12 statistics, due to the huge number, it still requires many resources to record the statistics, so we need to choose a suitable traffic sampling technique and use an efficient storage structure.

B. Traffic sampling

In the large-scale backbone network, processing the complete traffic is difficult and will consume a lot of resources. So traffic sampling has been used in many aspects of network management.

Traffic sampling is widely used in the field of intrusion detection[14][15] and SDN measurement[16]. And the sampling techniques can be classified into two types, including packet-based sampling and flow-based sampling. Three basic packet-based sampling techniques are mentioned in the research [24], including Systematic Sampling, Random n-out-of-N Sampling and Uniform Probabilistic Sampling. And Figure 5 illustrates these methods.

Compared with the other two sampling techniques, the systematic sampling technique has the smaller time and memory overhead. Therefore, we use the systematic sampling technique when conducting Tor bridge detection. The usability of this technique will be demonstrated in the following experiments.

Since we use systematic sampling, when inputting data packets, it is only necessary to store data packets according to the sampling interval.

C. Nested Count Bloom Filter

Although CBF achieves an increase in the counting value of the same counting cell, it cannot complete the recording of elements that contain more than one statistic.

Therefore, in this paper, we put forward the NCBF structure. It is used to implement the recording of packet statistics for computing the eigenvectors. The structure is shown in Figure 6.

Based on CBF, NCBF expands each counting cell to a counting block. Each counting block is one CBF.

In the initial state, NCBF is a structure containing m empty CBFs. During the insertion process, each x in set $S = \{x_1, x_2, \ldots, x_r\}$ contains more than one statistic, which means $x = \{I_1, I_2, \ldots, I_q\}$, we use part of the statistics as the input of k independent hash functions. The hash functions can map x to k different counting blocks, then the statistics of x is recorded in these blocks by increasing the value of counting cells.

The query process is similar to the classic BF. If the queried element y is processed by hash functions, and each block it mapped to has recorded statistics, then y is considered to be in NCBF.

Compared with CBF, if we need to store multiple statistcs of a packet, we only need to perform the hash function once.

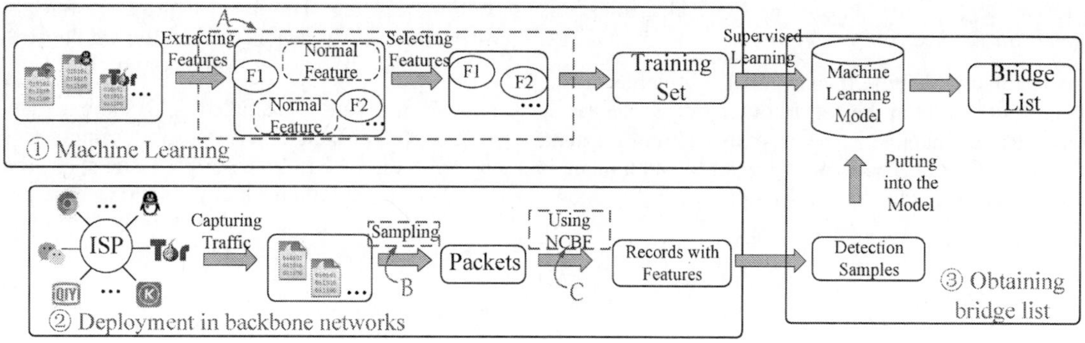

Fig. 4: The architecture of the detection method

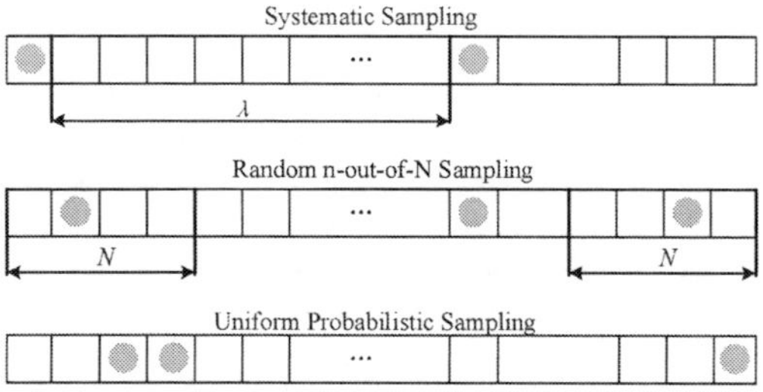

Fig. 5: Schematic figure of the basic sampling methods

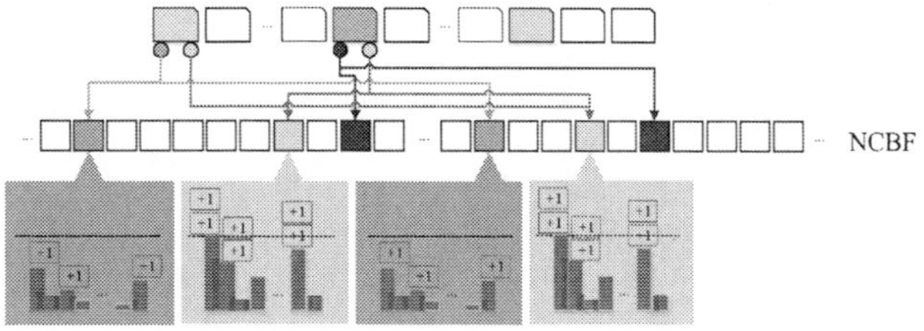

Fig. 6: The architecture of NCBF

Like Bloom Filter, NCBF also has false positive probability, that is, a hash collision occurs and the element is mapped to the wrong counting block.

The formula for calculating the false positive rate of NCBF is consistent with Formula 3. The difference lies in the meaning of the parameters. In NCBF, m represents the number of counting blocks, and r represents the number of different tuples entered.

Because the memory occupied by NCBF is limited, we cannot store elements in it without limitation. Once there are too many elements input, hash collisions may occur, resulting in a decrease in the storage efficiency and accuracy of the entire structure. Therefore, we need to determine the memory of NCBF through the above parameters.

When we storing the packet statistics using NCBF, the arriving packet's quintuple is used as the input of hash functions. Then the corresponding packet will be mapped to k different counting blocks and the statistics are stored in each block.

The ultimate purpose of using NCBF is to get the Record and calculate corresponding eigenvectors. Because there are so many packets with the same quintuple in the real network, we cannot classify all packets of the same quintuples into one Record. If we group all the packets of the same quintuple into one Record, we need to extract a lot of statistics when calculating the eigenvectors, which will consume a lot of memory of NCBF. That's why we set a threshold to get Records. This threshold is judged based on the value of a certain counting cell in the counting block. Because of hash collisions, we choose the minimum value of this certain counting cell. Then we use the statistics stored in the corresponding block to calculate the eigenvectors.

To improve the accuracy of eigenvectors calculation, we need to set a proper memory for the NCBF used for processing traffic to minimize the impact of hash collisions on the result of the calculation.

Considering the low ratio of Tor traffic in backbone networks, we need an NCBF structure that can process traffic for a long time to ensure that the statistics of Tor traffic packets stored in NCBF can reach the threshold and the Record can be extracted. At the same time, FPR of NCBF is also considered to prevent excessive hash collisions of the elephant flow and cause NCBF to be cleared. This means that we need to allocate a reasonable amount of memory to NCBF and get the traffic duration that can be processed by NCBF before being emptied. The NCBF parameters we need to consider include the number of counting blocks m, a reasonable value of FPR, and the number of hash functions k. The value of these parameters is related to the data scale and hardware environment, so we give the details of parameter setting in section V.

V. Experiment & Results

In this section, we describe how to adjust the parameters before the validation experiment, and the exact procedures of the validation experiment. Finally we analyze the sampling results and the detection results separately.

A. *Parameter adjustment before validation*

In the validation experiment, we use two types of parameters, one is the adjustable sampling ratio, and the other is the relevant parameters of NCBF structure. Both can be adjusted through the same preparation experiment.

We use the 15-minute backbone traffic collected by the MAWI working group[25] (https://mawi.wide.ad.jp/mawi/ditl/ditl2019-G/201904090000.html) as a large-scale data set for calculating the parameters.

When performing NCBF processing, we use SHA1 as the hash function, which outputs a 20 byte (160 bit) hash value. Supposing there are 2^n counting blocks in NCBF, n bits are needed to store the serial number of the counting block. k is the number of hash functions, so we need to calculate k hash values, each is n-bit. The method for obtaining the hash value of NCBF is to sequentially split the 160-bit hash value into k parts. If the value of k is large, the hash value of one output of SHA1 may not be enough to divide.

When we employ 4 hash functions, the hash value output by one SHA1 can obtain 4 hash values. At this time, the corresponding NCBF has 2^{40} counting blocks. According to the later experiment, 2^{40} counting blocks takes up enough memory.

Next, we obtain different numbers of quintuples by changing the sampling ratio, the quintuples are all obtained based on the 15-min backbone network traffic. And we use NQP to represent the Number of Quintuples from the Public traffic data set.

Compared with other traffic in the public traffic data set, Tor traffic mainly consists of mouse flows, which are more difficult to make hash collisions. So what we need to pay attention to is the hash collision that occurs when recording the elephant flow. In other words, we need to consider the FPR of the NCBF structure. Based on Formula 3, we can obtain the relationship between FPR and NQDM (the maximum Number of Quintuples that can be inserted when FPR is less than the threshold under Different Memories) when the number of counting blocks is different. As shown in Formula 4.

$$FPR \approx (1 - e^{\frac{-k*NQDM}{m}})^k \tag{4}$$

Where m indicates the number of counting blocks. k indicates the number of hash functions.

In the NCBF structure, k is generally a fixed value greater than 1, and will not be discussed here. In the case of the same memory, when NQDM increases, FPR will increase. When the FPR increases to a certain extent, the packets with the same quintuple input to NCBF will be mapped to the wrong counting block with probability, causing errors in the recording of packet statistics, and further affecting the calculation of eigenvectors. When using NCBF to process elephant flow, NQDM will increase, and FPR will increase accordingly. Therefore, we need to allocate appropriate memory for the NCBF structure during the design stage to keep FPR within a reasonable range and reduce the impact of hash collisions on eigenvectors calculations.

When we set the value of FPR to **1/100**, it means that when 100 different quintuples in the traffic have been inserted in NCBF, there may already be packet statistics in the block where the next packet from different quintuples should be mapped to. In this case, hash collisions have almost no effect on the result.

TABLE I: NQP with different sampling ratios

Sampling ratio	NQP
16:1	450344
64:1	178930
256:1	71204

What's more, based on Table III in Appendix A, we only need 12 counting cells for each block. So we set the memory of each block to **12 bytes** to calculate the total memory NCBF occupies. The memory of NCBF can be calculated by Formula 5.

$$Me = m * 12\ bytes \tag{5}$$

Where Me indicates the memory of NCBF.

By changing the sampling ratio, we get different NQP. When the sampling ratio is different, the number of packets we extract from the public traffic data set is different, which causes some quintuples to not be in the sampling results and NQP will change. The results calculated using the public data set are shown in Table I.

Based on the above preparation, we can use Formula 6 to get the traffic duration that can be processed by NCBF before being emptied under different memory conditions.

$$T \approx \frac{NQDM}{NQP} * 15\ min \tag{6}$$

Where T indicates the time NCBF required to be cleared. $NQDM$ indicates the maximum number of quintuples that can be inserted when FPR is less than the threshold under different memories. And NQP indicates the number of quintuples that can be obtained from the public traffic data set.

However, these NQPs are all obtained from the same public traffic data set, so the value does not change. We adjust the value of m, to get different Me and T under different memory of NCBF. The results are shown in Table II.

TABLE II: Traffic duration that can be processed by NCBF

Sampling ratio	m	Me	NQDM	T
16:1	2^{20}	12.0MB	1.00e+05	3.32min
	2^{22}	48.0MB	4.00e+05	13.28min
	2^{25}	384.0MB	3.00e+06	1.77hr
	2^{28}	3072.0MB	3.00e+07	14.16hr
	2^{30}	12288.0MB	1.00e+08	2.36d
64:1	2^{20}	12.0MB	1.00e+05	8.35min
	2^{22}	48.0MB	4.00e+05	33.41min
	2^{25}	384.0MB	3.00e+06	4.46hr
	2^{28}	3072.0MB	3.00e+07	1.49d
	2^{30}	12288.0MB	1.00e+08	5.94d
256:1	2^{20}	12.0MB	1.00e+05	20.99min
	2^{22}	48.0MB	4.00e+05	1.40hr
	2^{25}	384.0MB	3.00e+06	11.20hr
	2^{28}	3072.0MB	3.00e+07	3.73d
	2^{30}	12288.0MB	1.00e+08	14.93d

From the table, we can know that when the sampling ratio is 16:1, we set the memory of the NCBF to about 12288MB.

The NCBF can handle the backbone network traffic for 2 days, which means it is cleared every 2 days. After NCBF has continuously processed network traffic for 2 days, the probability of hash collision will increase. The next input data packet is more likely to be mapped to the wrong counting block, resulting in inaccurate statistical information. When the sampling ratio increases, NCBF of the same memory can be cleared for a longer time.

And during the 2 days of data collection, some Tor bridge may generate normal traffic, we can judge whether the traffic is normal based on features. The normal traffic won't affect the detection results.

Taking into account the actual traffic situation in the backbone network and the needs of network management, we need to establish NCBF with suitable memory for the detection of the Tor bridge.

B. Procedures of the validation experiment

In order to verify the method's usability in backbone networks, the validation experiment is divided into four main steps:1) collecting traffic data, 2) changing the ratio of Tor traffic to normal traffic, 3) sampling the traffic and using NCBF, 4) detecting and obtaining Tor bridge addresses.

(1) Collecting traffic data: Some Tor users use Tor bridge to access the network, disguising the Tor traffic as normal traffic. In the existing research, it is not mentioned whether bridges are used in the Tor traffic data set collected during the experiment.

Therefore, our experiments are conducted using a mixture of large public traffic datasets and self-gathered Tor traffic from known bridges.

We use the same traffic data set in sction V-A as the public traffic data set. The 15-minute backbone traffic was collected by the MAWI working group[25] at samplepoint-G on April 9, 2019. This data set contains more than 100 million packets and 72.93% of the packets are tcp packets. And samplepoint-G is one of the samplepoints monitored by WIDE. It monitors the 10Gbps link to an experimental IX in Tokyo.

When collecting Tor traffic, the bridges are applied via https and email. We use Wireshark to collect the traffic. The topology for Tor traffic collection is shown in Figure 7.

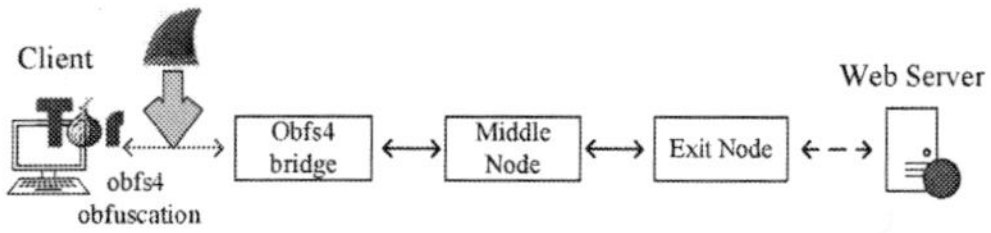

Fig. 7: Topology of Tor traffic collection

(2) Changing the ratio of Tor traffic to normal traffic: Since the percentage of Tor traffic in the actual network is very low, we change the ratio of Tor traffic to normal traffic during the experiment to verify that the method can still detect Tor bridge in the actual network environment where the percentage of Tor traffic is very low. The ratios are shown in Table III.

After adjusting the ratio, we used a random function to modify the time starting point of Tor traffic and inserted each

TABLE III: Different ratio of Tor traffic

Tor packets	Public data set packets	Ratio
17613	1418227476	0.01%
70197	1418227476	0.05%
140784	1418227476	0.10%
217314	1418227476	0.15%
282564	1418227476	0.20%
350600	1418227476	0.25%
425874	1418227476	0.30%

Tor traffic file into the different time points in the public traffic file.

(3) Sampling traffic and using NCBF: When a ratio of mixed traffic data is selected, the traffic needs to be sampled. We use systematic sampling techniques to obtain packets from the traffic, and change the number of samples by adjusting the value of λ. Then we use NCBF to process these packets to get Records and corresponding eigenvectors for detection.

(4) Detecting and obtaining the detection results: After the model outputs the detection results, the evaluation criteria related to the results can be calculated since the experiment is conducted under the premise of known bridges.

C. Analysis of results

Before proceeding to analyze the detection results, the sampling results are first analyzed. To reduce the storage size, we sample the complete traffic. Once the scale of Tor traffic is too small, the number of packets obtained after sampling is not enough to constitute Records. By adjusting the sampling ratio and traffic ratio, the numbers of Records in the detection sample are shown in Figure 8.

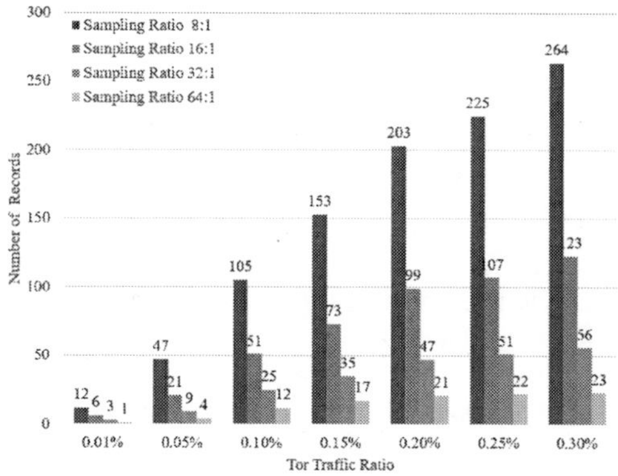

Fig. 8: The number of Records with different ratios

When Tor traffic only accounts for 0.01%, after sampling with a ratio of 8:1 and sending the data packet to NCBF for processing, 12 Records for detection can still be obtained. And the number of Records increases as the traffic ratio increases. This demonstrates that NCBF can process the sampled packets to obtain the Records in large-scale traffic environments with low Tor traffic ratios.

After the analysis of the sampling results, the detected results were evaluated using precision, recall and F1 score.

TABLE IV: Tor bridge detection results

Tor traffic ratio	Sampling ratio	Precision	Recall	F1 Score
0.01%	8:1	25%	100%	0.4
	16:1	23.08%	100%	0.375
	32:1	50%	100%	0.6667
	64:1	25%	100%	0.4
0.05%	8:1	57.32%	100%	0.7287
	16:1	54.05%	95.24%	0.6897
	32:1	50%	100%	0.6667
	64:1	33.33%	100%	0.5
0.10%	8:1	74.24%	93.33%	0.827
	16:1	75.38%	96.08%	0.8448
	32:1	73.33%	88%	0.8
	64:1	78.57%	91.67%	0.8462
0.15%	8:1	84.88%	95.42%	0.8985
	16:1	87.50%	95.89%	0.915
	32:1	89.19%	94.29%	0.9167
	64:1	93.75%	88.24%	0.9091
0.20%	8:1	84.48%	96.55%	0.9011
	16:1	82.30%	93.94%	0.8774
	32:1	85.19%	97.87%	0.9109
	64:1	91.30%	100%	0.9545
0.25%	8:1	86.48%	93.78%	0.8998
	16:1	84.43%	96.26%	0.8996
	32:1	87.72%	98.04%	0.9259
	64:1	75.86%	100%	0.8627
0.30%	8:1	86.69%	96.21%	0.912
	16:1	82.31%	98.37%	0.8963
	32:1	85.07%	98.28%	0.912
	64:1	81.48%	95.65%	0.88

Since the bridge addresses used in the experiment are in a known state, the precision, recall, and F1 score for Tor bridge detection with different traffic ratios and sampling ratios can be calculated, as shown in Table IV.

From the table, it can be seen that as the ratio of Tor traffic increases, the precision rate has increased significantly, and the recall rate has stabilized above 95%. When Tor traffic accounts for only 0.15%, the F1 score of the detection result stabilized at about 0.9. When the ratio of Tor traffic increased from 0.20% to 0.30%, the precision rate shows a downward trend. After analysis, we consider that it might be because when adjusting the ratio, Tor packets are randomly selected, resulting in the occurrence of deviations.

For network managers, what is needed is to detect as many correct Tor bridge addresses as possible. High recall rate means that the number of the real bridges which identified as bridge accounts for a high proportion of the number of the real bridge, which means that the detection results are relatively complete, and the real bridges are almost in the detection results. Therefore, when the detection is performed in the actual network, it is only necessary to perform a second identification based on the first detection result.

VI. Discussion

In this section, we first compare the advantages and disadvantages of our method with existing Tor bridge detection methods. Then we discuss the limitations of our method and possible countermeasures. Finally we suggest aspects that can be improved in future work.

A. Comparison

Compared with the Tor bridge detection method proposed by M. Yang et al.[10], our method is more practical. They suggested that there existed high correlations among the subscribed tuple of three bridges, so it is possible to expand the bridge set to get all bridges. This means that their approach requires constantly expanding the set of bridges, putting a lot of pressure on storage and computational resources. And to extract such correlations, their experiments must use complete traffic.

They run Tor bridges in the campus network environment and conduct experiments. They detect the bridge by analyzing the traffic between the campus network and the Internet, which is complete traffic.

Our method is mainly applied in backbone networks, so traffic sampling is performed first, breaking the continuity and correlation between flows. And we consider the low ratio of Tor traffic in the real network environment, so we conducted experiments under different Tor traffic ratios to prove the availability of this method in backbone networks with a low Tor traffic ratio.

In order to achieve Tor bridge detection in the backbone network, it is difficult to use the method based on the correlation between bridge tuples. Processing each flow in the massive traffic consumes a lot of resources. Therefore, our method has better adaptability.

In research[9], they used randomness and timing sequence detection to roughly distinguish the obfs4 traffic. The timing-sequence based detection method has strict requirements for the integrity and continuity of the traffic. This means that when using this method for obfs4 traffic detection, the traffic processed must be sequential. As the method in the study [10], this method is less usable in actual network.

We also compare our detection method with research[8]. Since we used random forest in our research and performed a 70-30 percentage split on the data set, we used random forest and the parameter settings are consistent with the research. The results of comparison experiment is shown in Table V.

The detection result shows that for the very low ratio of Tor traffic (0.01%, 0.05%), the method proposed by Soleimani et al.[8] cannot achieve the detection purpose, which may be because the low ratio was not considered in their experiment. In other ratios of Tor traffic, Soleimani's method achieves high precision rate, but the recall rate is not high compared with precision. Therefore, we can refer to their method in future research and adjust the parameters of the machine learning model to obtain better detection performance.

B. Limitations and Countermeasures

We did not use the latest version of Tor Browser when collecting Tor traffic. We collected traffic mainly around July 2020, and once the obfuscation protocol changed within six months, we needed to re-screen the features for our method.

TABLE V: The results of comparison experiment

Tor traffic ratio	Sampling ratio	Soleimani et al			Our paper		
		Precision	Recall	F1 Score	Precision	Recall	F1 Score
0.01%	8:1	null	0	null	25%	100%	0.4
	16:1	null	0	null	23.08%	100%	0.375
	32:1	null	0	null	50%	100%	0.6667
	64:1	null	null	null	25%	100%	0.4
0.05%	8:1	100%	91.70%	95.70%	57.32%	100%	0.7287
	16:1	100%	50%	0.667	54.05%	95.24%	0.6897
	32:1	null	0	null	50%	100%	0.6667
	64:1	null	null	null	33.33%	100%	0.5
0.10%	8:1	100%	83.30%	0.909	74.24%	93.33%	0.827
	16:1	100%	68.80%	0.815	75.38%	96.08%	0.8448
	32:1	75%	54.50%	0.632	73.33%	88%	0.8
	64:1	100%	25%	0.4	78.57%	91.67%	0.8462
0.15%	8:1	100%	93.80%	0.968	84.88%	95.42%	0.8985
	16:1	100%	76.90%	0.87	87.50%	95.89%	0.915
	32:1	85.70%	54.50%	0.667	89.19%	94.29%	0.9167
	64:1	100%	60%	0.75	93.75%	88.24%	0.9091
0.20%	8:1	94.50%	88.10%	0.912	84.48%	96.55%	0.9011
	16:1	100%	64.90%	0.787	82.30%	93.94%	0.8774
	32:1	100%	100%	1	85.19%	97.87%	0.9109
	64:1	100%	25%	0.4	91.30%	100%	0.9545
0.25%	8:1	98.50%	91.70%	0.95	86.48%	93.78%	0.8998
	16:1	96.60%	93.30%	0.949	84.43%	96.26%	0.8996
	32:1	100%	84.20%	0.914	87.72%	98.04%	0.9259
	64:1	100%	57.10%	0.727	75.86%	100%	0.8627
0.30%	8:1	98.80%	97.60%	0.982	86.69%	96.21%	0.912
	16:1	97.20%	97.20%	0.972	82.31%	98.37%	0.8963
	32:1	100%	94.70%	0.973	85.07%	98.28%	0.912
	64:1	87.50%	100%	0.933	81.48%	95.65%	0.88

In order to prevent detection, the obfuscation protocol can be improved based on the features proposed in this method. The features we extracted are most related to the length of packets. Once the obfuscation protocol has updated for obfuscating packet lengths, such as adding padding in the information control part, shielding ultra-small data packets, our method needs to be updated accordingly.

C. Future work

In this paper, we propose a method to detect Tor bridges in backbone networks. While the experimental results prove the feasibility of the method, the method still has some limitations mentioned above. In future work, we need to follow the update of the obfuscation protocol promptly, re-screen the features, and design a secondary detection method to maintain the practicability of this method.

VII. Conclusion

While the initial design purpose of the anonymous communication systems are only to enhance anonymity, the darknet market based on it has caused major hidden dangers to the network and even social security.

The use of bridges further obfuscates traffic and makes Tor traffic analysis more difficult. In order to exclude normal users using the bridge and identify criminals, the traffic passing through the bridge needs to be analyzed to identify the behavior. Therefore the use of bridges needs to be detected first.

In this paper, we have proposed a method to detect Tor bridges in backbone networks. Compared with other methods, our method samples the traffic to reduce the amount of data that needs to be processed and designs a new storage structure called NCBF for packet statistics recording. Taking into account the low ratio of Tor traffic in backbone networks, we mix the public backbone network traffic data set with different ratios of Tor traffic in experiments to verify the availability of this method in backbone networks. When Tor traffic accounts for only 0.15%, the F1 score of the detection result is maintained at about 0.9. And the recall rate stabilized above 95% all the time.

In future research, we will study how to design a secondary detection method, determine the new features and maintain the usability of the method when the obfuscation protocol update causes the old features to be unavailable.

Our research on bridge detection demonstrates to some extent that there is still room for improvement in Tor, and we believe there are other ways to defend against such attacks and strengthen anti-censorship capabilities besides the countermeasures briefly mentioned in this paper.

Acknowledgment

This work was supported by the National R&D Program of China (2020YFB1807503)

REFERENCES

[1] The chainalysis 2021 crypto crime report. [Online]. Available: https://go.chainalysis.com/2021-Crypto-Crime-Report.html

[2] Users. [Online]. Available: https://metrics.torproject.org/userstats-relay-country.html

[3] R. Dingledine, N. Mathewson, and P. Syverson, "Tor: The second-generation onion router," Naval Research Lab Washington DC, Tech. Rep., 2004.

[4] A. H. Lashkari, G. Draper-Gil, M. S. I. Mamun, and A. A. Ghorbani, "Characterization of tor traffic using time based features." in *ICISSp*, 2017, pp. 253–262.

[5] M. Kim and A. Anpalagan, "Tor traffic classification from raw packet header using convolutional neural network," in *2018 1st IEEE International Conference on Knowledge Innovation and Invention (ICKII)*. IEEE, 2018, pp. 187–190.

[6] J. Lingyu, L. Yang, W. Bailing, L. Hongri, and X. Guodong, "A hierarchical classification approach for tor anonymous traffic," in *2017 IEEE 9th International Conference on Communication Software and Networks (ICCSN)*. IEEE, 2017, pp. 239–243.

[7] Z. Rao, W. Niu, X. Zhang, and H. Li, "Tor anonymous traffic identification based on gravitational clustering," *Peer-to-Peer Networking and Applications*, vol. 11, no. 3, pp. 592–601, 2018.

[8] M. H. M. Soleimani, M. Mansoorizadeh, and M. Nassiri, "Real-time identification of three tor pluggable transports using machine learning techniques," *The Journal of Supercomputing*, vol. 74, no. 10, pp. 4910–4927, 2018.

[9] Y. He, L. Hu, and R. Gao, "Detection of tor traffic hiding under obfs4 protocol based on two-level filtering," in *2019 2nd International Conference on Data Intelligence and Security (ICDIS)*. IEEE, 2019, pp. 195–200.

[10] M. Yang, J. Luo, L. Zhang, X. Wang, and X. Fu, "How to block tor's hidden bridges: detecting methods and countermeasures," *The Journal of Supercomputing*, vol. 66, no. 3, pp. 1285–1305, 2013.

[11] K. C. Claffy, G. C. Polyzos, and H.-W. Braun, "Application of sampling methodologies to network traffic characterization," in *Conference proceedings on Communications architectures, protocols and applications*, 1993, pp. 194–203.

[12] B. Claise, G. Sadasivan, V. Valluri, and M. Djernaes, "Cisco systems netflow services export version 9," 2004.

[13] P. Phaal, S. Panchen, and N. McKee, "Inmon corporation's sflow: A method for monitoring traffic in switched and routed networks," 2001.

[14] A. N. Mahmood, J. Hu, Z. Tari, and C. Leckie, "Critical infrastructure protection: Resource efficient sampling to improve detection of less frequent patterns in network traffic," *Journal of Network and Computer Applications*, vol. 33, no. 4, pp. 491–502, 2010.

[15] W. Meng, W. Li, C. Su, J. Zhou, and R. Lu, "Enhancing trust management for wireless intrusion detection via traffic sampling in the era of big data," *Ieee Access*, vol. 6, pp. 7234–7243, 2017.

[16] L. Huo, D. Jiang, and Z. Lv, "A software-defined networks-based measurement method of network traffic for 6g technologies," *Transactions on Emerging Telecommunications Technologies*, p. e4172, 2020.

[17] R. Jang, "Towards scalable network traffic measurement with sketches," 2020.

[18] Servers. [Online]. Available: https://metrics.torproject.org/networksize.html

[19] Yawning/obfs4. [Online]. Available: https://github.com/Yawning/obfs4

[20] meek · wiki · legacy / trac. [Online]. Available: https://gitlab.torproject.org/legacy/trac/-/wikis/doc/meek

[21] T. Yang, J. Jiang, P. Liu, Q. Huang, J. Gong, Y. Zhou, R. Miao, X. Li, and S. Uhlig, "Elastic sketch: adaptive and fast network-wide measurements," 08 2018, pp. 561–575.

[22] B. H. Bloom, "Space/time trade-offs in hash coding with allowable errors," *Communications of the ACM*, vol. 13, no. 7, pp. 422–426, 1970.

[23] L. Fan, P. Cao, J. Almeida, and A. Z. Broder, "Summary cache: a scalable wide-area web cache sharing protocol," *IEEE/ACM transactions on networking*, vol. 8, no. 3, pp. 281–293, 2000.

[24] G. Androulidakis, V. Chatzigiannakis, S. Papavassiliou, M. Grammatikou, and V. Maglaris, "Understanding and evaluating the impact of sampling on anomaly detection techniques," in *MILCOM 2006-2006 IEEE Military Communications conference*. IEEE, 2006, pp. 1–7.

[25] C. Sony and K. Cho, "Traffic data repository at the wide project," in *Proceedings of USENIX 2000 Annual Technical Conference: FREENIX Track*, 2000, pp. 263–270.

APPENDIX A
FEATURE ENGINEERING

After capturing traffic from the backbone network, packets with the same quintuple (source address, source port, destination address, destination port, communication protocol) can be grouped into the same flow.

The first step is to extract the features from the complete traffic. Based on the existing research[6][7][9] and our observations on traffic, we extract five types of features that can be used for Tor traffic identification, which is shown in Table I.

TABLE I: Type and quantity of initial features

Type No.	Type of features	Number
1	the proportion of packets with different directions	6
2	the proportion of packets with different lengths	14
3	the proportion of packets with different intervals	5
4	the proportion of special packets	3
5	the related logarithmic calculation results	4
Total		32

Some of these features have been used in other Tor traffic identification researches, such as 600-byte packet frequency[6], and the usability of these features has been validated in the complete traffic.

To handle the backbone network traffic, the traffic will be sampled and only a portion of the packets can be obtained from each flow. A fixed number of packets of the same quintuple are called Record in the later feature statistics. Depending on the sampling ratio, the number of packets that can be extracted from a flow varies, resulting in a different number of Records. The packets that make up these Records are not time-dependent, so the proportion of packets with different intervals cannot be used as a post-sampling feature. The associated logarithm calculation results are also discarded for the same reason. The time-dependent packets do not affect the solution, because the features used in this method can also be extracted from such packets.

After the first filtering step, the remaining features are all proportional features, and the eigenvalues need further computation. In order to reduce the storage and computation consumption, as few packet statistics as possible need to be used. At the same time, these features also need to be of some importance to be useful in model training. Therefore, in this paper, the importance of features is evaluated using the Gini-index based method in the random forest algorithm. The final selection of features are shown in Table II.

TABLE II: The meaning and importance of features

Feature	Meaning	Significance score
Ca_1/C_d	The percentage of packets with a length of 0 to 61 to the total number of no-empty packets sent by the client	0.206592
Ca_4/C_d	The percentage of packets with a length greater than 1050 to the total number of no-empty packets sent by the client	0.15457
C_d/C_p	The ratio of non-empty packets to the total number of packets sent by the client	0.095711
C_{psh}/C_d	The percentage of PSH packets out of the total number of non-empty packets sent by the client	0.082727
Sa_4/S_d	The percentage of packets with a length greater than 1050 to the total number of no-empty packets sent by the server	0.07791
Ca_2/C_d	The percentage of packets with a length of 61 to 465 to the total number of no-empty packets sent by the client	0.07743
S_{psh}/S_d	The percentage of PSH packets out of the total number of non-empty packets sent by the server	0.073635
C_0/S_d	The ratio of empty packets sent by the client to non-empty packets sent by the server	0.050955
timestamp	Whether more than half of the packets have timestamp	0.044416
C_d/D_p	The ratio of non-empty packets sent by the client to the total number of bidirectional packets	0.03741
S_d/D_p	The ratio of non-empty packets sent by the server to the total number of bidirectional packets	0.033841
S_d/S_p	The ratio of non-empty packets to the total number of packets sent by the server	0.030836
Sa_2/S_d	The percentage of packets with a length of 61 to 465 to the total number of no-empty packets sent by the server	0.026115
S_0/C_d	The ratio of empty packets sent by the server to non-empty packets sent by the client	0.007852

TABLE III: Statistics to be recorded

Counter	Statistics recorded	Counter	Statistics recorded
C_1	The number of packets sent by the client	C_7	The number of client packets between 0 and 61 in length
C_2	The number of non-empty packets sent by the client	C_8	The number of packets between 61 and 465 in length sent by the client
C_3	The number of packets sent by the server	C_9	The number of packets longer than 1050 sent by the client
C_4	The number of non-empty packets sent by the server	C_{10}	The number of packets between 61 and 465 in length sent by the server
C_5	The number of PSH packets sent by the client	C_{11}	The number of packets longer than 1050 sent by the server
C_6	The number of PSH packets sent by the server	C_{12}	The number of packets with timestamp

An Analysis of First-Party Cookie Exfiltration due to CNAME Redirections

Tongwei Ren*, Alexander Wittman†, Lorenzo De Carli*, Drew Davidson†
*Worcester Polytechnic Institute, †University of Kansas

***Abstract*—DNS CNAME redirections, which can "steer" browser requests towards a domain different than the one in the request's URI, are a simple and oftentimes effective means to obscure the source of a web object behind an alias. These redirections can be used to make third-party content appear as first-party content. The practice of evading browser security mechanisms through misuse of CNAMEs, referred to as CNAME cloaking, has been recently growing in popularity among advertisers/trackers to bypass blocklists and privacy policies.**

While CNAME cloaking has been reported in past measurement studies, its impact on browser cookie policies has not been analyzed. We close this gap by presenting an in-depth characterization of how CNAME redirections affect cookie propagation. Our analysis uses two distinct data collection samples (June and December 2020). Beyond confirming that CNAME cloaking continues to be popular, our analysis identifies a number of websites transmitting sensitive cookies to cloaked third-parties, thus breaking browser cookie policies. Manual review of such cases identifies exfiltration of authentication cookies to advertising/tracking domains, which raises serious security concerns.

I. Introduction

The domain name system (DNS) is a fundamental part of the web infrastructure, allowing domain names to be used as identifiers throughout much of the web browser stack. The most obvious use of domain names is to serve as aliases to IP addresses, but more complex and subtle aliasing relationships can be constructed through DNS records. The entity that owns the domain controls the DNS records, and may either map a (sub)domain to an IP address via an A/AAAA record, or to another domain name—which the DNS will recursively look up—via a CNAME record. While CNAME redirections are invisible to higher layers of abstraction in the browser, they play a crucial role in informing identities and trust. A website may, for instance, legitimately map one of its subdomains to a domain name belonging to a content delivery network (CDN) so that scripts, images, and rich media served from the CDN can interact with content served from the first-party server without crossing a security boundary. By specifying, through DNS, that the CDN and first party content come from the same entity, a visiting browser will *identify and trust* the CDN content as coming from the website domain itself. However, CNAME records can also be used for less benign purposes.

Misuse of CNAME records to hide the source of advertising/tracking content is a recurring issue [30], [29] which has seen a resurgence [21]. Recently, several websites have been found to deploy redirections for this purpose [31], [19], [36]. This utilization of CNAME records allows advertisers to serve content that appears to come from the first-party, complicating the task of ad-blockers. CNAME use is by no means the only strategy to integrate advertising services into first-party code [29], but it has a notably problematic effect of weakening a core mechanism of web security, the same origin policy (SOP)—by causing browsers to treat third-party subdomains as part of the first party origin. Forgoing origin-based isolation gives scripts imported from the CNAME domain permissions that are potentially contrary to the intent of the website administrator, such as the capability to read and manipulate first-party cookies and the DOM. Due to their negative connotation, these CNAME redirections of advertising/tracking resources from a first- to third-party domain have been termed *CNAME cloaking*. We furthermore term a third-party domain which is used as a target of CNAME cloaking as a *cloaked domain*.

In this paper we focus on the implications of CNAME cloaking on browser cookie policies. For web developers, correctly configuring a cookie policy is a delicate balancing act between security and usability. Cookies set with incorrect configurations can have significant consequences, from major functionality breakdown to allowing malicious code to impersonate an authenticated user. CNAME redirections throw in an additional layer of complexity, as they entangle otherwise-distinct origins. In our work, we perform an analysis of cookie behavior across Alexa top-10000 websites. We identify numerous instances of CNAME cloaking and a significant number of cases where first-party cookies are sent to third-parties due to cloaking. Furthermore, we carry a manual, in-depth analysis on select websites, showing first-party authentication cookies being propagated to third-party advertisers. Propagation of authentication cookies to (non-authentication-related) third-parties serve no functional purpose, and is likely an unintended consequence of cloaking. At the same time, such events represent serious security lapses.

Mitigations against CNAME cloaking are still nascent, as the problem is not well-studied. Recent additions to ad-blocking tools including UBlock Origin and AdBlocker were introduced as recently as November 2019 [16]. Unfortunately, these tools rely on manually-curated blocklists, which have no guarantee of being exhaustive. 95 of the 101 distinct entities that we found to be the targets of CNAME cloaking were not covered in these lists. Despite previous anecdotal evidence of sensitive cookies being forwarded to cloaked domains [19], we believe our work to be the first to investigate the security/privacy impact of CNAME cloaking with respect to cookies. Integrated browser protections are also limited, and

Workshop on Measurements, Attacks, and Defenses for the Web (MADWeb) 2021
25 February 2021, Virtual
https://dx.doi.org/10.14722/madweb.2021.23018
www.ndss-symposium.org

those protections that do exist are quite new: Brave's CNAME cloaking mitigations for content blocking were announced as recently as October 27th, 2020 [17], and Apple's defenses were only released to Safari alongside the recent Big Sur update [14]. Furthermore, the popular Chrome, Firefox, and Edge browsers have no CNAME defenses.

Studying the threat of CNAME cloaking in practice is essential to inform the debate surrounding the security and privacy implications of online tracking and advertising. However, conducting a large-scale study of the impact of CNAME cloaking on cookie policies is challenging, due to the scale and complexity of the analysis. Identifying cloaking and cookie exfiltration requires sifting through all objects served by the large number of websites that can be conceivably construed as popular. To handle the scalability challenge, we leverage a custom-built analysis platform that allows us to analyze millions of HTTPS requests towards 95% of Alexa Top-10000 websites, identifying and reporting all instance of CNAME redirections. We augmented this automation platform with extensive manual analysis of exfiltrated cookies and the domains to which they are propagated. **Our main contributions are:**

- We track cookie creation and exfiltration for Alexa top-10000 websites, identifying a number of instances where first-party cookies are sent to unrelated advertising third-parties due to CNAME cloaking.
- We perform an in-depth manual analysis for a select sample of websites, which shows that sensitive content is exposed in practice to third-parties through CNAME cloaking, including authentication tokens that may allow for impersonation attacks.
- We perform our data collection and analysis in two experiments six months apart (June and December 2020), identifying trends that underscore the prevalence of the phenomenon.
- We make our dataset available for other researchers to investigate CNAME cloaking[1].

To the best of our knowledge, our work is the first to shed light on the impact of CNAME cloaking on cookie exfiltration.

II. Background

A. CNAME Redirections

A CNAME (Canonical Name) redirection is used to inform a DNS cache performing a resolution that the provided hostname is an alias for a different hostname. Upon receiving a CNAME answer, a DNS cache issues a second query for the canonical name, and subsequently packages (i) the original CNAME record, and (ii) the A (or AAAA) record for the canonical hostname, in a single response to the client. For example, consider a hostname $www.domainA.com$ whose resolution encounters a CNAME record pointing to $srv1.cloudprovider.com$. The answer received by the client will include both this $CNAME$ record, and an A record expressing the IP address of $srv1.cloudprovider.com$. In some cases, multiple CNAME records may be encountered on the path to an A/AAAA record.

[1]https://www.dropbox.com/sh/nd1b4bzjhlp1fr9/AABTMDV9OeeOoL4gu_TzATKga

CNAME redirections offer an additional layer of indirection on top of the one naturally provided by DNS, and simplify a number of benign use cases (e.g., redirecting requests towards the main hostname to an external cloud provider). Importantly, since DNS resolutions are low-level operations unconstrained by browser policy, a CNAME redirection may be to a completely distinct domain, as in the previous example wherein a request for $www.domainA.com$ was CNAME-redirected to $srv1.cloudprovider.com$.

B. Definitions

First, we define the **first-party domain** to be the domain of the website the user is visiting in a browsing session, i.e., the domain shown in the browser URL bar. Note that although *website* and *domain* are distinct concepts, for the purpose of our analysis a website corresponds to exactly one domain. A **first-party subdomain** is a subdomain of the first-party domain. A **third-party domain** is a domain, different from the first-party domain, from which content is fetched while browsing the first-party domain. For example, if the user is visiting *www.domainA.com* and the website includes an iframe with content from *domainB.com*, *domainA.com* is a first-party domain and *domainB.com* a third-party domain. A **third-party subdomain** is a subdomain of a third-party domain.

*A **first-party redirection** consists of a CNAME redirection from a first-party subdomain to a different domain.* As an example, consider a website at *www.domainA.com*, which includes some web resources which are fetched from *sd1.domainA.com*. In turn, this subdomain CNAME-redirects to *sd2.domainB.com*.

*A **third-party redirection** consists of a CNAME redirection from a third-party subdomain to a different domain.* For example, consider the situation where the website at *www.domainA.com* includes an iframe pulling content from *sd1.domainB.com*, and this subdomain CNAME-redirects to *sd2.domainC.com*.

In this study, we only consider first-party redirections. We consider this type of redirection to be particularly important, since it allows interactions between first- and third-party content. Therefore, we ignore third-party redirections and redirections that remain within the same domain, be it first- or third-party. As a CNAME redirection makes it difficult for the browser logic to identify the true source which serves an HTTP request, we refer to the domains at the end of first-party redirection chains as **cloaked domains**. We also refer to first-party redirections as **cloaking**.

C. Browser Cookie Policies

One of the most straightforward ways to maintain user identities on the web is to associate a stateful token to each browser in the form of a cookie. Cookies are text-based key-value pairs that can be set by a first- or third-party, and are managed by the browser. Cookies are popular for authentication, since an authentication token can be stored as a key-value pair. Cookies are also popular for user tracking, since they offer a means to re-identify a user across multiple web requests. In its most basic form, a first-party can track a user with a key-value pair representing a unique ID in a cookie, and then request that cookie from every visiting browser. On the first visit to that site, the cookie will not yet exist, so a unique identifier will be generated and sent to be managed by the browser. On subsequent visits, the first-party can retrieve the tracking ID from the cookie, and re-identify the user for whom the cookie was generated. Similarly, third-party entities can generate and serve cookies to users for a variety of purposes, including tracking across the web. Due to the security- and privacy-sensitive content of cookies, browser policies limiting propagation of cookies use a notion of origin-based isolation as part of the cookie policy: a cookie may specify the subdomain of servers that are allowed to see the cookie (by default the domain of the URL serving the cookie will be used if no subdomain is set). The cookie policy works in cooperation with the well-known same-origin policy (SOP) [33] to ensure that data is not leaked through cookies: the browser can prohibit access to a cookie from other origins even if it within the cookie's domain. These mechanisms are important security measures, since cookies can contain authentication data and personally-identifiable information.

Indeed, a use of CNAME cloaking is to allow a third-party to set tracking cookies that appear to come from the first-party domain. The effect of CNAME Cloaking is to obscure the true origin of a web request for a resource like a cookie. In the process, the cloaked domain can subvert the cookie policy for the purpose of more invasive interactions, such as user tracking. Since cookies can be used for authentication, weakening the distinction may also lead to information leakage to third parties, such as credential stealing.

D. Browser-based Countermeasures

In recognition of the threat of CNAME cloaking, several client-side solutions have been proposed or implemented to mitigate the threat. Since the CNAME record is a part of DNS, it is sufficient for a browser to recursively check CNAME records that are encountered as part of the request. In effect, this approach uncovers the true provenance of a domain obscured by the CNAME record. This approach, which is implemented natively in the Brave browser and in UBlock Origin on Firefox, is particularly effective in allowing block-lists to transcend the threat of CNAME cloaking. However, without a re-implementation of the browser cookie policy that is CNAME-cloaking aware, cloaked third parties that do not appear on a blocklist can still access first-party resources.

E. Object of Study

The goal of our work is to characterize first-party cloaking which causes cookies to propagate beyond the first-party domain which sets them. However, not all such propagations are significant. In particular, we focus on instances where cookies propagate to advertising- and tracking-related third-party domains which bear no direct relation to the first party setting the cookie. Such redirections are problematic because they reveal potentially sensitive data belonging to the first party. In some cases, evidence strongly suggests that cookies are exfiltrated by mistake, i.e., as an unintentional consequence of cloaking (ref. Section IX-B).

III. Methodology

In this section, we outline our data collection infrastructure and methodology.

Our goal is to measure the extent to which CNAME cloaking affects the propagation of first-party cookies to third-parties. We limit the scope of our measurements to the Alexa top-10,000 websites. This is necessary as our analysis (detailed below) involves complex, time-consuming manual steps. This decision is further discussed in Section IX-D.

Our analysis is structured in four steps: (a) bulk data collection; (b) domain classification; (c) cookie lifecycle analysis; and (d) manual website analysis. We further performed a high-level evaluation of browser defenses (e). In the following, we detail each step.

A. Data Collection

Cookies are set and transmitted by HTTP(s) responses and requests; therefore, studying the lifecycle of cookies for a website requires logging all requests/responses generated while visiting a website. Furthermore, the DNS resolution chain associated with the hostname in each request must also be logged. Due to the volume of data, we limit bulk data collection to the homepage of each website in the Alexa Top-10,000 list (we discuss why we consider this an acceptable limitation in Section IX-D).

To collect bulk website data, we use a custom crawler/logger based on a current version of the Firefox browser, the Selenium web testing framework [9], and the mitmproxy HTTPS proxy [7]. As neither Selenium nor mitmproxy provide insight into DNS resolutions, immediately after each request we issue a DNS resolution for the respective subdomain using dnspython (unless we previously encountered the subdomain during the same visit). Changes in DNS records between resource fetching and DNS resolution are unlikely: the interval between the two operations remains below a second, while DNS updating frequencies tend to be minutes to hours.

We encapsulate our tooling in a Singularity container and spawn multiple instances on an HPC cluster at the University of Kansas. A separate container running MongoDB server is used as log storage. During data collection, our Singularity cluster is configured to spawn 20 concurrent instances. Each container is short-lived, and receives a list of 500 websites to visit on startup. It visits each website's homepage for 30 seconds, to ensure complete loading of dynamic and delayed content. The container logs the content of all HTTP requests and responses, including header and request/response body. Browser caches are cleared between each visit.

In order to obtain an historical perspective on cloaking we repeated the collection in June and December 2020, in both cases using the infrastructure described above. The raw data upon which we perform our analysis consist of HTTP requests and responses, and DNS responses associated to the URI in each request.

1) Isolating Candidate Redirections: Our object of study concerns redirections that cause cookies to be sent to third-party advertisers/trackers. Before further analyzing our dataset, we begin by isolating a set of candidate redirections that are likely to be advertising-/tracking-related, and we restrict further analysis to those. We use two approaches:

Domain-based: We extract all domains in the EasyList [4] and EasyPrivacy [6] lists, which are popular blocklists used by browser-based ad-blockers. We only extracted domains that explicitly appear in blocking rules, e.g., the rule `||myfinance.com^$domain=cnn.com|marketwatch.com` would cause us to extract the domain `myfinance.com`. We then select all first-party redirections ending in one of such domains.

URL-based: The lists introduced above also include rules that identify advertising and tracking content based on the presence of specific byte patterns in the URL (regardless of domain). We extract all such patterns and we select all first-party redirections affecting requests that match those patterns.

Together, the redirections collected via the methods above constitute 19% of all first-party redirections. Note that the above methods are prone to false positives, as not all identified domains are solely used to distribute advertising/tracking content. In practice this does not constitute a problem, as identified domains are further manually analyzed, as discussed below. We characterize our dataset (pre- and post-filtering) in Section IV.

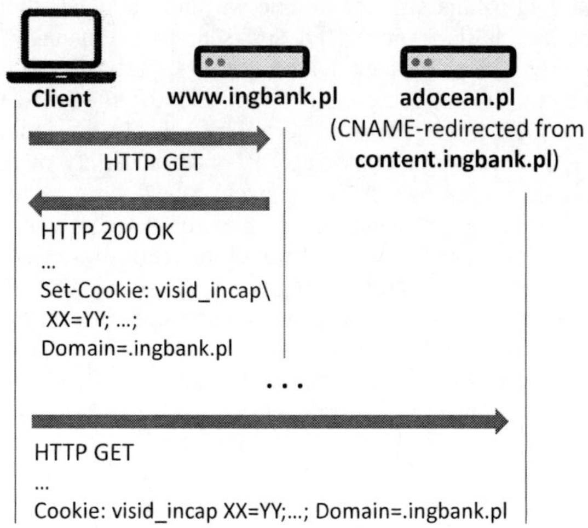

Fig. 1: Cross-domain cookie transmission

B. Domain Classification

Philosophically, the issue under study is propagation of cookies to domains whose ownership has been misrepresented due to CNAME redirections. However, redirections can be deployed in a variety of ways, not all of which misrepresent the entity to which cookies are transmitted.

For example, redirecting a first-party domain to an ad provider which is also owned by the first-party, is arguably not a misrepresentation. Such redirections are deployed often and as a matter of traffic optimization, and data exchanged across the two domains remain within control of the user and the first-party. On the opposite end of the spectrum, a first-party redirecting requests to an external tracking company is concerning, since the user may not wish to expose its private information to such a third party. In between these extremes there are a number of ambiguous cases, which include redirections towards a number external CDNs and PaaS which are sometimes used for advertising/tracking (and therefore appear in blocklists). These entities host content upon which the first party retains varying degrees of control.

Given the considerations above, we implemented a high-level taxonomy based on manual investigation of each *(source domain, destination domain)* pair in the dataset, and we make sources for each labeling decision publicly available in our dataset (ref. Section I). We include the following categories:

Same-organization: includes redirections in which source and target domain are broadly part of the same organization. An example is *msn.com* redirecting to *microsoft.com*. We put a redirection in this category if two domains can be determined to belong to the same organization either via publicly available data, or by using the "adns" methodology by Krishnamurthy and Wills [29]. The latter puts two domains under the same ownership if they declare the same authoritative DNS server (we manually reviewed the output to filter out false positives).

External ad/tracking: This category includes redirections which do not fall under **Same-organization**, and whose destination domain belongs to an organization whose primary business is online advertising and/or tracking. In order to make this determination we: (i) reviewed whether the destination domain advertises itself as a provider of advertising services; and (ii) reviewed company information aggregators such as *crunchbase.com*. Conservatively, we only put a domain in this category if the information sources described above unambiguously identify the domain as belonging to an advertiser/tracker.

Other 3rd-Parties: This category includes all redirections which do not fall under either **Same-organization** or **External ad/tracking**. Most first-party redirections not meeting this condition are directed towards CDNs and cloud providers.

We report the results of our domain analysis in Section V.

C. Cookie Lifecycle Analysis

After having performed domain classification, we specifically focus our analysis on the lifecycle of cookies set by first parties. In both the June and December datasets, we isolate browsing sessions, among those in our dataset, in which the first-party domain issues a *Set-Cookie* for a cookie which is later transmitted to a third-party via a first-party redirection. During the process, we filter out cookies that are set by first-party domains which consist of cloaked third-party ones, as those cookies are not truly set by a first-party. For example, Figure 1 presents a situation (extracted from our June 2020 dataset) in which what appears to be a first-party tracking cookie set during a visit to *www.ingbank.pl* is later transmitted to *adocean.pl*, despite browser design forbidding explicit cross-domain cookie transmissions.

In practice, the first-party may issue multiple *Set-Cookie* directives across several responses; however, the browser coalesces these cookie key/value pairs into a single string when they are sent back in HTTP request headers via a *Cookie:* field. To avoid ambiguities, here we consider the content of a single *Cookie:* HTTP request header field as one cookie. This analysis is automated and at the end of it we map each cookie to the label (*Same organization*, *External ad/tracking*, *Other 3rd-parties*) assigned to the third-party domain to which it gets transmitted. Results are reported in Section VI.

D. Manual Cookie Analysis

In order to gain insight on inter-domain cookie transmission beyond each website's homepage, we performed a second experiment focused on exfiltration of sensitive cookies. Our definition of *sensitive cookie* is provided below; intuitively, those are cookies which store information pertaining the user identity and/or authentication. We further define the implication of these cookies being exfiltrated in Section IX.

For this experiment, we selected 62 websites, among those found perform redirections towards domains in the External Ad/Tracking category (roughly 14% of all sites in this group). We selected these sites at random, excluding those which require payment for creating an account. We then created user accounts on each of them and recorded authenticated browsing sessions using our *mitmproxy* setup. Finally, we repeated this analysis for the same websites in December 2020 (we used the same set of sites in both sessions).

Collecting candidate cookies: in each experiment, during the login process we manually identified candidate cookies via the Firefox network console. Using the console UI, we identified first-party cookies set in the HTTP traffic generated in response to logging into the website (we also verified that each of these cookies is set by the actual first-party, and not by a cloaked third-party). We then searched HTTP session logs to determine whether each candidate had been transmitted to a cloaked domain falling in the "External Ad/Tracking" category. We retained only candidates for which at least one such transmission was observed.

In the next step, we analyzed each candidate cookie to determine if it is to be considered *sensitive*. Note that here a candidate cookie is intended as a key/value pair, and not the whole *Cookie* field in the HTTP header. We define a cookie sensitive if it matches one of the following conditions (or both):

a) Cookie stores sensitive content: We consider this condition matched if the cookie visibly contains one or more of the following data: user name, user email, user website ID, geographical location, profile data, account status, and timestamp. We manually analyzed each candidate to attempt to determine its content. We found this to be a complex process, due to the fact that cookie content is not bound to follow any standardized format. Many cookies appear to be textual serializations of internal backend state; without knowledge of the backend logic, it is impossible to make sense of them. Luckily, however, some cookies are formatted according to standards (e.g., JWT, OpenAM), and/or have easily recognizable structure. Overall, decoding was an empirical, heuristic process where we used our own domain knowledge to determine the appropriate decoding technique. For example, apply base64 decoding if the content appears to be base64-encoded data; apply an OpenAM decoder if the cookie is in OpenAM format, etc. (OpenAM [8] is an access management platform). As a result, the analysis is conservative: it may exhibit false negatives, but not false positives. We term cookies belonging to this category as "information cookies".

b) Cookie is necessary for user identity/authentication: We verified each candidate by visiting the website again after manually deleting the candidate from the browser cookie storage. A website requiring the user to re-authenticate themselves after deleting a cookie strongly suggests the cookie plays a role in the authentication process (we also verified that the website recognizes the user if the cookie is not deleted). We termed such cookies "authentication cookies". We also noted that in some cases, after deleting a cookie it was possible to log back in by confirm the user identity without entering a password. A brief analysis suggests that server-side logic may be recovering the session via data in other cookies and/or local storage. We term cookies leading to this behavior as "identity cookies".

	June 2020	December 2020
Websites	9,578	9,683
HTTP Requests	1,576,505	1,554,789
HTTP Responses	1,552,791	1,533,379
Avg Req size [B]	1,364	1,428
Avg Resp size [B]	104,535	102,566
First-party redirections	188,300	203,957
Redirections after filtering	28,250	46,745

TABLE I: Summary of main dataset

Note that information cookies and identity/authentication cookies are not disjoint sets, since some cookies may match both conditions above. The results of our manual analysis are reported in Section VII.

E. Browser Blocklist Evaluation

As described in Section II-D, some client-side security mechanisms exist to prevent CNAME cloaking from evading blocklists. These mechanisms, embedded in the browser or loaded via extensions, are implemented by recursively dereferencing CNAME records to check for entities on a blocklist. However, cookie leaks through CNAMEs (inadvertent or otherwise) may still occur when the cloaked domain is not blocked.

To verify the behavior of cookie sharing between sites that are not blocklisted, we arranged a simple experiment: we created two sites with distinct domains, to simulate a third party and a collaborating first party. We added a DNS record containing a CNAME record for a subdomain of the first party to the third party site, and embedded the third party page into a first party page. This basic experiment is sufficient to observe the behavior of browsers' cookie policies when neither site is on a blocklist. We verified that no browser prevents cookie sharing through CNAME records, including those browsers that implement recursive CNAME lookups for blocklists: in every major browser, the simulated third party had access to all cookies not otherwise prevented by the cookie policy.

This preliminary analysis encouraged us to perform a further experiment. We selected the Safari and Brave browsers as these have explicitly advertised their ability to prevent CNAME cloaking [3], [10]. We then evaluated whether the instances of authentication cookie exfiltration identified in our analysis of the December 2020 dataset (ref. Section III-D) happen under these browsers. Results are provided in Section VIII.

IV. Data Collection Results

Our Dataset is characterized in Table I, rows 1-5. In the June and December sessions, our data collection infrastructure successfully processed **9578** (June) and **9683** (December) websites among those in the Alexa Top-10,000 list. The remaining

	June 2020	December 2020
First-party redirections	3,330	3,417
Same-organization:	416	249
External Ad/Tracking:	509	513
Other 3rd-Parties:	2,405	2,655
Source domains	1,509	1,597
Same-organization:	176	154
External Ad/Tracking:	453	459
Other 3rd-Parties:	998	1,207
Destination domains	135	133
Same-organization:	29	24
External Ad/Tracking:	31	33
Other 3rd-Parties:	78	77

TABLE II: First-party redirections and domains in each category

websites failed to return any content, or returned various types of HTTP error codes. This data was then processed to isolate all requests for which the DNS answer included a first-party CNAME redirection (row 6 in Table I). We ignored redirections starting and ending within the same domain, which are extremely common and irrelevant to this study.

The set of first-party redirections was further filtered according to the methodology described in Section III-A1. The remaining redirections (detailed in row 7 of Table I) constitute approximately **19%** of all first-party redirections.

V. Domain Classification Results

We isolated all the *unique* first party redirections within the set described in Section IV (i.e. we collapsed redirections appearing more than once into one). For each unique redirection, we classified the target domain according to the categories of Section III-B. Figure 2 breaks down first-party redirections into the three categories above, for June and December data. Each square represents 2.5% of the total redirections.

Table II shows details of the set of redirections. In particular, it presents breakdowns by category for both the redirections themselves, and domains that appear as sources and target of such redirections. Note that some domains appear in multiple categories. The number of unique source domains deploying first-party redirections, across our two data collection sessions, is **2818** (There are **1527** overlapping domains between the sets of June and December domains). The number of unique domains appearing as target of redirections is **101** (There are **31** overlapping domains between the sets of June and December domains). Interestingly, **95 of 101** such domains did not appear in public CNAME cloaking blocklists [36] at the time of writing.

The set of domains appearing as source of advertising-related first-party redirections is far larger than that of destinations, and there are no domains belonging to both sets. Analysis of the graph defined by source and destination domains suggests that there exist multiple communities of websites using CNAME cloaking, each clustered around a highly popular content provider. At the same time, most websites which redirect their users to third-parties via CNAME cloaking depend on a single provider of cloaked content. The

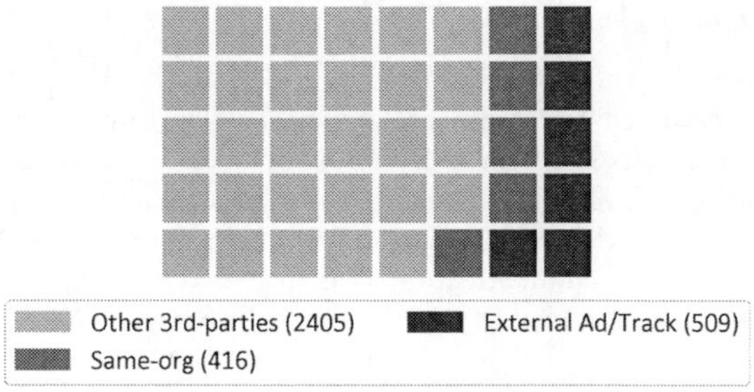

(a) June 2020

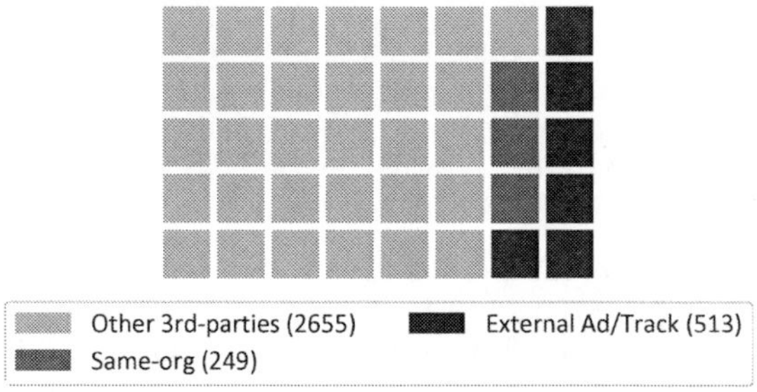

(b) December 2020

Fig. 2: Categorization of first-party redirections by category of destination domain

average outdegree for redirection sources in June (December) is **1.04** (**1.05**) and the average indegree for targets is **15.22** (**14.58**). For example, the most popular provider, *omtrdc.net*, served requests from **325** sources in the June dataset and **361** sources in the December dataset.

A. CNAME Redirections Chains

An iterative DNS resolution may include multiple CNAME redirections; we encountered **49** (**508**) redirections of length greater than 2 in the June (December) dataset. To categorizing these, we use the following labeling heuristic: first, if the first and last domain share ownership, we apply the "same-organization" label. Otherwise, if $>= 1$ domains in the chain are labeled as "External Ad/Tracking", we label the entire redirection as such. Otherwise, we label the redirection as "Other 3rd-parties". We also identified **85** (**318**) cases where the source domain redirects to an external one, which then redirects back to the original domain. These appear to be related to DNS-based load-balancing, and we ignored them.

VI. Cookie Lifecycle Analysis Results

In this section we demonstrate that CNAME-based cross-domain cookie transmission happens in the wild. In particular, we isolate all instances of first-party cookies transmitted to cloaked third-parties from website homepages, according to the methodology described in Section III-C.

In the June dataset, the analysis results in **89** cookies that appear in cross-domain transmissions (for a total of **521** key/value pairs). In December, we identify **108** cookies representing **914** key/value pairs. Next, we classify the third-party domains receiving first-party cookies according to the

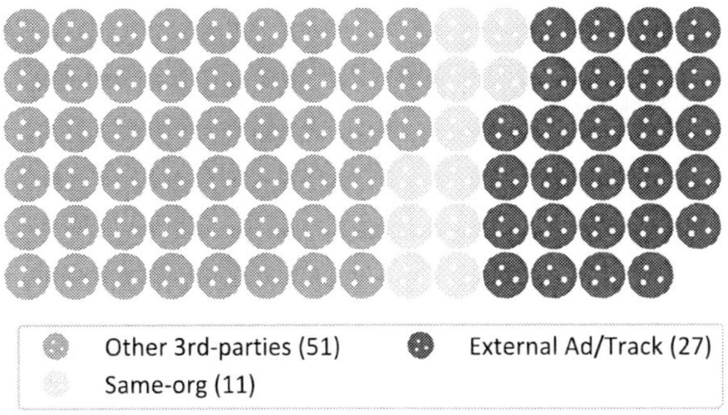

(a) June 2020

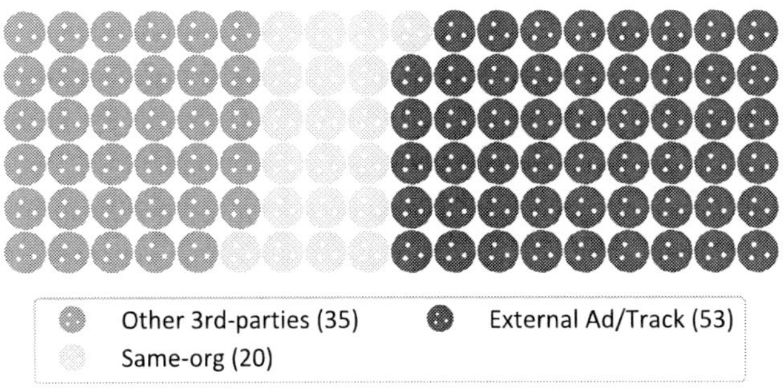

(b) December 2020

Fig. 3: Categorization of cross-domain cookie transmission instances by category of destination domain

	June 2020	Dec. 2020
First-party (source) domains	28	26
Sends to Same-organization:	5	5
Sends to External Ad/Tracking:	6	9
Sends to Other 3rd-Parties:	18	12
Third-party (destination) domains	10	12
Belongs to Same-organization:	1	2
Belongs to External Ad/Tracking:	4	4
Belongs to Other 3rd-Parties:	5	6

TABLE III: Number of domains involved in cross-domain cookie transmission

categories of Section III-B; results are presented in Figure 3. Table III further breaks down the number of source/destination domains in each category.

VII. Manual Cookie Analysis Results

As discussed in Section III-D, this experiment involves manually creating accounts in a select sample of 62 websites, and isolating cookies which are (1) generated in response to authentication; (2) sent to a cloaked third-party in the "External Ad/Tracking" category; and (3) contain user information and/or are necessary to conduct an authenticated session.

Table IV summarizes the results of the analysis. The table lists all domain found to leak sensitive cookies. For each domain, we specify if exfiltration happened in the June (column 2) and December (column 3) analysis. We furthermore list the type and number of leaked key/value cookie pairs ("cookies" for brevity in the following) (column 4). Cookies listed under the **I** label are Information cookies; cookies listed under the **A** label are Authentication cookies; and cookies listed under the **D** label are iDentity cookies (refer to Section III-D for a detailed description of each category). Some cookies are both information cookies and authentication (or identity) cookies. Finally, for each domain we provide a few relevant details in regards to exfiltrated cookie content (column 5).

While determining if a cookie belongs to the authentication/identity category is simple (deleting the cookie results in a user logout), determining whether a cookie contains personal information is more complex. Despite our efforts, some cookies had no obvious plaintext meaning. Other used open, reversible standards that are amenable to decoding. Figure 4 summarizes the analysis of two such cookies. *realestate.com.au* transmits three cookies storing JSON data. One contains, among other things, the semi-obfuscated user email. Another stores a JWT token [26]; such tokens are used to encode website and user identity in single sign-on systems (contextual clues suggests that this website uses Amazon Cognito). *sas.com* transmits an OpenAM session cookie. OpenAM [8] is an access management platform; the purpose of an OpenAM cookie is to facilitate single-sign on [5]. Indeed, Figure 4 shows that it contains internal server-side session identifiers. Other authentication-related cookies contain opaque data which is probably only meaningful in the context of the server-side logic. For example, *carsales.com.au* sends an ".XdmAuth" cookie, which contains 644 bytes of binary data, to advertisers. Data appears to be a randomly generated token according to entropy analysis. Removing this cookie fully logs out the user.

VIII. Browser Blocklist Evaluation Results

In this section, we used the Brave and Safari browsers to visit all websites found to exfiltrate authentication cookies in our December 2020 dataset (ref. Table IV). When using Safari, **2 out of 7** instances of exfiltration were blocked (cookies were blocked on *autotrader.com* and *carsales.com.au*). When using Brave, **6 out of 7** instances of exfiltration were blocked (cookies were exfiltrated on *mathworks.com*).

IX. Discussion

A. Summary of Results

Our analysis shows that despite recent press coverage of CNAME cloaking, the practice is still observable, even on popular sites. Overall, data in Section V shows that the practice is uncommon, but not rare: more than **4%** of Alexa-10000 websites perform first-party redirections towards destination domains which can be unambiguously identified as third-party advertisers/trackers. Analysis of the historical data show a negligible decrease (**1%**), between June and December 2020, in the number of domains performing first-party redirections to destinations that are unambiguously classified as third-party advertisers/trackers. Interestingly, the decrease in the number of domains acting as destination of such redirections is more significant (**7%**). We speculate that some advertisers may be renouncing the practice due to community pressure; however, there is no conclusive evidence.

Domain	June 2020	Dec. 2020	#Key/Value Pairs	Content found in cookies
autotrader.com	✗	✓	**A/I:1**	HEX data; user email address
carsales.com.au	✓	✓	**A:1**	Opaque HEX data
cheaptickets.com	✓	✓	**A:1**; I:1	Opaque encoded data; username
childrensplace.com	✓	✓	**A:5**; I:9	Base64 data; user's name, location, ZIP, account n., reg. date
denik.cz	✓	✓	D:2; D/I:1	User email address
everydayhealth.com	✗	✓	**A:3**; I:3	Opaque HEX data; user email, username, name, birthday, ZIP
intel.com	✗	✓	**A:1**	Opaque Base64 data
mathworks.com	✗	✓	**A:1**; I:1	HEX data; username and profile-picture filename
realestate.com.au	✓	✗	D/I:1	JWT token (see Figure 4); user email address
royalcaribbeans.com	✓	✗	**A:1**	OpenAM authentication cookie
sas.com	✓	✗	D:1; I:1	OpenAM-formatted cookie (see Figure 4); username
startribune.com	✓	✓	D:5; D/I:5	JWT token; user email address, registration date and ZIP code
travelzoo.com	✓	✗	**A:1**	Opaque HEX data
vagaro.com	✗	✓	I:1	City-level user location and ZIP code

TABLE IV: Categorization of sensitive key/value cookie pairs exfiltrated to third parties (**I**: information cookie; **A**: Authentication cookie; **D**: iDentity cookie; **A/I**: Authentication and Information cookie; **D/I**: iDentity and Information cookie). In column 4, items in bold represent authentication cookies exfiltrated to third parties.

The analysis of Section VI shows that these redirections have an impact on cookie policies. A number of websites were found exfiltrating cookies to advertising/tracking third-parties on their homepage. The number is small, but increasing (**9** in the December dataset, vs **6** in the June dataset). The number of first-party cookies transmitted in such events also increased slightly (from **89** in June to **108** in December 2020). Likewise, the percentage of such cookies which is sent to advertisers/trackers increased from **30%** to **49%**. It should be pointed out, however, that these exfiltrations involve cookies generated simply in response to a non-authenticated users browsing a website homepage. Upon close analysis, most cookies appear to be related to session and/or user identification and geolocation (based the presence of keys such as "visid", "sid", "Country", and similar). A few (containing the key "ak_bsmc") appear to be related to Akamai's bot detection platform. Unfortunately, without knowledge of each specific website design rationale, it is impossible to determine whether such cookies were intended to be exposed to third-parties. It is also worth noting that the practice of having first-parties set tracking cookies on behalf of advertisers is well-documented [29]. At least some cases identified above may be instances of this practice.

In order to evaluate the extent of cookie exfiltration beyond each site's homepage, we performed the manual analysis of Section VII. The analysis focused on a sample of websites known to perform first-party redirections, and found that roughly one every seven websites analyzed exfiltrates cookies which are generated in response to user authentication, and contain sensitive information. Through this process, we identified **9** domains exfiltrating authentication/identity cookies to third-parties in June, and **10** in December. Only **5** domains appears in both sets, suggesting churn in the websites suffering from this type of issues. Overall, the identified domains exfiltrated **46** cookies. Among those, we identified **15** authentication-related cookies which are particularly interesting. We further discuss those in the following section.

Our final experiment (Section VIII) looked at the effectiveness of browser-based blocklist in preventing sensitive cookie exfiltration. At high level, the experiment suggests that neither Safari nor Brave prevents cookie sharing through CNAME records, unless the redirection target is explicitly included in a blocklist.

B. Security Implications of our Findings

The impact of any individual instance of CNAME cloaking is difficult to predict; although a first party site may expose cookies to a given third party, as discussed above in some cases that behavior may be intentional. Without visibility into the behavior of the third party, it is likewise impossible to determine how the cookie is being used (if at all). Nevertheless, CNAME Cloaking as an aggregate phenomenon has undesirable implications for user security and privacy. In a broad, theoretical sense, origin-based isolation is one of the most recognized security principles of web browsers, which is muddied by CNAME cloaking. As our work shows, third parties and first parties are willing to collaborate in ways that blur origin-based security. Regardless of the parties' intent, browser protections that would prevent incidental data collection (i.e. cookies) are rendered less effective.

Identity and authentication-related cookies are particularly interesting for studying the impact of weakening browser protections. These cookies are generated by a website in response to a user login, and may contain authentication tokens (or similar values) whose purpose is to recognize the user as authenticated, and/or various classes of user- and session-related data. The exfiltration of authentication cookies as those detailed in Table IV carries direct practical implications, as it may open the door to impersonation and account takeover. The most direct mean to impersonate the user involve an attacker directing requests to the first-party website, presenting the obtained authentication cookies in an attempt to pose as the victim user. Note that access to authentication cookies alone may not be sufficient. First, authenticated sessions may be operated with mechanisms beyond cookies (e.g., header-based tokens). Also, some frameworks deploy countermeasures, like CSRF tokens, which are designed to ensure authentication cookies are used within a legitimate browsing session. We also point out that the domains on the receiving end of exfiltrated sensitive cookies receive them as a matter of standard browser

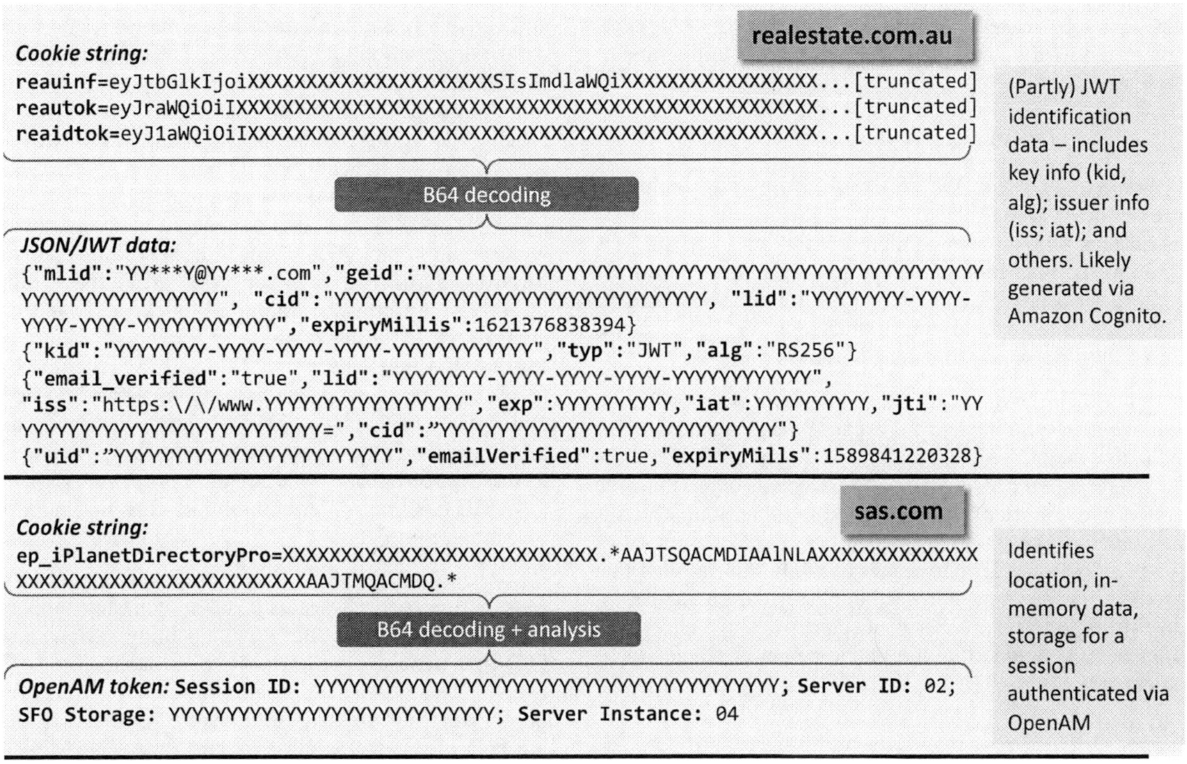

Fig. 4: Examples of sensitive cookies transmitted across domains

cookie policies; most likely, the exfiltration we identified are not performed maliciously, and the third parties receiving those simply ignore them. However, exfiltration of authentication material such as tokens beyond the boundary of the first-party website still constitutes a significant relaxation of security, and can simplify attacks. In this case, exfiltrated information is directed to third-parties which are also, at the same time, injecting content into the first-party website. Thus exfiltration can be construed as extending the first-party attack surface, and therefore we believe it constitutes a significant finding.

From the point of view of our study, such exfiltrations are also relevant because they may not be intentional. A number of websites set authentication/identity cookies with either the "Secure" or "HttpOnly" flag, or both (**7** out of **9** websites in both dataset). These flags respectively instruct the browser to only transmit the cookie over encrypted connection, and to negate access to the cookies from JavaScript code; their presence further suggest that these cookies are considered at least somewhat security sensitive by the website maintainers. Fine-grained data pertaining to authenticated sessions is not necessary for user tracking; as such, we suspect these cookies are broadcasted to third-parties as an unintended consequence of CNAME cloaking.

In terms of incentives, CNAME cloaking appears to be a feasible means for advertisers to evade blocklists when they have the cooperation of first parties. Ours and previous analyses [31], [19] suggests that evading blocklists is the main incentive for employing advertising-related CNAME cloaking. Furthermore, there is no apparent technical disincentive from employing CNAME cloaking.

C. Possible Remediations

As we showed in Sections III-E and VIII, no browser or security mechanism attempts to detect or prevent illegitimate use of CNAME records, nor prevent cookie sharing through CNAME records, including those browsers that implement recursive CNAME lookups for blocklists. Rather, tools simply appear to explore CNAMEs to find blocklist hits. This design decision is unsurprising, since preventing cookie sharing across CNAME subdomains would break functionality where the subdomain is a legitimate part of the main domain. This is a fundamental limitation of blocklists, which are agnostic to the *intent* of the website designer, and therefore cannot discriminate between legitimate and illegitimate cookie propagation. For the same reason, it is unclear that detecting misuse of CNAMEs is technically achievable without additional information from the first-party, though it may be an area for possible area for future work. However, enhancing any DNS-based content blocking mechanism with recursive CNAME lookups may be sufficient to end the widespread use of CNAME cloaking, since it will no longer be useful for cloaking advertising.

We also emphasize that a first-party that employs CNAME cloaking can still prevent cookie sharing with third-parties by creating a cookie policy that explicitly names the subdomains from which a cookie can be accessed. The cookie policy can thus allow the cloaked domain to be excluded from the cookie's domains, without breaking other functionality. Unfortunately, explicitly naming subdomains is more onerous than using an implicit wildcard to allow access on all subdomains. An administrator that would agree to enable CNAME cloaking may be unlikely to expend extra effort in locking down cookie policies. In such cases, clients rely entirely on blocklists to prevent CNAME cloaking as a vector for (unintentional) cookie leaks.

D. Threats to Validity

A threat to *external validity* stems from only including the Alexa top-10,000 websites. As pageview distribution is understood to follow a heavy-tailed distribution [12], analysis of the top websites is enough to capture a significant portion of daily internet activity. Therefore, we do not believe including additional websites would return a clearer or more useful picture of the impact of cloaking on cookie policies.

In terms of *internal validity*, limiting bulk data collection to each website's homepage may cause false negatives, i.e. a conclusion that CNAME cloaking is not performed while in fact it is deployed on parts of the website other than the homepage. We consider this an acceptable limitation, which is compensated by the in-depth analysis of a select number of websites in Section VII. Furthermore, while this implies that our results may represent a lower bound for the prevalence of cookie exfiltration, the number of instances that we uncovered is sufficient to conclude that the phenomenon continues to be a problem.

E. Ethical Disclosure

Prior to submitting this paper, we contacted maintainers for the seven websites that were found to exfiltrate authentication cookies in our December 2020 dataset (ref. Table IV), and informed them of the issue.

X. Related Work

a) CNAME Cloaking: The risk of DNS aliases as an origin-obfuscation tool has been previously highlighted. Krishnamurthy and Wills identify *hidden third-parties* (CNAME-cloaked domains) as one of multiple means advertisers use to avoid blocklists [30], [29]. These studies are more than 10 years old and they do not characterize DNS redirections in-depth, as they focus chiefly on user privacy loss. Olejnik and Castelluccia [37] also identify a specific instance of cloaking, but do not investigate the phenomenon on a larger scale. More recently, Dao et al. characterize the landscape of advertising-related cloaking on the web [21]. Their work, which constitutes the inspiration for ours, investigate the prevalence of redirections but does not analyze their impact on cookie policies and exfiltration. Our work was also informed by a number of expert blog posts [31], [19] describing a recent rise in first-party redirections. Members of the community and commercial providers were quick to propose solutions for blocking suspicious cloaked domains [39], [2], [1], [3], [10] and build public blocklists [36]. However, we are concerned that without a comprehensive view of the phenomenon, those who deploy countermeasures risk to be "flying blind" and failing to identify all ramifications of the problem (a concern supported by our results).

b) Online Advertising and Tracking: Characterizing the impact of online advertising [15], [25] and tracking [18], [22], [29], [11], [43] has received much attention from the security and measurement communities. Most works find a continued and concerning impact of advertising on user privacy, elaborate and constantly evolving tracking technology, and rampant user data sharing among advertisers. Advertising and tracking also extend beyond web browsing. Razaghpanah et al. [41] identify thousands of advertising and tracking services. Andreou et al. [13] show similar widespread and invasive tracking and targeting on Facebook. Other work investigates the use of browser-based blocklists specifically to block online ads. Pujol et al. [40] find that use of ad-blocking technology is widespread, although it seems to be rooted more in annoyance towards ads than privacy concerns. Wills and Uzunoglu [45] investigate differences among ad-blockers. Gomer et al. [24] analyze the exposure of users to tracking cookies specifically for search. Englehardt et al. [23] show the potential for cookies to be used to violate user privacy in the context of tracking and mass surveillance. Despite this significant amount of prior work on online advertising, tracking, and ad-blockers, to the best of our knowledge the impact of advertising-related CNAME cloaking on cookie policies has not been previously investigated in detail.

c) DNS Security: DNS is an aging protocol, and efforts to improve its security have been slow and marred by deployment mistakes [32], [20], enabling various attacks [28], [27] and misuse by ISPs [44]. New technologies like DNS-over-HTTPS [34] have been proposed for remediation, but deployment has only recently begun. As CNAME redirections are part of the DNS infrastructure (and CNAME cloaking is not clearly distinguishable *prima facie*), none of the existing countermeasures affect it. Pearce et al. [38] investigate the role of DNS manipulations in internet censorship; while relevant, this work is orthogonal to advertising-related manipulations.

d) Website Security: Several large-scale analyses of website security focus on the presence of potentially vulnerable code (e.g., [42], [35]). Cavalier CNAME redirections (as the one uncovered in this paper) can enable unwanted access from third-party code to sensitive resources without the need of exploiting pre-existing vulnerabilities.

XI. Conclusions

In this paper, we presented the results of a large-scale analysis of the impact of advertising-related CNAME redirections on cookie propagation. Our data confirm that a non-negligible fraction of the Alexa-10,000 websites perform such redirections, consistent with prior studies. Furthermore, we show that in a number of sites, the deployment of first-party redirections causes sensitive cookies—which include personal information and/or authentication data—to leak to third-party advertising domains. While exfiltration of these cookies is likely unintentional, it is also problematic as it facilitates impersonation and takeover attacks. We also find that the ability of blocking these exfiltrations vary between browsers.

Overall, these results show that CNAME cloaking has serious ramifications, affecting cookie propagation in unexpected ways. A combination of more sophisticated browser-based blocking strategies, and more fine-grained website policies, may be necessary to tackle the problem.

References

[1] "Address 1st-party tracker blocking · Issue #780 · uBlockOrigin/uBlock-issues," 2019. [Online]. Available: https://github.com/uBlockOrigin/uBlock-issues/issues/780

[2] "Apply Pi-Hole blocking to CNAMEs," Nov. 2019. [Online]. Available: https://discourse.pi-hole.net/t/apply-pi-hole-blocking-to-cnames/25445/95

[3] "Cname cloaking and bounce tracking defense — webkit," 2020. [Online]. Available: https://webkit.org/blog/11338/cname-cloaking-and-bounce-tracking-defense/

[4] "easylist/easylist/ at master," May 2020. [Online]. Available: https://github.com/easylist/easylist/tree/master/easylist

[5] "Faq: Cookies in am/openam," 2020. [Online]. Available: https://backstage.forgerock.com/knowledge/kb/article/a19829000

[6] "https://easylist.to/easylist/easyprivacy.txt," May 2020. [Online]. Available: https://easylist.to/easylist/easyprivacy.txt

[7] "mitmproxy - an interactive https proxy," May 2020. [Online]. Available: https://mitmproxy.org

[8] "Openam - open access manager," 2020. [Online]. Available: https://www.openidentityplatform.org/openam

[9] "Seleniumhq browser automation," May 2020. [Online]. Available: https://www.selenium.dev

[10] "What's brave done for my privacy lately? episode #6: Fighting cname trickery," 2020. [Online]. Available: https://brave.com/privacy-updates-6/

[11] G. Acar, C. Eubank, S. Englehardt, M. Juarez, A. Narayanan, and C. Diaz, "The web never forgets: Persistent tracking mechanisms in the wild," in *CCS*, 2014.

[12] L. A. Adamic and B. A. Huberman, "Zipf's law and the internet." *Glottometrics*, vol. 3, no. 1, pp. 143–150, 2002.

[13] A. Andreou, M. Silva, F. Benevenuto, O. Goga, P. Loiseau, and A. Mislove, "Measuring the facebook advertising ecosystem," in *NDSS*, 2019.

[14] Apple, "Tracking prevention in webkit," Nov. 2020. [Online]. Available: https://webkit.org/tracking-prevention/#intelligent-tracking-prevention-itp

[15] P. Barford, I. Canadi, D. Krushevskaja, Q. Ma, and S. Muthukrishnan, "Adscape: Harvesting and analyzing online display ads," in *WWW*, 2014.

[16] D. Bradbury, "Ad-blocking companies block 'unblockable' tracker," Nov. 2019. [Online]. Available: https://nakedsecurity.sophos.com/2019/11/25/ad-blocking-companies-block-unblockable-tracker/

[17] Brave, "What's brave done for my privacy lately? episode #6: Fighting cname trickery," Oct. 2020. [Online]. Available: https://brave.com/privacy-updates-6/

[18] J. M. Carrascosa, J. Mikians, R. Cuevas, V. Erramilli, and N. Laoutaris, "I always feel like somebody's watching me: measuring online behavioural advertising," in *CoNext*, 2015.

[19] R. Cointepas, "CNAME Cloaking, the dangerous disguise of third-party trackers," Dec. 2019. [Online]. Available: https://medium.com/nextdns/cname-cloaking-the-dangerous-disguise-of-third-party-trackers-\\195205dc522a

[20] T. Dai, H. Shulman, and M. Waidner, "Dnssec misconfigurations in popular domains," in *International Conference on Cryptology and Network Security*. Springer, 2016, pp. 651–660.

[21] H. Dao, J. Mazel, and K. Fukuda, "Characterizing CNAME Cloaking-Based Tracking on the Web," in *TMA*, 2020.

[22] S. Englehardt and A. Narayanan, "Online tracking: A 1-million-site measurement and analysis," in *CCS*, 2016.

[23] S. Englehardt, D. Reisman, C. Eubank, P. Zimmerman, J. Mayer, A. Narayanan, and E. W. Felten, "Cookies that give you away: The surveillance implications of web tracking," in *Proceedings of the 24th International Conference on World Wide Web*, 2015, pp. 289–299.

[24] R. Gomer, E. M. Rodrigues, N. Milic-Frayling, and M. Schraefel, "Network analysis of third party tracking: User exposure to tracking cookies through search," in *2013 IEEE/WIC/ACM International Joint Conferences on Web Intelligence (WI) and Intelligent Agent Technologies (IAT)*, vol. 1. IEEE, 2013, pp. 549–556.

[25] S. Guha, B. Cheng, and P. Francis, "Challenges in measuring online advertising systems," in *IMC*, 2010.

[26] M. Jones, J. Bradley, and N. Sakimura, "RFC 7519 - JSON Web Token (JWT)," May 2015. [Online]. Available: https://tools.ietf.org/html/rfc7519

[27] A. Klein and B. Pinkas, "Dns cache-based user tracking," in *NDSS*, 2019.

[28] A. Klein, H. Shulman, and M. Waidner, "Internet-Wide Study of DNS Cache Injections," in *INFOCOM*, 2017.

[29] B. Krishnamurthy and C. Wills, "Privacy diffusion on the web: a longitudinal perspective," in *WWW*, 2009.

[30] B. Krishnamurthy and C. E. Wills, "Generating a privacy footprint on the internet," in *IMC*, 2006.

[31] J. Leyden, "Web trackers using CNAME Cloaking to bypass browsers' ad blockers," Nov. 2019. [Online]. Available: https://portswigger.net/daily-swig/web-trackers-using-cname-cloaking-to-bypass-browsers-ad-blockers

[32] W. Lian, E. Rescorla, H. Shacham, and S. Savage, "Measuring the practical impact of DNSSEC deployment," in *USENIX Security Symposium*, 2013.

[33] J. R. Mayer and J. C. Mitchell, "Third-party web tracking: Policy and technology," in *2012 IEEE Symposium on Security and Privacy*. IEEE, 2012, pp. 413–427.

[34] P. McManus and P. Hoffman, "RFC 8484 - DNS Queries over HTTPS (DoH)," Oct. 2018. [Online]. Available: https://tools.ietf.org/html/rfc8484

[35] M. Musch, C. Wressnegger, M. Johns, and K. Rieck, "New kid on the web: A study on the prevalence of webassembly in the wild," in *International Conference on Detection of Intrusions and Malware, and Vulnerability Assessment*. Springer, 2019, pp. 23–42.

[36] nextdns, "nextdns/cname-cloaking-blocklist," May 2020. [Online]. Available: https://github.com/nextdns/cname-cloaking-blocklist

[37] L. Olejnik and C. Castelluccia, "Analysis of openx-publishers cooperation," in *HotPETs*, 2014.

[38] P. Pearce, B. Jones, F. Li, R. Ensafi, N. Feamster, N. Weaver, and V. Paxson, "Global Measurement of DNS Manipulation," in *USENIX Security Symposium*, 2017.

[39] O. Poitrey, "NextDNS added CNAME Uncloaking support, becomes the first cross-platform solution to the problem," Nov. 2019. [Online]. Available: https://medium.com/nextdns/nextdns-added-cname-uncloaking-support-becomes-the-first-cross-\\platform-solution-to-the-problem-e3f437f84342

[40] E. Pujol, O. Hohlfeld, and A. Feldmann, "Annoyed users: Ads and ad-block usage in the wild," in *Proceedings of the 2015 Internet Measurement Conference*, 2015, pp. 93–106.

[41] A. Razaghpanah, R. Nithyanand, N. Vallina-Rodriguez, S. Sundaresan, M. Allman, C. Kreibich, and P. Gill, "Apps, trackers, privacy, and regulators," in *NDSS*, 2018.

[42] G. Richards, C. Hammer, B. Burg, and J. Vitek, "The eval that men do," in *ECOOP*, 2011.

[43] F. Roesner, T. Kohno, and D. Wetherall, "Detecting and defending against third-party tracking on the web," in *NSDI*, 2012.

[44] N. Weaver, C. Kreibich, and V. Paxson, "Redirecting dns for ads and profit." in *FOCI*, 2011.

[45] C. E. Wills and D. C. Uzunoglu, "What ad blockers are (and are not) doing," in *IEEE HotWeb*, 2016.

What Remains Uncaught?: Characterizing Sparsely Detected Malicious URLs on Twitter

Sayak Saha Roy
The University of Texas at Arlington
sayak.saharoy@mavs.uta.edu

Unique Karanjit
The University of Texas at Arlington
unique.karanjit@mavs.uta.edu

Shirin Nilizadeh
The University of Texas at Arlington
shirin.nilizadeh@uta.edu

Abstract—**Twitter maintains a blackbox approach for detecting malicious URLs shared on its platform. In this study, we evaluate the efficiency of their detection mechanism against newer phishing and drive-by download threats posted on the website over three different time periods of the year. Our findings indicate that several threats remained undetected by Twitter, with the majority of them originating from nine different free website hosting services. These URLs targeted 19 popular organizations and also distributed malicious files from 9 different threat categories. Moreover, the malicious websites hosted under these services were also less likely to get detected by URL scanning tools than other similar threats hosted elsewhere, and were accessible on their respective domains for a much longer duration. We believe that the aforementioned features, combined with the ease of access (drag and drop website creating interface, up-to-date SSL certification, reputed domain, etc.) provides attackers a fast and convenient way to create malicious attacks using these services. On the other hand, we also observed that the majority of the URLs which were actually detected by Twitter remained active on the platform throughout our study, allowing them to be easily distributed across the platform. Also, several benign websites in our dataset were detected by Twitter as being malicious. We hypothesize that this is caused due to a blocklisting procedure used by Twitter, which detects all URLs originating from certain domains, irrespective of their content. Thus, our results identify a family of potent threats, which are distributed freely on Twitter, and are also not detected by the majority of URL scanning tools, or even the services which host them, thus making the need for a more thorough URL blocking approach from Twitter's end more apparent.**

I. Introduction

Over the last decade, social networking websites, such as Twitter, Facebook and Instagram have seen a steady increase with respect to the presence of malicious URLs that are posted on these platforms, especially phishing websites [1]. Attackers find these platforms alluring because of the easy propagation of information through users' networks which also increases the exposure of these URLs to users as well [2]. The detection and prevention solutions against these types of attacks are provided by social media platforms themselves, as well as third-party URL scanning tools. Twitter, in particular, takes a blackbox approach towards detecting malicious URLs [3]. There is a huge body of work studying the problem of malicious web attacks on Twitter. However, the majority of them attempt to measure the prevalence of malware and phishing attacks spreading through the user networks [4], [5], [6], [7], [8]. Some studies have also replicated phishing attacks [9], [10] to study their characteristics and how Twitter detects them. In contrast, our work focuses mostly on determining and characterizing malicious URLs which are not detected on Twitter for an extended period of time, as well as benign URLs which are incorrectly detected due to several factors.

In this work, we aim to find the effectiveness of Twitter's URL detection mechanism against several Phishing and Drive-by URL threats found on the platform through three different time periods of the year, and in turn, determine the features of the URLs which do not get detected by Twitter. In particular, this paper (i) evaluates Twitter's response towards both Phishing and Drive-by URLs that are posted on their platform; (ii) categorizes the URLs that are not detected by Twitter based on their characteristics and also identifies certain features that can used to recognize them in the wild; and (iii) examines the characteristics of *benign* URLs that are detected as malicious by Twitter.

We collected and analyzed more than 132k unique URLs, which had been collected from over 3 million posts, spread out over three different time periods of the year (January, June and November 2020). Using VirusTotal, an online tool to scan websites with multiple scanning engines at the same time, which is used by both regular users and the research community alike [11], [12], [13], [14], [15], [16]. We initially labelled 4.5k URLs as 'malicious' based on the scores provided by VirusTotal, and then manually investigated each of them to check if they were indeed so. The URLs which were confirmed to be malicious were then analyzed to find the patterns and obfuscation tactics used by the attackers to make these websites remain undetected by both Twitter and popular anti-phishing engines over extended periods of time. Finally, we also determined the characteristics for the benign URLs in our dataset that were detected by Twitter as malicious.

Our findings can be summarized as below:

1) Twitter was unable to detect about 66% of the malicious

Workshop on Measurements, Attacks, and Defenses for the Web (MADWeb) 2021
25 February 2021, Virtual

https://dx.doi.org/10.14722/madweb.2021.23028
www.ndss-symposium.org

URLs in our dataset over the course of our study, most of which utilized one of nine different website creation services. These malicious URLs also targeted 19 popular organizations (phishing websites) and distributed malicious files from 9 different threat categories (drive-by downloads).
2) Twitter exhibited inconsistent protection behaviour against phishing websites in our dataset that it was able to detect, only generating a warning for the majority of them, instead of removing them outright. Over the course of our study which spanned nearly 11 months, we found that a substantial amount of these URLs were still alive on the platform and could be freely redistributed (shared or retweeted).
3) We also found that more than 60% of these URLs were still accessible on their respective hosting domains even after a month of their first appearance in our dataset. They also got detected by very few URL scanning engines, with none of these tools being able to flag even half of the phishing URLs, that had not been detected by Twitter throughout our study in our dataset, as malicious.
4) Several URLs in our dataset which exhibited no malicious behaviour were detected by Twitter. Our results indicate that the majority of these incorrect warnings were due to Twitter blocklisting websites which utilized several URL shortening and web hosting domains.

II. Background and Related Work

Phishing Websites. They are websites which attempt to imitate legitimate organizations in order to trick users into sharing their personal or financial information. The scale of damage done by these attacks is massive, with more than 1.4 million such websites being created every month [17] which leads to losses of half a billion dollars to American businesses every year [18]. Established academic literature is plentiful in this regard, with researchers tracking several techniques used by these attackers [19], [20], [21], [22], [23], [24], determining how prevalent phishing detection measures fare against these attacks [25], [26], [27], [28], [29], as well as a myriad of obfuscation strategies used by the attackers to prevent their attacks from being detected by these tools. Significant progress has also been made towards detecting phishing websites, by bringing improvements to URL blocklists [30], [31], [32], [33], [34], [35], as well as developing novel machine learning based approaches [36], [37], [38], [39], [40], [41], [42], [43] which utilize several features derived from the characteristics of these websites. Considering the resulting improvements that have been made in detecting phishing attacks over the last few years, our work focuses mainly on a single, yet popular platform for spreading phishing and other malicious URLs alike - Twitter - and we aim to evaluate Twitter's performance against several URL threats posted on its platform.

VirusTotal. VirusTotal [44] is an online URL scanning tool which scans both files and URLs for malicious content. After a user submits a file (or URL), VirusTotal checks with 80 different scanning engines and returns the aggregated total and name of the tools which detected the resource as a threat. In addition to an online web interface [44], VirusTotal also provides an API [45] for scanning larger volume of URLs. Researchers frequently use VirusTotal to label URLs in their dataset, with several published literature depending on it to create their ground truth for malicious URLs [46], [12], [47], [11], [48], [49]. We use VirusTotal in a similar way to determine what portion of scanners detect the URLs in our dataset in Section III-A, and later on in Sections IV-A and V-A to compare the detection statistics between phishing and drive-by URLs which were and were not detected by Twitter.

III. Data Collection and Processing

We collected one million tweets from each of three time periods which consist of January (Dataset 1 or D1), June (Dataset 2 or D2) and November 2020 (Dataset 3 or D3) using the Twitter API [50]. Our unconventional approach towards spreading out the data collection over the entire year was to a) determine if our findings were consistent over a large period of time, and conversely, b) to check if Twitter had improved on the issues raised during an earlier time. We only collected tweets which had URLs embedded in them. Since all URLs posted on Twitter are enclosed under the t.co URL shortening banner, we resolved each of them such that we were able to collect the next URL in the redirection chain. We then removed the URLs that were links to other tweets or images/videos posted on Twitter. This was to make sure we only preserved the tweets in our dataset, which contained URLs which linked to third-party websites.

After this filtering procedure, we were able to retain 43,605 URLs for D1, 51,129 URLs for D2 and 37,951 URLs for D3, for a total of 138k URLs across the three datasets. Note that sometimes, similar URLs were found between these three datasets, and we only considered these URLs to belong to the dataset that they first appeared in.

A. *Identifying Malicious URLs*

For the purposes of our study, we first had to reliably identify the URLs in our dataset which might be malicious. To do this, we at first used VirusTotal [44] to scan all the unique URLs in our datasets. We initially considered URLs which were detected by at least one engine on Virustotal as being *'malicious'*.

Prior work in [51] has found that it is common for URL scanning engines to change their detection from malicious to benign within a short period of time. Also the label provided by VirusTotal for a particular engine also sometimes lags behind that engine's actual label. Since a majority of our URLs have only one detection, it is possible for these detections to be removed for a short time, (thus resulting in the URL being classified as benign in our dataset, as per our threshold) only for a detection to be added back to that URL, a few hours later. Thus, to avoid this inconsistency, the URLs in our datasets that had at least one detection by VirusTotal on the first day were scanned regularly for a month. If a URL turned out to have zero detections in newer scans, it was separated from the *malicious* URLs set and was again scanned after a week.

In the event that it gained detections in the weekly scan, it was put back in the *malicious* URLs set again. On the other hand, URLs which did not get detected in the first scan were considered as benign initially, and then scanned every week, and if they gained at least one detection during these weekly scans, were then moved to the *malicious* set, and scanned daily from thereon. After the conclusion of a month for the respective time frames of our dataset, we obtained 1,318 URLs from D1 (from 1,421 tweets), 1,827 URLs (from 2,082 tweets) from D2 and 1,401 URLs from D3 (from 1,650 tweets), which were still detected by one or more engines on VirusTotal. To identify whether the URLs are indeed malicious, and to further characterize them, we investigated these URLs manually as described in the next section.

B. Categorization of 'Malicious' URLs

The 4,546 URLs across our datasets which had one or more detection on VirusTotal were evaluated manually by two security researchers, who labelled them independently. The researchers were advised about the risks associated with visiting the malicious URLs and took necessary precautions to prevent getting their systems infected. These precautions included using a virtual machine to visit the websites and using dummy account credentials for websites which required login information to be properly evaluated. Since malicious websites (especially those that are phishing) generally have a very short lifespan [52], all the URLs included in our study were evaluated on the day of their collection itself. We provided certain guidelines for the researchers, such as features to observe inside the website which helped them label each URL as one of the four pre-defined categories: Phishing, Drive-by Download, Benign, and Unknown. These categories are briefly explained below.

1) Phishing: These websites imitate legitimate organizations and ask the victim for sensitive and private information, such as account passwords, social security numbers, payment information, etc. The majority of phishing websites are usually hosted on independent domains, lack SSL certification (though this phenomenon is changing slowly [53]) and/or are part of a larger phishing campaign.

2) Drive-by Download: Websites of this category usually claim to offer a legitimate software, which is not easily available otherwise, enticing the user to download files (usually executable programs), which come bundled with trojan-horses, ransomwares, spyware or potentially unwanted programs (such as adwares) [54]. However, a drive-by download attack might also occur without the user's knowledge, by exploiting vulnerabilities in the victim's browser or operating system [55]. Unlike phishing URLs which are usually detected by frequently updated blocklists, file based malware detection is much more complex, and depends on several factors beyond simple signatures, such as file heuristics and other sophisticated behaviour based detection procedures, something which VirusTotal does not consistently emulate in their scans [56][57][58][48]. Also several malicious files bundled in seemingly benign software do not create executables (such as malicious browser extensions, fileless malware, miscellaneous PuP, etc.) and thus cannot be easily uploaded and scanned on VirusTotal. Thus, for websites which asked to download a file, coders were prompted to scan the downloaded file using the desktop versions of four top rated antivirus engines (Bitdefender, Kaspersky, Avast and AVG) according to AV-Comparatives [59] and if at least two of these engines detect it as a threat, the coders labelled the URL as a *Drive-by Download* website. The threshold of detection for identifying the downloaded file as malicious is set to at least two engines to reduce the possibility of a false positive. For the files which did not pick up any detections or had only one detection, we keep re-scanning them throughout our study to check if it gained any more detections. The real-time protection modules of these products were also able to detect malicious web-browser plugins and file-less malware, and other software exploits.

3) Benign websites: Websites in our datasets, which i) did not imitate any organization, ii) did not ask for any unwarranted data which was sensitive in nature, and iii) did not ask to download a file, and even if it did, the said file(s) did not show any detections from the four antivirus engine scans, were labelled as *benign* URLs.

4) Unknown websites: Websites which could not be reliably determined to have any malicious intent. This included the URLs which could not be accessed, and several websites which appeared to be e-commerce portals, or even those which redirected the coders to online advertisements or third party websites. The e-commerce websites did not imitate any other legitimate organization but asked for sensitive data, such as credit card information, residential address, etc. with the promise of delivering some product/service at a later date. Thus, it is hard to evaluate whether these websites had any malicious intent. Findings in [60] shows that several popular and legitimate websites and domains become the source of unknowingly promoting malicious advertisements due to CDNs as well. Thus, the coders were asked to label websites, which otherwise behaved benignly, but provided suspicious advertisements as *Unknown*. We did not include websites in this category for any further analysis in our study.

4) Label agreement: After labeling the URLs by two coders, we computed their inter-rater agreement, which was 96% with a Cohen's kappa of 0.72, indicating substantial agreement. For inconsistent results, coders discussed how to resolve disagreements and assigned a final label to the URLs. Table I provides a descriptive statistic of the URLs for each category.

IV. PHISHING URLS ON TWITTER

Based on our manual evaluation, we found 950 URLs across our datasets which exhibited phishing behaviour. Table III illustrates the statistics of the URLs which were detected by Twitter over the course of a month. By *'detected'*, we refer to one of two situations. The first one is that the tweet was no longer available, suggesting Twitter might have removed the tweet(s) containing the URL, but, there remains the possibility

Dataset	Time Period	Unique URLs	detection rate≥1	Phishing	Drive-by-download	Benign	Unknown
1	Jan 2020	43,605	1,318	186 (14%)	67 (5%)	879 (66%)	139 (11%)
2	June 2020	51,129	1,827	471 (25%)	109 (6%)	1041 (56%)	206 (11%)
3	Nov 2020	37,951	1,401	293 (21%)	91 (6%)	896 (63%)	121 (9%)

Table I: Distribution of the categories of the URLs across the three datasets.

that the author of the tweet removed it as well. To clarify this situation, for every URL that we could not access, we retried posting the same URL using one of our private accounts(which for ethical purposes, could not be accessed by any other user on Twitter), and only considered the URL as *'detected'* if Twitter prevented us from posting it or provided an explicit warning. The second scenario is when the URL was still accessible on Twitter, but it provided a warning indicating that the URL might be harmful to visit, as seen in Fig 11. About 62% of these URLs were still active, on average, across the three datasets after the month of their first appearance in our dataset, with around 57% of them still being accessible on Twitter even after the conclusion of the study. Thus, a total of 544 phishing URLs remaining undetected on Twitter which warrants a closer look into the characteristics of these threats.

A. Comparing Detected and Undetected Phishing URLs

To check how other URL scanning tools fared against these undetected URLs *(n=544)*, we compared their detection statistics with the 406 URLs which had been detected by Twitter during our study. We did this by scanning each of these URLs using VirusTotal to determine how many scanning engines detected them. The descriptive statistics for this analysis is illustrated in Table II. We found that the undetected phishing URLs were detected on average by 2.95 engines (σ=0.94), whereas those which had been detected by Twitter at some point during the duration of the study maintained an average detection rate of 9.66 (σ=4.21). The undetected URLs were also caught by only 17 unique engines on VirusTotal, compared to 38 engines for the detected URLs. Figure 1(a) shows the cumulative distribution of number of times each engine detected these URLs throughout the duration of our study. We observe that nearly 80% scanning engines were unable to detect even 10% of all the undetected URLs, with none of the engines being able to detect half of them. This is in stark contrast with these tools' performance against the phishing URLs which were detected by Twitter, for which 10 engines were able to detect half of the URLs, and three of them even managed to detect 80% of them. Thus, this difference in detection patterns indicates the undetected URLs (on Twitter) might have different characteristics than those which were detected (on Twitter) and so we dedicate Section IV towards closely investigating the former.

B. Analyzing the Undetected Phishing URLs

We found 544 phishing URLs which were not detected by Twitter throughout the course of our study. Also, after scanning these URLs using VirusTotal, we found that they had significantly lower detection rates by URL scanning tools compared to URLs which had been detected by Twitter.

URL Set	Total	AD	Median	Min/Max	Std. Dev	Engines
Undetected Set	544	2.95	3	0/12	0.94	17
Detected Set	406	9.66	10	1/21	4.21	38

Table II: URL Scanning Tool detection statistics for Detected and Undetected(on Twitter) Phishing URLs in our datasets. *AD=Average engine detections, Engines=Total number of unique engines.*

Dataset	Total	Detected after a month	Detected throughout the study
D1	186	79 (42%)	85 (46%)[1]
D2	471	182 (38%)	209 (44%) [2]
D3	293	107 (36%)	112 (38%) [3]

Table III: Descriptive stats for Phishing URLs detected across the three datasets. **Time periods 1=Jan to Dec 2020, 2=June to Dec 2020, and 3=Nov to Dec 2020**

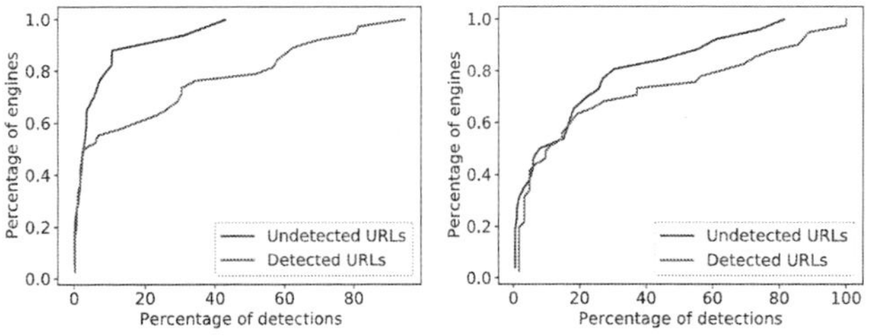

(a) Phishing URLs (b) Drive-by download URLs

Figure 1: CDF of the percentage of detected and undetected (a) phishing and (b) drive-by download URLs that were flagged by the anti-phishing engines.

Through our manual investigation, we found that 435 (80%) of these URLs are hosted by one of six different free website creation services: Google Forms, Microsoft Forms, Wordpress, Micrsoft Sharepoint, Wix, Weebly and one API interface: Google APIs. In comparison, out of the 406 phishing URLs that were detected by Twitter, only 28 of them are originated from these services.

Websites hosted under these services always have SSL certification, the lack of which is often considered by regular users as a sign that a website might be malicious [53]. Table IV shows the distribution of the URLs in our dataset across these website hosting services. Regular phishing URLs are often removed by the domain hosting services or registrars themselves very quickly upon their appearance [61]. However, we found that only a small number of URLs hosted under these domains had been removed on the day after their appearance on Twitter, with 87% of the phishing attacks still active across all the different hosting services combined. This number drops to only about 57% even after a month of their appearance in our dataset. It is also observed that these attacks are predominantly present across all three of our datasets, signifying that phishing attacks having these features were carried out throughout the entire year. Moreover, these attacks primarily targeted 19 popular organizations including AT&T, eBay, Amazon, Facebook, etc. as illustrated in Figure 2. We thus dedicate the next few paragraphs towards discussing the characteristics of the phishing websites hosted under each of these services and also discuss possible features that can be observed to identify them in the wild.

Category	D1	D2	D3	A_{d1}	A_M
Google Forms	43	88	54	163 (88%)	139 (75%)
Microsoft Forms	16	41	23	73 (91%)	39 (49%)
Wordpress	12	9	20	31 (74%)	23 (55%)
Wix	6	15	21	35 (83%)	13 (31%)
Google APIs	10	29	18	52 (94%)	12 (21%)
Weebly	2	17	11	26 (86%)	21 (70%)
Total	**89**	**199**	**147**		
	435 (100%)			**380 (87%)**	**253 (57%)**

Table IV: Distribution of undetected phishing URLs across the 3 datasets. A_{d1}= phishing URLs still active, i.e., they can be visited on day one, and A_M= phishing URLs active after a month of their first appearance in our datasets.

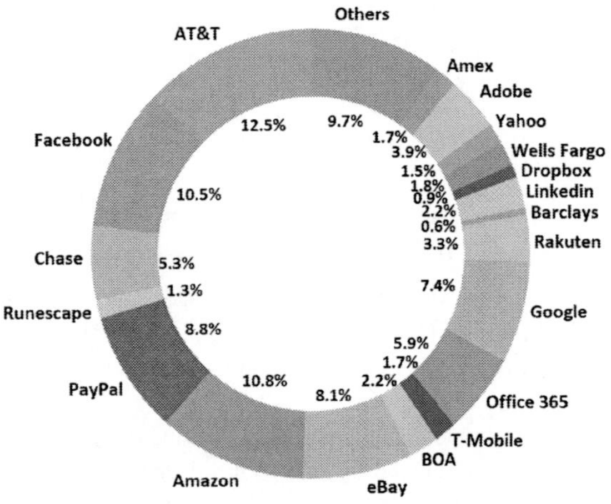

Figure 2: Organizations targeted by the Phishing URLs *(n=544)* which remained undetected on Twitter.

C. Google and Microsoft Forms URLs

From our datasets, we found 34% of the URLs were hosted on Google Forms and 15% of the URLs hosted on Microsoft Forms. These services allow for easy point to click interfaces for creating web-forms, where users can submit data by entering information in the provided form fields. However, we found that attackers frequently utilized these services to create websites which imitated legitimate organizations and asked for sensitive information, such as account passwords, credit card information, Social Security Numbers, etc. Form URLs created under both these services are hosted under Google's *(https://docs.google.com/forms/..)* and Microsoft's *(https://forms.office.com/...)* own domains. In fact, unlike domains which host regular phishing websites, we find that both these services are not very efficient at detecting these phishing forms, with around 75% and 49% of them still active on Google Forms and Microsoft respectively after the first month of their appearance. However, websites created using these services are very limited with respect to design and only allow users to change the background colour and add images/videos in pre-defined field areas. This lack of customization separates these two website services from the others which hosted undetected phishing URLs in our dataset. However, we found that attackers were able to creatively construct phishing URLs which could partially imitate the organizations they were targeting and also remain undetected for extended periods. We discuss these strategies below.

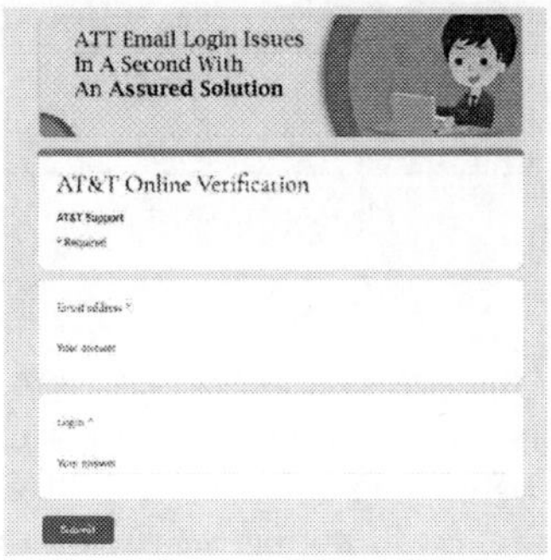

Figure 3: A simple phishing websites hosted on Google Forms which uses text for its form fields.

1) Obfuscation approaches used by attackers: A large portion of these phishing forms hosted on both the services used images for creating the form fields instead of regular text as shown in Figures 4(a) and 4(b). We found that all 17 of the Google Form URLs that were removed after one day consisted of text only form fields. In contrast, out of the 139 URLs that remained alive, 111 of them used images for form-fields, out of which 21 were removed after a month. Twenty-eight URLs used special characters in between the malicious form text (e.g., PA***WORD* instead of PASSWORD) as shown in Figure 4(c). Only 10 of these URLs were removed after a month. Similarly, all 73 of the Microsoft Form URLs, which were active after a day, consisted of images as form fields, though we found no URLs using special characters inside form fields. Microsoft fared a bit better than Google, removing 45% of these URLs with image based fields after a month of their appearance in our dataset. Thus, our findings indicate that attackers often use images and special characters for obfuscating these phishing URLs, which ensures that these attacks remain online longer.

D. Wix and Weebly URLs

Eight percent of the URLs in our dataset were hosted on Wix, while 30 URLs were hosted on Weebly, two free hosting websites, and were not detected by Twitter throughout the course of our study. Unlike Google and Microsoft Forms, however, these services provide far more options for

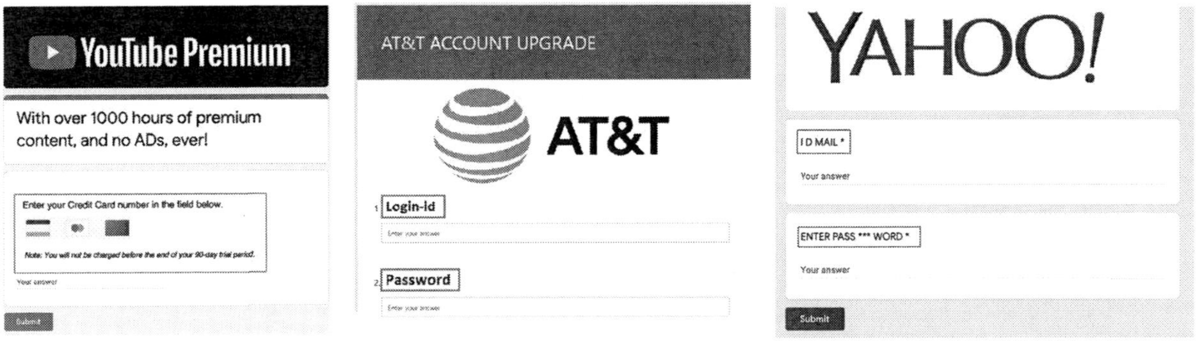

(a) Image-based (Google) (b) Image based (Microsoft) (c) Character based (Google)

Figure 4: (a) and (b) Google and Microsoft Forms phishing with images as form fields (highlighted in red), (c) Google Forms phishing with special characters for form fields (highlighted in blue). These websites are removed at a much slower pace than similar websites with text-based form fields.

(a) (b)

Figure 5: (a) Phishing website hosted on Wix, (b) Phishing website hosted on Weebly.

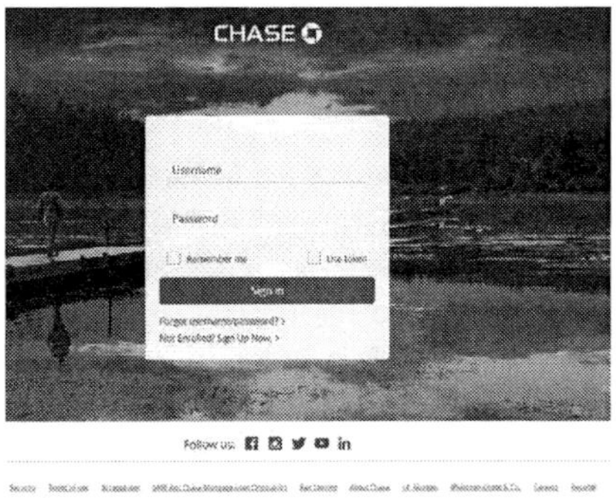

Figure 6: Phishing website hosted on wordpress.com. The bottom nav bar at the bottom contains links to the real JPMorgan Chase website.

customization including layout themes and sophisticated web designing objects, all bundled in easy drag and drop interfaces. Attackers thus leveraged these features to create phishing websites which were much harder to recognize based on appearance than the form URLs we have discussed in IV-C, as is apparent in the illustrations shown in Figure 5(a) and (b). We found that 70% and 31% of the URLs hosted on Weebly and Wix respectively were alive even after a month of their appearance in our datasets.

E. Wordpress URLs

We found around 7.5% of the phishing URLs in our datasets, which were hosted on Wordpress' own free web-hosting domain (wordpress.com). Users of wordpress.com have access to several customizability options and feature rich plugins, which resulted in attackers creating phishing websites which were practically indistinguishable in appearance from organizations that they were targeting, with little to no indication of them being a free website hosted on wordpress.com. Figure 6 shows one such website, which very accurately imitates the JP Morgan Chase login page. In addition, similar to the Wix and Weebly phishing URLs, these websites also included navigation bars containing links which lead to legitimate resources on the targeted organization's website.

F. Google APIs

Google's Cloud Storage API is an online repository offered by Google to host web applications created using Firebase. We found 10% of the URLs in our dataset which utilized this service to host phishing web applications. Prior work in [62] has noted that scammers utilize this service to implement web applications which imitate popular organizations. We also found that 36% of the URLs target some form of Microsoft Outlook or 365 suite of login page. We found that Google was able to remove only 6% of these applications after a day, but went on to get rid of 79% of these URLs over the course of a month.

G. Identifiable characteristics

While we do not analyze how often these phishing attack URLs were distributed across Twitter, nor have any data of how often users fall victim to these attacks, their continuing prevalence across all of our datasets suggests that they might be effective, considering that attackers kept using them. We discuss some of their identifiable characteristics in this paragraph. For the phishing attacks hosted on Google and Microsoft Forms, along with the restrictive structure of designing these websites, both vendors also provide specific warnings to not enter private or sensitive information on

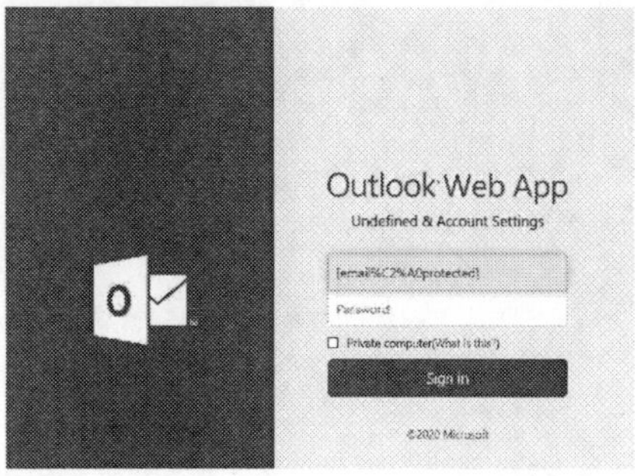

Figure 7: Phishing web application targeting Outlook Email login hosted on Google Cloud Storage API

websites hosted by them. Microsoft specifically states that it is not affiliated with the owner of the form websites they host, and that all data entered on the forms will be sent directly to the author. These phishing attacks could be prevented if users pay attention to these disclaimers. For the Wix and Weebly URLs, based on their appearance alone, these websites appear to be much harder to recognize than Google and Microsoft's form URLs, and unlike the latter, neither Wix nor Weebly provide any disclaimer to the user against entering sensitive information on these websites. Additionally, these websites often contained navigation bars location at either the header or footer of the websites, which contained links leading to the targeted organization's website, thus further improving the case for their false credibility. However both these vendors have a watermark which identifies that the respective service has been used to create these websites either at the top (for Wix URLs) or bottom (for Weebly URLs) of the website, which can be noticed accordingly in Figure 5. The phishing attacks on wordpress.com are much more sophisticated which makes them very difficult to detect based on appearance. Thus, the only way to identify them is to carefully study the URL string. Finally, the phishing attacks hosted on Google API are the most sophisticated and feature rich across all the approaches we have discussed so far, since the attacker has complete control over the front and back-end code of the phishing applications. There are also no indicators or disclaimers for the user to not enter their sensitive information on any applications hosted under this domain Figure 7. It is worth mentioning that the websites hosted across all these services come with up-to-date SSL certifications. Thus, the only way to recognize all these threats is to pay close attention to the URL strings and be able to recognize they are different from their legitimate target organizations.

V. Drive by Downloads on Twitter

Based on our manual evaluation in Section III-B, we found 267 URLs in our dataset, which hosted malicious drive-by downloads. We found that Twitter was able to detect an average of 17% of them at the end of the month across all the datasets and only 23% overall till the end of the study. Thus, 205 URLs were not detected by Twitter throughout the entire duration of our work. As illustrated in Table VI, 169 (82%) of the 205 undetected URLs originated from one of three services: Microsoft Sharepoint, Wordpress and Blogspot. In comparison, out of the 62 drive-by download URLs that were detected by Twitter, only 2 of them are originated from these services. Similar to the phishing URLs that we observed in Section IV, all websites hosted under these services had up-to-date SSL certification. We used four popular antivirus vendors (as mentioned in Section III-B), whose detection label was used to categorize each file into one of nine different threat categories as illustrated in Fig 8. We found more than 71% of the threats targeted Microsoft Windows systems (including Trojans, Ransomware and Spyware), and 11% of these URLs included malicious Android APK files. Also nearly 15% of the downloads included malicious plugins (extensions) that were compatible with Google's Blink engine (used in the Chromium family of web-browsers) and Gecko/Quantum (used in Mozilla's Firefox web-browser and other similar open source alternatives).

A. Comparing Detected and Undetected Drive-by Download URLs

To check how other anti-phishing engines fare against these undetected drive-by URLs, we selected the 62 URLs which had been detected by Twitter and compared them with the 205 URLs which remained undetected throughout our study, then scanned them using VirusTotal. The descriptive statistics for this analysis is illustrated in Table VII. We found the undetected drive-by URLs were caught by an average of 5.92 engines (σ=2.20), whereas those which had been detected by Twitter at some point during the duration of the study maintained an average detection rate of 11.01 (σ=2.92). The undetected set of URLs were detected by 26 unique scanning engines on VirusTotal, compared to 41 engines for the detected URLs. Fig 1(b) shows the cumulative distribution of engine detections towards these URLs. We find that nearly 40% of the engines were unable to catch 90% of the undetected drive-by download URLs. Only 4 engines were able to detect at least half of them, with 11 engines detecting less than 5% of these URLs, compared to 12 engines which were able to achieve the same feat for the drive-by URLs which were detected on Twitter. We also observed that nearly 83% of the undetected drive-by URLs remained active on Twitter after a month (and 76% at the end of our study) and are also detected by very few URL scanning engines. Additionally, from Table V, we found that 63% of these URLs remained alive on their respective hosting services even after a month. Again, similar to phishing URLs, we also observed these attacks are consistently present across all three of our datasets, signifying they have remained prevalent throughout the entire year that we conducted our experiments. We thus dedicate the following paragraphs to discuss the characteristics of these websites.

B. Microsoft Sharepoint

Microsoft Sharepoint is often used as a collaborative platform for sharing and working on documents or presentations online. We found that 18% of the URLs in our datasets,

Category	D1	D2	D3	A_{d1}	A_M
Sharepoint	18	38	41	93 (96%)	81 (83%)
Wordpress	5	9	11	25 (100%)	15 (60%)
Blogspot	13	15	17	37 (82%)	12 (27%)
Total	**36**	**62**	**69**		
	167 (100%)			**155 (91%)**	**108 (63%)**

Table V: Distribution of undetected drive-by downloads URLs. A_{d1}= Active on day one, and A_M= Active after a month.

Dataset	Total	Detected after a month	Detected throughout the study
1	67	21(31%)	23(34%)[1]
2	109	17(16%)	31(28%)[2]
3	91	8(9%)	8(9%)[3]

Table VI: Descriptive stats for Drive-by download URLs detected across the three datasets. **Time periods 1=Jan to Dec 2020, 2=June to Dec 2020, and 3=Nov to Dec 2020**

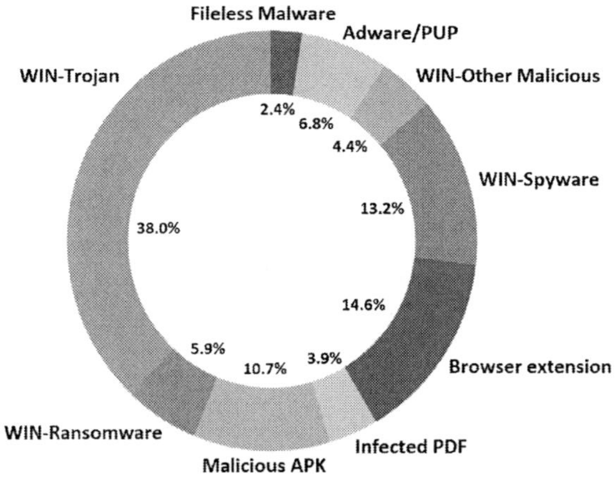

Figure 8: Categories of threats distributed by the Drive-by download URLs *(n=205)*, which remained undetected on Twitter.

which distributed malicious downloads used this service, out of which more than 83% remained active even after a month. Nearly 76% of the Sharepoint URLs led directly to documents hosted on Microsoft OneNote containing links to the malicious downloads, which were usually executable files (Windows) disguised as a PDF or Microsoft Word documents. We also observed a unique two step attack vector in the remaining 24% of the URLs, which asks users to enter sensitive login information to get access to download a malicious file. The attack was usually carried out in the following manner: first, the user was asked to enter their account login information on a login form page created used Microsoft Office Online, which imitated one of several different legitimate organizations, as shown in Fig. 9(a), so that the user can gain access to the file. If the user complies and enters their information, they are provided with a download link for the document distributed using Microsoft OneNote as shown in Fig 9(b). Thus these URLs might also be classified as a hybrid phishing/drive-by download attack.

URL Set	Total	AD	Median	Min/Max	Std. Dev	Engines
Undetected	205	5.92	6	1/17	2.20	26
Detected	62	11.01	12	3/24	2.92	41

Table VII: URL Scanning Tool detection statistics for Detected and Undetected(on Twitter) Drive-by download URLs in our datasets. *AD= average engine detections. Engines=Total number of unique engines.*

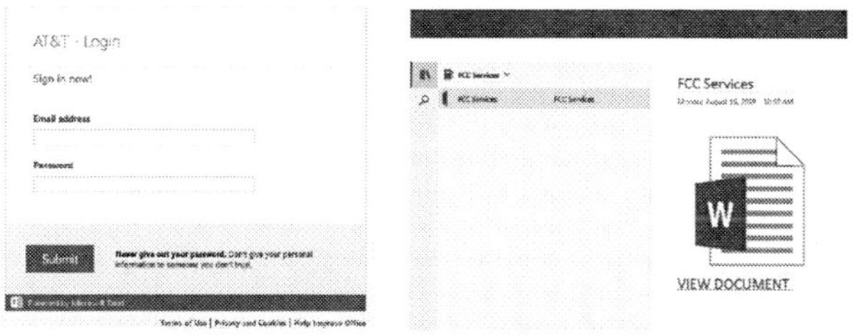

(a) (b)

Figure 9: Two step attack hosted on Sharepoint, (a) Webform hosted using Microsoft Excel, which leads to (b) a malicious download on OneNote

Note that forms created using Microsoft Excel Online have very low customizability, even when compared with the URLs we discussed in IV-C. Users are only allowed to edit the title of the form page, and the text of the field prompts, and there is no functionality for inserting additional images/video content, or even changing the design theme. Also, Microsoft provides a detailed disclaimer similar to the one found in IV-C, urging users to not enter any sensitive information in these web forms. Interestingly, the majority of these two step attacks appear in D3, which suggests that it is a newer threat.

C. *Wordpress*

We found about 4.5% of the URLs hosted on wordpress.com distributed malicious downloads. Despite the appearance of these websites being far more sophisticated (similar to URLs discussed in 6) than the Sharepoint URLs, all of them were one step attacks, which distributed malicious executable files directly via a link embedded on the webpage and did not ask for any sensitive information. Wordpress was able to remove only 40% of these URLs over the course of a month. One such attack is illustrated in Figure 10. It is possible that, similar to the phishing URLs hosted on wordpress.com, these websites are not detected on Twitter due to the reputation of the domains.

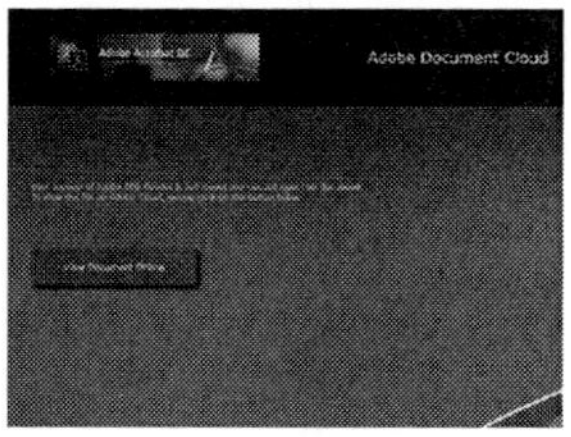

Figure 10: Example of a malicious Drive-by download URL imitating an Adobe Document reader page and hosted on Wordpress)

D. Blogspot

Eight percent of the URLs which distributed malicious domains and remained undetected by Twitter for over a month were hosted under Blogspot. Blogspot is Google's free hosting service for creating online blogs. Attackers exploited this service by consistently posting malicious executable files which masqueraded as software or other downloadable resources. Based on our observation, the majority of the malicious downloads tried to tempt visitors by offering a 'free' or 'patched' version of a commercial software which could be downloaded at no additional cost. Our data suggests that Google is efficient at detecting these URLs, as they removed 79% of them over the period of the period of a month.

VI. Twitter's Reaction Towards Detected Malicious URLs

Among the 406 phishing URLs that were detected by Twitter, 48% of the tweets were no longer accessible on the website at the end of the study. However, 52% of the URLs still remained active on the platform, despite generating a warning similar to the one in Figure 11. These tweets could be retweeted and sent as direct messages to other twitter users, despite them containing phishing URLs. These visible tweets were posted by 185 unique accounts who had 274.2 followers on average (σ=103.9). A similar trend was seen for the 62 URLs in our dataset which distributed drive-by downloads and were detected by Twitter. Twenty-nine of them were still active on Twitter at the end of our study, which could again be distributed freely across the platform and were posted by the same number of unique user accounts. These accounts had 563.8 followers on average (σ=321.7). We believe that this approach can encourage the easy distribution of malicious URLs across the platform, and since we have already found several malicious URLs in our dataset which were able to remain alive for a significant period of time, users can be exposed to these threats even months after their initial appearance in the wild. Our experiment in this regard, however, is not conclusive, and should be pursued with more rigor to generalize our limited findings. Also considering that the accounts which posted these malicious URLs had several followers, a future study can be dedicated to determine how Twitter reacts to accounts which frequently post malicious URLs and re-distributes them as well among their network.

VII. Benign URLs on Twitter

During our manual investigation in Section III-B , coders found 2,816 (62%) of the all URLs across our three datasets (that had been flagged by at least one engine on VirusTotal) to be benign in nature. Twitter detected 293 (11%) of these benign URLs over the course of our study. The distribution of the detected benign URLs on Twitter is illustrated in Table VIII. We analyzed the characteristics of these URLs and our subsequent findings suggest that Twitter blocked websites from 6 URL shortening services and 4 free web hosting domains irrespective of whether the content of these websites

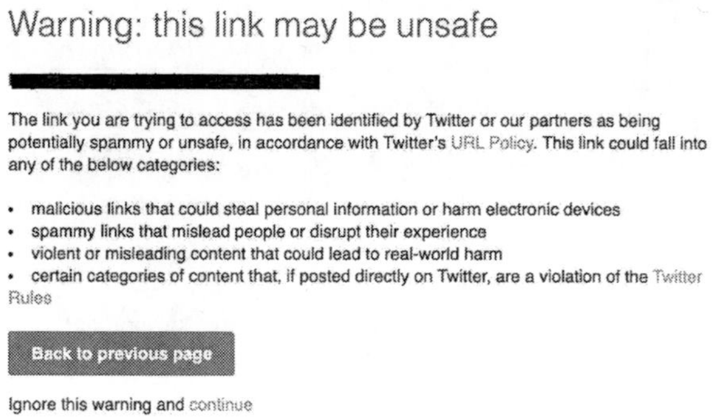

Figure 11: Warning message generated by Twitter when it detected the URL as malicious.

were malicious or not. We elaborate more on this in the proceeding sections.

Dataset	Total	Detected after a month	Detected throughout the study
1	879	63(7%)	76(8%)[1]
2	1041	153(15%)	189(18%)[2]
3	896	24(3%)	32(4%)[3]

Table VIII: The distribution of benign URLs detected by Twitter as malicious (False positives). Time periods 1= Jan to Dec 2020, 2= June to Dec 2020, and 3= Nov to Dec 2020

A. URL Shortening services

A 178 URLs in datasets D1 and D2 were shortened by 7 different URL shortening services, which included *bitly.com*, *forms.gle*, *rebrand.ly*, *ow.ly*, *us.to*, *chng.it*. Anti-phishing tools often block the entire top/sub level domains of websites from which several malicious URLs originate from [63], [64]. We assume Twitter takes a similar approach, since we found that it provides a warning for any URL which uses one of several URL shortening services, irrespective of whether they are malicious or not. The distribution of the benign URLs by Twitter across the 7 different URL shortening services in D1 and D2 are shown in Table IX. In fact, to further confirm our suspicion that Twitter was detecting the URL based on the name of the domain only, we performed a small experiment where we created some URL strings which do not exist (for example, *forms.gle/this-is-not-a-real website*). We found that Twitter immediately detected these non-existent URLs as malicious ('potentially harmful') by providing a warning similar to Fig. 11.

During the collection of our final dataset in November 2020 (D3), we found that Twitter had stopped detecting benign URLs hosted by 4 of these services but were still detecting URLs from the remaining three services consisting of forms.gle (17), bitly.com (8) and chng.it (3).

Web Hosting Domains. We found 117 URLs being hosted across 4 free web hosting domains, including *000webhost*,

URL Shortener	URLs
bitly.com	54
rebrand.ly	26
ow.ly	23
chng.it	35
forms.gle	31
us.to	9

URL Shortener	URLs
000webhost	63
hpage	28
freehostia	20
Atspace	6

Table IX: **(On left)** URL Shortening services detected as malicious by Twitter throughout D1 and D2. **(On right)** Web Hosting services detected by Twitter

hpage, *freehostia*, and *atspace* which had been detected by Twitter as malicious. We assume these free web-hosting services are detected for the same reason that URL shortening services were detected, i.e. reputation of the domain. Indeed, similar to the URL shortening services, Twitter warns against even nonexistent URLs if they are using one of these three services. The distribution of the detected URLs across the four hosting domains are illustrated in Table IX. Similar to the URL shortening services, this area too saw an improvement on Twitter's end towards the final stages of our study, with Twitter no longer detecting URLs generated from 000webhost and Atspace; however, it still detected websites hosted under hpage (3) and freehostia (1).

To summarize, our findings in this section indicate that Twitter detected URLs hosted by 6 URL shortening services, and 4 free web hosting domains over at least the first half of the year (up until the analysis of D2), irrespective of the content of these websites. We assume that Twitter did so based on the reputation of these services, though it is hard to ascertain it because of the former's blackbox nature of detection. We do find that they are improving their allowlist towards not detecting several URLs hosted by these services towards the end of our study (in dataset D3). This further justifies that a similar improvement is required in updating their blocklist to better protect against the threats that we have discussed in Sections IV and V.

VIII. Limitations and Future Work

Age of malicious URLs. For the URLs in our dataset that turned out to be malicious, we considered the day the URL first appeared online as the day the tweet containing it was posted. This may not always be the case, as the URL might have appeared in the wild at an earlier time and also possibly in an older tweet that was not part of our dataset.

Effectiveness of undetected malicious URLs. The majority of the malicious websites (61%) in our study did not invoke any warnings from Twitter, and it would be interesting to observe how users interact with them and if they are more likely to be affected by the attacks we have illustrated in IV and V. In Section IV-G, we mentioned several features that help users in identifying the URLs as phishing, but there is a need to determine if users are actually able to recognize these indicators.

Impact of warnings against Benign URLs. More than 11% of the benign URLs were detected by Twitter. Adherence to these warnings might deter the users from visiting genuine and useful resources which might be inconvenient for them or for the owners of the website (for example lower traffic for an e-commerce websites). In the future, we plan to extend these nascent findings into a concrete analysis to determine how users react to these warnings and if there is significant decrease of traffic to the affected websites.

IX. Conclusion

In this work, we evaluated and characterized more than 1.2k unique malicious URLs that remained undetected on Twitter for a significant period of time from the date of their first appearance in our dataset. We have been able to establish the majority of these URLs are hosted over nine different website/web application creation services. Our findings indicate that these services are favorable to attackers for the following reasons: **1)** Twitter's apparent inability to detect and block several of the URL threats in our dataset, which originated from these website creation services. On average 80% of the URLs that Twitter was initially unable to detect originated from these services. On the flip side, it was only able to detect 7% of the phishing URLs and 3% of the drive-by download URLs hosted by these services. Twitter's poor pattern of detection against these URLs is also shared by many other anti-phishing tools and blocklists, with nearly 80% of them unable to block above 90% of phishing threats in our dataset. Additionally, the website creation services themselves are not very efficient at removing these URLs, with more than 57% of phishing URLs and 63% of drive-by download URLs remaining active even after a month of these URLs appearing in our dataset. Both of these factors can allow attackers to organize successful phishing campaigns over extended periods of time.**3)** Additionally, we found Twitter did not remove several malicious URLs which it had detected, allowing for them to be easily redistributed over the platform at a later time. **4)** All the website creation services in consideration have simple drag and drop interfaces to create webpages, are free to use and come with up-to date SSL certification.

Though Twitter and several URL scanning tools use blackbox approaches which are unknown to us, our findings strongly hint towards the fact the sparse detection of the majority of the malicious URLs in our dataset can be contributed to the reputation of the domains that the website creation services hosting them provide. Thus, from Twitter's or the URL scanning tools' end, allowlisting websites using these services, without considering their content is far from an ideal practice. On the other hand Twitter also detected websites using one of 6 URL shortening services and 4 web hosting domains, irrespective of their content. But, their improvement in this regard towards the end of our study indicates that Twitter has improved their allowlisting approach towards benign URLs, when compared to their blocklisting implementations towards real malicious websites.

References

[1] "Why Social Media is Increasingly Abused for Phishing Attacks]," https://info.phishlabs.com/blog/how-social-media-is-abused-for-phishing-attacks, 2020.

[2] E. D. Frauenstein and S. V. Flowerday, "Social network phishing: Becoming habituated to clicks and ignorant to threats?" in *2016 Information Security for South Africa (ISSA)*. IEEE, 2016, pp. 98–105.

[3] S. Bell, K. Paterson, and L. Cavallaro, "Catch me (on time) if you can: Understanding the effectiveness of twitter url blacklists," *arXiv preprint arXiv:1912.02520*, 2019.

[4] A. Sanzgiri, A. Hughes, and S. Upadhyaya, "Analysis of malware propagation in twitter," in *2013 IEEE 32nd International Symposium on Reliable Distributed Systems*, 2013, pp. 195–204.

[5] C. Chen, S. Wen, J. Zhang, Y. Xiang, J. Oliver, A. Alelaiwi, and M. M. Hassan, "Investigating the deceptive information in twitter spam," *Future Generation Computer Systems*, vol. 72, pp. 319–326, 2017.

[6] A. Sanzgiri, J. Joyce, and S. Upadhyaya, "The early (tweet-ing) bird spreads the worm: An assessment of twitter for malware propagation," *Procedia Computer Science*, vol. 10, pp. 705–712, 2012.

[7] D. A. Broniatowski, A. M. Jamison, S. Qi, L. AlKulaib, T. Chen, A. Benton, S. C. Quinn, and M. Dredze, "Weaponized health communication: Twitter bots and russian trolls amplify the vaccine debate," *American journal of public health*, vol. 108, no. 10, pp. 1378–1384, 2018.

[8] A. Javed, P. Burnap, and O. Rana, "Prediction of drive-by download attacks on twitter," *Information Processing & Management*, vol. 56, no. 3, pp. 1133–1145, 2019.

[9] M. Bossetta, "A simulated cyberattack on twitter: Assessing partisan vulnerability to spear phishing and disinformation ahead of the 2018 us midterm elections," *arXiv preprint arXiv:1811.05900*, 2018.

[10] J. Seymour and P. Tully, "Weaponizing data science for social engineering: Automated e2e spear phishing on twitter," *Black Hat USA*, vol. 37, pp. 1–39, 2016.

[11] Y. Tanaka, M. Akiyama, and A. Goto, "Analysis of malware download sites by focusing on time series variation of malware," *Journal of computational science*, vol. 22, pp. 301–313, 2017.

[12] R. Masri and M. Aldwairi, "Automated malicious advertisement detection using virustotal, urlvoid, and trendmicro," in *2017 8th International Conference on Information and Communication Systems (ICICS)*. IEEE, 2017, pp. 336–341.

[13] F. Wei, Y. Li, S. Roy, X. Ou, and W. Zhou, "Deep ground truth analysis of current android malware," in *International Conference on Detection of Intrusions and Malware, and Vulnerability Assessment*. Springer, 2017, pp. 252–276.

[14] F. O. Catak and A. F. Yazı, "A benchmark api call dataset for windows pe malware classification," *arXiv preprint arXiv:1905.01999*, 2019.

[15] P. Prasse, L. Machlica, T. Pevný, J. Havelka, and T. Scheffer, "Malware detection by analysing encrypted network traffic with neural networks," in *Joint European Conference on Machine Learning and Knowledge Discovery in Databases*. Springer, 2017, pp. 73–88.

[16] N. Alshahwan, E. T Barr, D. Clark, G. Danezis, and H. D Menéndez, "Detecting malware with information complexity," *Entropy*, vol. 22, no. 5, p. 575, 2020.

[17] "1.4 million phishing websites are created every month]," https://www.zdnet.com/article/1-4-million-phishing-websites-are-created-every-month-heres-who-the-scammers-are-pretending-to-be/l, 2020.

[18] "Phishing Scams Cost American Businesses Half A Billion Dollars A Year]," https://www.forbes.com/sites/leemathews/2017/05/05/phishing-scams-cost-american-businesses-half-a-billion-dollars-a-year/#7a1b70773fa1, 2020.

[19] K. L. Chiew, K. S. C. Yong, and C. L. Tan, "A survey of phishing attacks: their types, vectors and technical approaches," *Expert Systems with Applications*, vol. 106, pp. 1–20, 2018.

[20] A. Aleroud and L. Zhou, "Phishing environments, techniques, and countermeasures: A survey," *Computers & Security*, vol. 68, pp. 160–196, 2017.

[21] S. Gupta, A. Singhal, and A. Kapoor, "A literature survey on social engineering attacks: Phishing attack," in *2016 international conference on computing, communication and automation (ICCCA)*. IEEE, 2016, pp. 537–540.

[22] M. Butavicius, K. Parsons, M. Pattinson, and A. McCormac, "Breaching the human firewall: Social engineering in phishing and spear-phishing emails," *arXiv preprint arXiv:1606.00887*, 2016.

[23] B. B. Gupta, A. Tewari, A. K. Jain, and D. P. Agrawal, "Fighting against phishing attacks: state of the art and future challenges," *Neural Computing and Applications*, vol. 28, no. 12, pp. 3629–3654, 2017.

[24] A. Sumner and X. Yuan, "Mitigating phishing attacks: An overview," in *Proceedings of the 2019 ACM Southeast Conference*, 2019, pp. 72–77.

[25] A. Tewari, A. Jain, and B. Gupta, "Recent survey of various defense mechanisms against phishing attacks," *Journal of Information Privacy and Security*, vol. 12, no. 1, pp. 3–13, 2016.

[26] B. B. Gupta, N. A. Arachchilage, and K. E. Psannis, "Defending against phishing attacks: taxonomy of methods, current issues and future directions," *Telecommunication Systems*, vol. 67, no. 2, pp. 247–267, 2018.

[27] S. P. Chorghe and N. Shekokar, "A survey on anti-phishing techniques in mobile phones," in *2016 International Conference on Inventive Computation Technologies (ICICT)*, vol. 2. IEEE, 2016, pp. 1–5.

[28] H. Sharma, E. Meenakshi, and S. K. Bhatia, "A comparative analysis and awareness survey of phishing detection tools," in *2017 2nd IEEE International Conference on Recent Trends in Electronics, Information & Communication Technology (RTEICT)*. IEEE, 2017, pp. 1437–1442.

[29] A. Oest, Y. Safei, A. Doupé, G.-J. Ahn, B. Wardman, and G. Warner, "Inside a phisher's mind: Understanding the anti-phishing ecosystem through phishing kit analysis," in *2018 APWG Symposium on Electronic Crime Research (eCrime)*. IEEE, 2018, pp. 1–12.

[30] M. Moghimi and A. Y. Varjani, "New rule-based phishing detection method," *Expert systems with applications*, vol. 53, pp. 231–242, 2016.

[31] J. Mao, W. Tian, P. Li, T. Wei, and Z. Liang, "Phishing-alarm: robust and efficient phishing detection via page component similarity," *IEEE Access*, vol. 5, pp. 17 020–17 030, 2017.

[32] G. Sonowal and K. Kuppusamy, "Phidma–a phishing detection model with multi-filter approach," *Journal of King Saud University-Computer and Information Sciences*, vol. 32, no. 1, pp. 99–112, 2020.

[33] C. L. Tan, K. L. Chiew, K. Wong, *et al.*, "Phishwho: Phishing webpage detection via identity keywords extraction and target domain name finder," *Decision Support Systems*, vol. 88, pp. 18–27, 2016.

[34] H. Shirazi, B. Bezawada, and I. Ray, "" kn0w thy doma1n name" unbiased phishing detection using domain name based features," in *Proceedings of the 23nd ACM on Symposium on Access Control Models and Technologies*, 2018, pp. 69–75.

[35] H. Y. Abutair and A. Belghith, "Using case-based reasoning for phishing detection," *Procedia Computer Science*, vol. 109, pp. 281–288, 2017.

[36] O. K. Sahingoz, E. Buber, O. Demir, and B. Diri, "Machine learning based phishing detection from urls," *Expert Systems with Applications*, vol. 117, pp. 345–357, 2019.

[37] T. Peng, I. Harris, and Y. Sawa, "Detecting phishing attacks using natural language processing and machine learning," in *2018 ieee 12th international conference on semantic computing (icsc)*. IEEE, 2018, pp. 300–301.

[38] R. S. Rao and A. R. Pais, "Detection of phishing websites using an efficient feature-based machine learning framework," *Neural Computing and Applications*, vol. 31, no. 8, pp. 3851–3873, 2019.

[39] P. Yi, Y. Guan, F. Zou, Y. Yao, W. Wang, and T. Zhu, "Web phishing detection using a deep learning framework," *Wireless Communications and Mobile Computing*, vol. 2018, 2018.

[40] R. Hassanpour, E. Dogdu, R. Choupani, O. Goker, and N. Nazli, "Phishing e-mail detection by using deep learning algorithms," in *Proceedings of the ACMSE 2018 Conference*, 2018, pp. 1–1.

[41] N. Abdelhamid, F. Thabtah, and H. Abdel-jaber, "Phishing detection: A recent intelligent machine learning comparison based on models content and features," in *2017 IEEE international conference on intelligence and security informatics (ISI)*. IEEE, 2017, pp. 72–77.

[42] E. Buber, Ö. Demir, and O. K. Sahingoz, "Feature selections for the machine learning based detection of phishing websites," in *2017 international artificial intelligence and data processing symposium (IDAP)*. IEEE, 2017, pp. 1–5.

[43] A. Subasi, E. Molah, F. Almkallawi, and T. J. Chaudhery, "Intelligent phishing website detection using random forest classifier," in *2017 International Conference on Electrical and Computing Technologies and Applications (ICECTA)*. IEEE, 2017, pp. 1–5.

[44] "VirusTotal]," https://www.virustotal.com/gui/home/, 2020.

[45] "VirusTotal API]," https://support.virustotal.com/hc/en-us/articles/115002100149-API, 2020.

[46] J. Charlton, P. Du, J. Cho, and S. Xu, "Measuring relative accuracy of malware detectors in the absence of ground truth," in *MILCOM 2018 -*

2018 IEEE Military Communications Conference (MILCOM), 2018, pp. 450–455.

[47] B. Sun, M. Akiyama, T. Yagi, M. Hatada, and T. Mori, "Automating url blacklist generation with similarity search approach," *IEICE TRANSACTIONS on Information and Systems*, vol. 99, no. 4, pp. 873–882, 2016.

[48] S. Zhu, J. Shi, L. Yang, B. Qin, Z. Zhang, L. Song, and G. Wang, "Measuring and modeling the label dynamics of online anti-malware engines," in *29th {USENIX} Security Symposium ({USENIX} Security 20)*, 2020.

[49] H. Wang, J. Si, H. Li, and Y. Guo, "Rmvdroid: towards a reliable android malware dataset with app metadata," in *2019 IEEE/ACM 16th International Conference on Mining Software Repositories (MSR)*. IEEE, 2019, pp. 404–408.

[50] "Twitter Developer]," https://https://developer.twitter.com/en/docs, 2020.

[51] P. Peng, L. Yang, L. Song, and G. Wang, "Opening the blackbox of virustotal: Analyzing online phishing scan engines," in *Proceedings of the Internet Measurement Conference*, 2019, pp. 478–485.

[52] "84% of Phishing Sites Last for Less Than 24 Hours]," https://www.infosecurity-magazine.com/news/84-of-phishing-sites-last-for-less/, 2020.

[53] "More Than Half of Phishing Sites Now Use HTTPS]," https://info.phishlabs.com/blog/more-than-half-of-phishing-sites-use-https, 2020.

[54] "What is a drive by download]."

[55] "How malware works: Anatomy of a drive-by download web attack]."

[56] "Why do not you include statistics comparing antivirus performance?]," https://support.virustotal.com/hc/en-us/articles/115002094589-Why-do-not-you-include-statistics-comparing-antivirus-performance-, 2020.

[57] "VirusTotal is not a Comparative Analysis Tool!]," https://www.welivesecurity.com/2008/09/12/virustotal-is-not-a-comparative-analysis-tool/, 2008.

[58] "VirusTotal += Behavioural Information]," https://blog.virustotal.com/2012/07/virustotal-behavioural-information.html/, 2012.

[59] "AV-Comparatives Summary Report 2019]," https://www.av-comparatives.org/tests/summary-report-2019/, 2019.

[60] Z. Li, K. Zhang, Y. Xie, F. Yu, and X. Wang, "Knowing your enemy: understanding and detecting malicious web advertising," in *Proceedings of the 2012 ACM conference on Computer and communications security*, 2012, pp. 674–686.

[61] "Hosting malicious sites on legitimate servers: How do threat actors get away with it?]," https://blog.malwarebytes.com/cybercrime/malware/2019/01/hosting-malicious-sites-legitimate-servers-threat-actors-get-away/, 2020.

[62] "How scammers are hiding their phishing trips in public clouds]," https://blog.checkpoint.com/2020/07/21/how-scammers-are-hiding-their-phishing-trips-in-public-clouds/, 2020.

[63] "Block that top level-domain]," https://bluecatnetworks.com/blog/block-that-top-level-domain, 2020.

[64] "Blacklisted URL Shorteners - Stop Using Them in Emails!]," https://support.rebrandly.com/hc/en-us/articles/228632488-Blacklisted-URL-Shorteners-Stop-Using-Them-in-Emails- , 2020.

A First Look at Scams on YouTube

Elijah Bouma-Sims
North Carolina State University
erboumas@ncsu.edu

Bradley Reaves
North Carolina State University
bgreaves@ncsu.edu

***Abstract*—YouTube has become the second most popular website according to Alexa, and it represents an enticing platform for scammers to attract victims. Because of the computational difficulty of classifying multimedia, identifying scams on YouTube is more difficult than text-based media. As a consequence, the research community to-date has provided little insight into the prevalence, lifetime, and operational patterns of scammers on YouTube. In this short paper, we present a preliminary exploration of scam videos on YouTube. We begin by identifying 74 search queries likely to lead to scam videos based on the authors' experience seeing scams during routine browsing. We then manually review and characterize the results to identify 668 scams in 3,700 videos. In a detailed analysis of our classifications and metadata, we find that these scam videos have a median lifetime of nearly nine months, and many rely on external websites for monetization. We also explore the potential of detecting scams from metadata alone, finding that metadata does not have enough predictive power to distinguish scams from legitimate videos. Our work demonstrates that scams are a real problem for YouTube users, motivating future work on this topic.**

I. Introduction

As the most popular video sharing and streaming platform and the second most popular website on the Internet according to Alexa [1], YouTube is a natural target for the perpetration of online fraud and other computer crimes. While there is a large body of work looking at other misuse on the platform such as harassment [2], extremism [3], [4] , video spam [5], hate [6] , disinformation [7], [8], and more [9], to the best of our knowledge no paper has examined how scammers use video sharing sites.

To this end, we present a preliminary analysis of scam videos on YouTube. We begin by collecting 3,700 YouTube videos from search queries likely to lead to scams based on authors' experiences on the platform. We then manually analyze these videos to determine if they meet our criteria for a scam video; we derived these criteria from YouTube's content policy and Terms of Service and United States law. We determined 668 videos met these criteria, with examples including a video that pretends to provide the user with "free" Walmart gift cards by "hacking" Walmart, a video that pretends to "generate" free Fortnite currency, and a video that claims to provide free Door Dash credits to viewers. We then collect metadata about the video, including user interactions and lifetime, as well as captions when available. We also collect metadata on the YouTube channel of the scam video owner. Finally, we revisit these videos five months later to determine liveness.

In this paper, we use the collected dataset to address the following research questions:

RQ1 *How does the metadata differ between scam and non-scam videos?* Scam videos are younger than non-scam videos, have fewer views and less comment engagement, and are posted by accounts with less activity than non-scam videos.

RQ2 *How do scammers monetize scams on YouTube?* The vast majority of scammers redirected to external websites, many of which use "Cost per action" (CPA) monetization tools like surveys to make money. Further, most scams in our dataset were on search terms related to gift cards or mobile games.

RQ3 *Can a classifier use metadata alone to distinguish scam and non-scam videos?* Statistical fields related to channel size and popularity provided the most mutual information. Additionally, the presence of gift card and mobile game-related words in metadata was found to be significant in discriminating between videos.

The remainder of this paper proceeds as follows. Section II describes the methodology used to answer our research questions and our data collection system. Section III describes our data and the results of our analysis. Section IV describes several important case studies observed in the process of completing this study. Section V provides discussion and future work.

II. Methods

We begin our methods discussion by describing our definition of a scam video before discussing data collection and initial analysis, then finally describing our follow-up data collection and analysis. We also discuss the limitations of our methodology. An overview of our analysis process can be seen in Figure 1

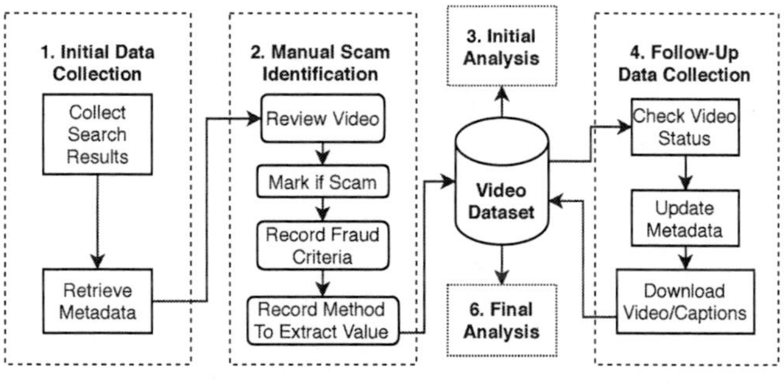

Fig. 1. Overview of Analysis Process

Workshop on Measurements, Attacks, and Defenses for the Web (MADWeb) 2021
25 February 2021, Virtual

https://dx.doi.org/10.14722/madweb.2021.23001
www.ndss-symposium.org

A. Definition of Scam Video

Before we collected or analyzed data, inspired by Pouryousefi et al. [10] we defined a video scam as *a video that attempts to attract viewers through misrepresentation, including fraudulently offering tangible, intangible, or financial awards.* Since a video view by itself may provide ad revenue, it is not necessary that there be an external profit source in our definition of a scam; however, we expected that many scams would attempt to direct users off-site to extract revenue.

To operationalize this definition of scam videos, we conservatively identify criteria based strictly on United States law and YouTube's Terms of Service. If a video falls into any of the following criteria, it was considered a scam for our purposes:

- Content which purports to commit a crime on behalf of the user (whether it actually does or not)
- Content which purports to provide an "unbounded" giveaway that offers unlimited free items without rules, limit or end
- Content which violates the following points from YouTube's content policy on "Spam, misleading metadata, and scams" [11]:
  - "Promises viewers they'll see something but instead directs them off-site."
  - "Gets clicks, views, or traffic off YouTube by promising viewers that they'll make money fast."
  - "Sends audiences to sites that spread malware, try to gather personal information or other sites that have a negative impact."
  - "Offering cash gifts, 'get rich quick' schemes, or pyramid schemes (sending money without a tangible product in a pyramid structure)."
- Content that impersonates another person, company, or organization.
- Any video whose claimed effect is demonstrably invalid.

B. Initial Data Collection

With a clear definition of scam videos, we then moved to collect data. The first challenge in creating a dataset was the likely sparsity of scams. With over 500 hours of videos uploaded to YouTube per minute [12], the amount of scam content is likely to only make up a very small fraction of a random sample of videos on the website. Thus, while a web crawler style approach may provide a representative sample, any sample small enough to be viewed in its entirety would contain virtually no offending content. Additionally, a random sample of all videos on the website would not accurately reflect the behavior of users. A viewer using the website normally does not have an equal chance of finding any given video. Rather, they will be directed to videos related to their interests based on search queries and YouTube's recommended video algorithm.

Rather than collect a random sample of all videos on the website, we collected videos using the "search.list" function of the YouTube Data API [1]. The search queries were chosen based on patterns that were expected to produce scam videos. We had previously found videos under similar queries during normal YouTube browsing. Table I shows a list of search query patterns and the source used to fill the pattern. Generally speaking, the 74 search queries fell into four categories: tech support (48), mobile game currency (8), bank support (8), and gift cards (24). In each search query pattern, the character * substitutes for the company or software name. The first 50 videos were retrieved for each search query.

TABLE I. SEARCH QUERIES USED TO GENERATE DATASET

Category	Pattern	Source	# of queries
Gift Card	"Free * Gift Card"	Amazon top 100 gift cards [13]	24
Tech Support	"* Tech Support"	Top Tech Companies on Forbes Global 2000 List [14]	8
Bank Support	"* Support"	Top 10 Private Banks According to Investopedia [15]	10
Tech Support	"* Tech Support"	Alexa Top 50 Websites (in English) [1]	24
Mobile Games	"Free * Currency"	Top Mobile Games (available in the US) by Worldwide Revenue for January 2020	8

Once a full list of videos was collected—with a total of 3700 videos—the dataset was filled out with information from the "video.list" and "channel.list" methods of the YouTube API. The final dataset has 21 fields, including video statistics (number of views, likes, dislikes, and comments), channel statistics (number of views, videos, and subscribers), video creation date, channel creation date, and user-created metadata (title, description, tags, and video description).

The final step of initial data collection was to manually categorize the content of each video. As the videos were evaluated, three data points were recorded: a boolean value corresponding to whether the video is a scam or not, a list of fraud criteria that were violated by the video, and the method(s) which the video used to extract value from viewers. Methods to extract value include redirecting to a website, providing a software download, and providing a phone number. We ultimately identified 668 scams out of the 3700 videos. These two categories of videos were then analyzed and compared using statistical tests to determine if there was a meaningful difference between scam and non-scam videos (RQ1). The additional two variables collected while viewing videos were used to determine the most common methods used to make money (RQ2). The exact methods and results are described in section III.

C. Follow-Up Analysis

After 5 months, in September 2020, we reviewed the status of videos from our initial crawl using the YouTube API to determine which videos had been removed. We did not consider these removed videos in secondary data analysis as their captions or videos could not be downloaded. The Python library PyTube[2] was used to download the MP4 file and English caption files for all videos that had not been removed and which had English captions. Some videos were unable to be downloaded despite being still available, including several videos which had been changed to be restricted to channel members since initial data collection. Ultimately, 322 out of the 3032 non-scam videos were removed,

[1]https://developers.google.com/youtube/v3

[2]https://pypi.org/project/pytube/

while 201 out of the 668 scam videos were removed. Of those 3165 videos remaining, we were able to download 3078 of the videos and get English captions from 2026 of the videos.

The YouTube Data API was also used to update metadata fields which had changed since the dataset was initially created. Although the vast majority of the videos did not have changes in their metadata fields, this updated metadata was used along with the aforementioned video data to analyze which metadata and statistical fields may provide the most information for video classification (RQ3). The exact methods and results are described in section III.

D. Limitations

Like all measurement studies, this work does have some limitations. As described above, our dataset is intentionally biased and cannot be said to be representative of the general population of non-scam or scam videos. Our findings are necessarily limited to the search queries used to seed the dataset. Additionally, our method for identifying scam videos was based on subjective and contextual manual analysis. Classification was done by a single person to reduce variance in how these rules were applied. Finally, our searches returned some non-English videos that could not be evaluated. Our data, thus, applies only to content in English.

III. Results

We begin by discussing video statistics before moving to look at the type of scams in our dataset and then finally describing our analysis of different variables for classification.

A. RQ1: How does the metadata differ between scam and non-scam videos?

After creating our dataset, our initial goal was to evaluate the properties of both scams and non-scam videos and determine whether such differences were statistically meaningful. To this end, we used a two-sample t-test to compare the median age, the median number of views, the median rating, and the channel statistics of scam and non-scam videos. While we cannot necessarily assume the normality of the data or the underlying distribution, the t-test is resilient to non-normal data [16]. These tests are all based on the initial data collection and are summarized in table II. For each test, the null hypothesis was that there was no difference between the two datasets with an alpha of 0.05.

This experiment led to the following findings:

Finding 1: *Non-scam videos had much more activity than the scam videos in our dataset, but like-dislike was not shown to be a reliable indicator of whether a video is scam or not.* Both the number of views and number of comments on scam videos were less than those on non-scam videos ($p < 0.001$). While the median like to dislike ratio of scam videos was less than that of the non-scam videos, the t-test did not show a statistically significant difference ($p = 0.21$). This test did not include videos that had the like and dislike function disabled or videos with no dislikes, but the finding is notable since it means that users may not be able to rely on the ratings as an indication of a video's accuracy.

Finding 2: *Scam videos are newer than non-scam videos but can still have a long life.* The median age of non-scam videos was nearly twice the median age of scam videos ($p < 0.001$). Notably, the median age of scam videos was still 268 days, with ages ranging from 0 to 4440 days. This finding does not necessarily mean that scam videos have been posted more recently than non-scam videos. It is possible that older scam videos are more likely to be flagged and removed from YouTube. Additionally, several of the search terms reference video games that were released within the last two years. However, this does show that scam videos are still being posted, even as soon as several days before the data was collected.

TABLE II. Comparison of Scam and Non-scam Video Statistics

Statistic	Median Scam Value	Median Non-Scam Value	P-Value
Age in Days	268	507	$1.2 * 10^{-10}$
# of Views	2519	5816	$4.3 * 10^{-7}$
Like-Dislike Ratio	8.5	20.6	0.21
# of Comments	8.0	23.5	$2.1 * 10^{-4}$
# of Channel Videos	9	339	$2.2 * 10^{-29}$
# of Channel Views	16112.5	3990403.0	$3.3 * 10^{-16}$
# of Channel Subscribers	35	20400	$9.8 * 10^{-33}$

Finding 3: *scam hosting channels have less activity than non-scam channels.* The median number of views, videos, and subscribers were significantly lower for channels that hosted scams as compared to channels without scam videos. This finding was expected, as it is likely hard for scam channels to gain popularity on YouTube. This also suggests that channels may be created or used for individual fraud campaigns before being abandoned. During analysis, we noticed some evidence of channels being taken over for the purposes of disseminating scams, such as channels used for home videos uploading scam videos after years of inactivity.

B. RQ2: How do scammers monetize scams on YouTube?

As mentioned in the previous section, as the videos in the dataset were viewed, scams were classified based on the method they used to extract value and the rule they violated. We also recorded the search term they were found using. These stats lead to the next three findings:

Finding 4: *Most scams in the dataset redirected users to other websites to extract value.* Out of the 668 scams, 526 (78.7%) directed viewers to visit an external website. It is possible that they led to an app download or phone number; however, the immediate point of redirection was a web address. 45 (6.74%) videos directed viewers immediately to download an application, and 44 (6.59%) videos directed users to call a phone number.

Finding 5: *Most scams in the dataset were found with search queries related to mobile game currency or gift cards.* Of the 668 scams, 393 (58.8%) were found with searches relating to gift cards, and 218 (32.6%) were found with searches relating to mobile games. The latter case is even more significant than its magnitude suggests, considering that only 8 search queries were related to mobile games. *All of those 8 search queries contained scams.* There were 57 (8.53%) scams on tech support search terms and no scams on bank support-related search terms. Table III shows more detail, providing the number of scams for the eleven search results with at least as many scam videos as non-scam videos in the top 50.

TABLE III.
OF SEARCH TERMS WITH AT LEAST AS MANY SCAM AS NONSCAMS

Rank	Search Term	# of Scams
1	'Free Gardenscapes Coins'	42
2	'Free PUBG Battle Points'	38
3	'Free Candy Crush Gold Bars'	34
4	'Free Mastercard Gift Card'	33
5	'Free Netflix Gift Card'	32
6	'Free AFK Arena Diamonds'	29
7	'Free iTunes Gift Card'	26
8	'Free Fortnite V-Bucks Gift Card'	26
9	'Free Google Play Gift Card'	26
10	'Free Starbucks Gift Card'	25
11	'Free Roblox Robux'	25

Finding 6: *Most scams in the dataset violated the rule on unbounded giveaways.* 534 (79.9%) of the scams in the dataset presented some form of unbounded giveaway, including the "gift card generators" which will be discussed in section IV. 54 (8.08%) violated the rule on misrepresentation. 54 (8.08%) others violated the rule on demonstrably invalid effects. Finally, 26 (3.89%) others claimed to commit some sort of crime.

C. RQ3: Can a classifier use metadata alone to distinguish scam and non-scam videos?

During our follow-up analysis, we explored the feasibility of automatically distinguishing scam and non-scam videos using metadata. All analysis was done using the Python package sci-kit learn [17].

The simplest features to analyze were the univariate numerical statistics, like those analyzed in subsection III-A. We used scikit-learn's mutual information estimation to measure the dependency between it and the boolean corresponding to whether a video is a scam or not. It is equal to zero if the two are totally independent, with greater values indicating a greater dependency. The results are summarized in figure 2. This led to the first finding:

Finding 7: *The video statistics related to channel size and popularity have the greatest predictive power.* This included channel video count, channel view count, and channel subscriber count. All other features seem to provide virtually no information about whether a video is a scam, with mutual information values below 0.02. Even the peak value of 0.17 for mutual information for channel video count is not very significant. This low level of information contained within statistics was somewhat expected, as these variables are probably similar among all videos which appear high on search rankings.

Analyzing the text-based metadata was more complicated, as text must be represented in some numerical form before analysis can be done. A word frequency or "bag of words" representation is the simplest, but it does not adjust for the relative significance of words; 'text' may occur many times within a document, but that high magnitude is not significant if the word appears many

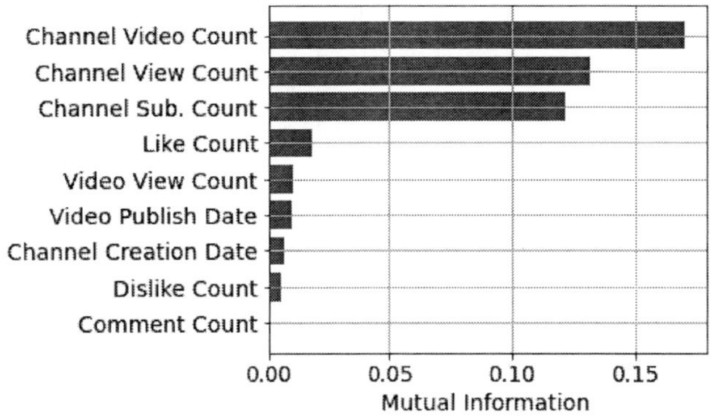

Fig. 2. Mutual information estimates for the relationship between video statistics and video scam status show that statistics related to channel popularity are the most descriptive.

times in all documents. By contrast, term frequency-inverse document frequency (TF-IDF) encoding has been shown to be a robust way to ensure word magnitude is considered relative to the entire corpus of documents. [18] [19] Each document is represented by the frequency of each word's occurrence in the document multiplied times the inverse of the magnitude of the word's occurrence across all documents. Sci-kit Learn's English stop words and the search terms were removed from all metadata before encoding. This representation was used for our analysis.

From this point, our analysis for meta-data was very similar to the analysis of other fields. For each field, we calculated the mutual information for each TF-IDF unigram and ranked the most significant words across all videos. These results are summarized in table IV. This analysis led to our next findings:

Finding 8: *The most predictive title unigrams reflect the high prevalence of gift card and mobile game-related scams.* The key words "code(s)," "promo," "android," and "ios" appear in the top 10 for title unigrams. Other more generic terms appear as well, including the year and words like "hack," "unlimited," and "New."

Finding 9: *The most predictive description unigrams appear to indicate that the use of links could be used as a distinguishing features.* The top ten unigrams include artifacts from links, including "com," "https," "www" and "http." This is slightly unusual as many of the scam videos seemed to obfuscate links or only display them in image form.

The most predictive tag unigrams are largely unhelpful, as most tags in the dataset were related to search terms, so excluding them removed many potentially high mutual information tags. Finally, channel title unigrams are also not very useful, as particular channels which appeared many times in the dataset had an outsized influence on this experiment.

English captions were present on roughly 2/3 of the remaining videos in the dataset. Their prevalence was roughly equal between scam and non-scam videos. Most captions were automatically generated and, therefore, not extremely reliable. We attempted dimensionality reduction on the captions using singular value decomposition (SVD) for the sparse matrix of captions, but it was not possible to reduce the data efficiently. As shown in figure 3, over 1700 components were still required to explain 90% of the variance in the captions between scam

TABLE IV.
UNIGRAMS WHICH HAVE THE HIGHEST MUTUAL INFORMATION IN EACH META-DATA FIELD

	Field			
Rank	Title	Description	Tags	Channel Title
1	hack	com	5mp	setup
2	2019	https	52	offer
3	codes	video	38aujwy	gaming
4	2020	www	1k	sivaji
5	android	http	basics	stuff
6	ios	like	appreciated	code
7	unlimited	channel	asksebby	new
8	new	subscribe	capital	wired
9	code	youtube	channels	today
10	promo	follow	appbounty	game

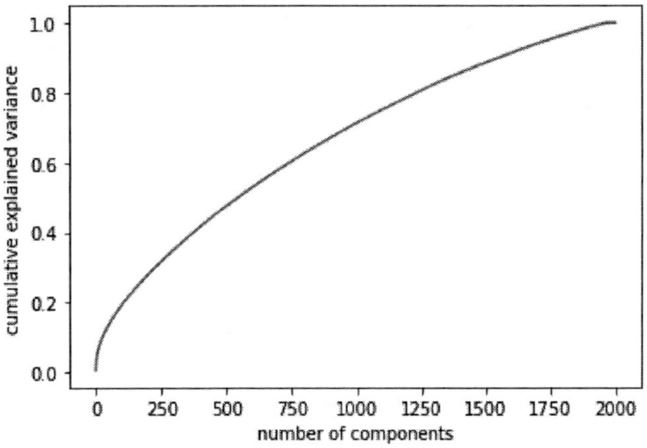

Fig. 3. This graph shows the cumulative explained variance per number of components for captions after SVD. It shows that significant dimensionality reduction is not possible without loosing a large amount of descriptive power

and non-scam videos. We determined that this reduction was not large enough to make it possible to analyze captions further.

The final part of our dataset which has not been discussed is video information, including the video file and the audio captions. Unfortunately, due to the sparsity of our dataset, we did not have enough data to explore classification on a high-dimensional space like video.

Leaving video analysis for future work, we looked for simple heuristics which may help with the classification task. Video and audio statistics like bit rate, frame rate, creation date, and resolution did not seem to contain any useful information. Ultimately, this simple analysis of video data did not prove it to be useful for classification, but more may be found with a larger dataset or if the more accurate transcription is used in future work.

IV. CASE STUDIES

The first case study described in subsection IV-A is a distinct type of fraud which we have termed "gift card generators." The second case study relates to tech support scams that use misrepresentation to fool users into calling a phone number or visiting a website. These are discussed in subsection IV-B. The final case study discussed in subsection IV-C involves the clickbait scam videos created by several moderately large YouTube channels.

A. Gift Card Generators

Finding 10: *Of the 668 scam videos in our dataset, 414 (62.0%) of them redirected to websites which claim to "generate" gift cards or mobile game resources, usually by "hacking".* We have termed these "gift card generators." Before these gift card generators provide the currency or gift cards that they claim they can produce, they state that "human verification" is required to prevent overuse of the tool. This "verification" is achieved through a web survey or application download, likely providing a stream of income to scammers. The videos try to increase the realism of these scams by showing a gift card being redeemed or in-game currency rapidly increasing.

Gift card generators often pretend to try automatic verification before requiring a survey or app download. In this way, these scams take advantage of fake feedback to try to fool users into thinking the scam is legitimate. While this particular type of scam does not seem to harm a user's device or extract private information, it does mislead users and uses them to earn money. Additionally, with the scam's prevalence on terms related to mobile games, young adults and even children may be particularly vulnerable.

Finding 11: *Some scams may be facilitated by crimeware vendors.* Many of the scam landing pages share similarities or even identical graphics (see an example in figure 4). We traced these back to a forum centered around creating websites for "cost-per-action" monetization or CPA.[3] While CPA can be a legal business practice employed to avoid risk and improve return on investment for advertisers [20], those in the CPA communities behind these gift card generators employ unethical or illegal tactics to convince users to complete actions—in this case, the "human verification" task—and gain profit. For these gift card generator websites, YouTube is another vector for spreading the scam, and discussion on the aforementioned community includes buying YouTube views and interaction to boost return on investment.

B. Tech Support Scams

Finding 12: *We found very few videos falsely claiming to be a legitimate company's tech support, and many of those that did exist were on just two search terms.* While 33 of the 74 search terms used to generate our dataset were related to tech support, only 8 of these search terms contained a scam video. 65% of the scams were on just two tech support search terms: "Office.com Tech Support" and "Yahoo.com Tech Support." Other search terms related to tech support were filled with legitimate tech support advice or videos completely unrelated to tech support. Tech support search queries related to social networking sites like "Facebook.com Tech Support" or "Twitter.com Tech Support" were filled with unrelated videos due to the search engine presenting videos with metadata linking to social media accounts.

The scams that do exist appear to be tech support scams like those discussed by Miramirkhani et al. [21] While it

[3] https://www.cpaelites.com/

Fig. 4. Example of a gift card generator animation which was seen on several websites. The graphic shows a loading bar and simulated console output to increase its perceived validity. One the "loading" completed, the website prompted the user to complete a survey or task.

is possible that some of the providers listed in these videos are legitimate, they cross the ethical line by fraudulently pretending to be a company which they are not. Indeed, there were several videos in the dataset which were clearly third party tech support, and therefore were not considered scams.

It is not immediately clear why most of the tech support scams were on only two search terms. It is noted that Yahoo does not have a support number that you can call, nor do they have a way to request that support calls you. It is possible that this gap allows scammers to fill the void that might otherwise be filled by legitimate support.

C. Clickbait Scams

Finding 13: *There were several cases of large YouTube creators which used clickbait to scam their audience.* While viewing videos under the search term "Free Fortnite V-Bucks Gift Card," several highly similar scams were found. These videos all had titles suggesting they could teach the viewer how to generate V-Bucks—the in-game currency of the game Fortnite. Most of the video would continue the ruse, with the narration describing how the viewer needs to watch until the end to learn the trick. Many of these videos would instruct the viewer to add a "Creator Code" to their Fortnite game in order to execute the trick, referring to the Epic Games "Support-a-Creator Program"[4] which provides money to online content creators when their viewers spend V-bucks. The end of the video would reveal that the title is misleading, either showing a fake glitch that fails to do anything or suggesting that players can sell promotional items to earn V-bucks.

While this may be considered simply benign clickbait, the suggestion that paying the creator is necessary pushes this over the edge into fraud. This scam is particularly insidious when one considers that 1) the game is frequently played by children and young teens, and 2) the creators hosting these scams have a large fan base and may be trusted. Since the initial dataset creation, these particular videos are still hosted on YouTube.

[4]https://www.epicgames.com/affiliate/en-US/overview

V. Discussion and Future Work

While to the best of our knowledge, we are the first to analyze this question in the research literature, we surely expect that engineers at YouTube are aware of the problems of scams on their platform. While YouTube provides no details on scam detection and removal, we suspect the high number of videos taken down between our two data collection periods may at least partially reflect an automated or manual detection process. We have also found a discussion of evading YouTube's anti-fraud system on CPA forums. As a consequence, the scams that we analyze are likely "survivors" of whatever processes are in place. It may be the case that the scams we study remained because they succeeded in maintaining a reasonable like/dislike ratio, making their metadata similar to legitimate content, or because they had not yet met some popularity threshold that would trigger a review. Our finding that metadata alone is unlikely to identify scams may only apply to these videos because videos that *could* be detected easily have already been removed. Our limited sample also focused primarily on topics likely to have associated fraud in order to acquire a large enough number of scam videos. Because of this selection bias and survivor bias, we are likely seeing only a narrow window into a larger phenomenon.

Future work should look at collecting larger datasets and using additional features beyond those analyzed in this work, including multimedia video and audio analysis. Additionally, future work could look more deeply into the world of fraudulent CPA practices, as many of the scams on YouTube are based upon those revenue streams. It may be possible to focus on identifying the crimeware used for these scams to better detect them automatically. Future work could also look more deeply at potential connections between campaigns to more accurately capture the ecosystem. Finally, we observe that individuals, consumer advocates, and regulators would benefit from greater transparency from YouTube and other video platforms about the quantity and tactics of scams on their platforms.

Acknowledgements

The authors thank our anonymous reviewers for their helpful insights. This material is based upon work supported by the National Science Foundation under Grant No. CNS-1849994.

References

[1] "Alexa - Top sites." [Online]. Available: https://www.alexa.com/topsites

[2] N. Aggarwal, S. Agrawal, and A. Sureka, "Mining youtube metadata for detecting privacy invading harassment and misdemeanor videos," in *2014 Twelfth Annual International Conference on Privacy, Security and Trust*, July 2014, pp. 84–93.

[3] A. Sureka, P. Kumaraguru, A. Goyal, and S. Chhabra, "Mining youtube to discover extremist videos, users and hidden communities," in *Information Retrieval Technology*, P.-J. Cheng, M.-Y. Kan, W. Lam, and P. Nakov, Eds. Berlin, Heidelberg: Springer Berlin Heidelberg, 2010, pp. 13–24.

[4] M. Conway and L. McInerney, "Jihadi video and auto-radicalisation: Evidence from an exploratory youtube study," in *Intelligence and Security Informatics*, D. Ortiz-Arroyo, H. L. Larsen, D. D. Zeng, D. Hicks, and G. Wagner, Eds. Berlin, Heidelberg: Springer Berlin Heidelberg, 2008, pp. 108–118.

[5] F. Benevenuto, T. Rodrigues, V. Almeida, J. Almeida, C. Zhang, and K. Ross, "Identifying video spammers in online social networks," in *Proceedings of the 4th International Workshop on Adversarial Information Retrieval on the Web*, ser. AIRWeb '08. New York, NY, USA: Association for Computing Machinery, 2008, p. 45–52. [Online]. Available: https://doi.org/10.1145/1451983.1451996

[6] S. Agarwal and A. Sureka, "A focused crawler for mining hate and extremism promoting videos on youtube." in *Proceedings of the 25th ACM Conference on Hypertext and Social Media*, ser. HT '14. New York, NY, USA: Association for Computing Machinery, 2014, p. 294–296. [Online]. Available: https://doi.org/10.1145/2631775.2631776

[7] M. N. Hussain, S. Tokdemir, N. Agarwal, and S. Al-Khateeb, "Analyzing disinformation and crowd manipulation tactics on youtube," in *2018 IEEE/ACM International Conference on Advances in Social Networks Analysis and Mining (ASONAM)*, Aug 2018, pp. 1092–1095.

[8] S. Mohammed, "Conspiracy theories and flat-earth videos on youtube," *The Journal of Social Media in Society*, vol. 8, no. 2, pp. 84–102, 2019. [Online]. Available: https://www.thejsms.org/index.php/TSMRI/article/view/527

[9] K. Papadamou, A. Papasavva, S. Zannettou, J. Blackburn, N. Kourtellis, I. Leontiadis, G. Stringhini, and M. Sirivianos, "Disturbed youtube for kids: Characterizing and detecting disturbing content on youtube," *CoRR*, vol. abs/1901.07046, 2019. [Online]. Available: http://arxiv.org/abs/1901.07046

[10] S. Pouryousefi and J. Frooman, "The consumer scam: An agency-theoretic approach," *Journal of Business Ethics*, vol. 154, no. 1, pp. 1–12, Jan 2019. [Online]. Available: https://doi.org/10.1007/s10551-017-3466-x

[11] Spam, deceptive practices & scams policies - YouTube help. [Online]. Available: https://support.google.com/youtube/answer/2801973?hl=en

[12] Youtube for press — youtube.com. [Online]. Available: https://www.youtube.com/about/press

[13] Amazon best sellers: Best gift cards store. [Online]. Available: https://www.amazon.com/Best-Sellers-Gift-Cards-Store/zgbs/gift-cards/2864120011

[14] M. Parietti. The world's top 10 tech companies. [Online]. Available: https://www.investopedia.com/articles/markets/030816/worlds-top-10-technology-companies-aapl-googl.asp

[15] D. Kurt. Which are the world's 10 largest private banks? [Online]. Available: https://www.investopedia.com/articles/investing/060915/which-are-top-10-private-banks.asp

[16] M. B. Editor. What should i do if my data is not normal? [Online]. Available: https://blog.minitab.com/blog/understanding-statistics-and-its-application/what-should-i-do-if-my-data-is-not-normal-v2

[17] F. Pedregosa, G. Varoquaux, A. Gramfort, V. Michel, B. Thirion, O. Grisel, M. Blondel, P. Prettenhofer, R. Weiss, V. Dubourg, J. Vanderplas, A. Passos, D. Cournapeau, M. Brucher, M. Perrot, and E. Duchesnay, "Scikit-learn: Machine learning in Python," *Journal of Machine Learning Research*, vol. 12, pp. 2825–2830, 2011.

[18] G. Salton and C. Buckley, "Term-weighting approaches in automatic text retrieval," *Information Processing Management*, vol. 24, no. 5, pp. 513 – 523, 1988. [Online]. Available: http://www.sciencedirect.com/science/article/pii/0306457388900210

[19] S. Robertson, "Understanding inverse document frequency: on theoretical arguments for idf," *Information Processing Management*, vol. 60, no. 5, pp. 503 – 520, 2004. [Online]. Available: https://www-emerald-com.prox.lib.ncsu.edu/insight/content/doi/10.1108/00220410410560582/full/html

[20] H. Nazerzadeh, A. Saberi, and R. Vohra, "Dynamic cost-per-action mechanisms and applications to online advertising," in *Proceedings of the 17th International Conference on World Wide Web*, ser. WWW '08. New York, NY, USA: Association for Computing Machinery, 2008, p. 179–188. [Online]. Available: https://doi-org.prox.lib.ncsu.edu/10.1145/1367497.1367522

[21] N. Miramirkhani, O. Starov, and N. Nikiforakis, "Dial one for scam: Analyzing and detecting technical support scams," *CoRR*, vol. abs/1607.06891, 2016. [Online]. Available: http://arxiv.org/abs/1607.06891